SUCCESSFUL
GARDENING

ON THE
NORTHERN PRAIRIE

Gaie Bergersen

Other books by Eric Bergeson:

Down on the Farm
Still on the Farm
Off the Farm
Back on the Farm
Pirates on the Prairie
A Treasury of Old Souls

SUCCESSFUL
GARDENING

ON THE
NORTHERN PRAIRIE

ERIC BERGESON

Country Scribe Publishing
4177 County Highway 1
Fertile, MN 56540
ericbergeson.com

Cover art and design by Lance Thorn

Printed in USA.

Second Edition, 2018
First Edition, 2017

ISBN 978-1-64255-486-1

CONTENTS

CHAPTER 1   **The Northern Prairie**   **1**

CHAPTER 2   **Getting Through Winter**   **8**

CHAPTER 3   **Basic Yard Design**   **16**

CHAPTER 4   **Soils and Fertilizer**   **32**
Soils   32
Fertilizer   38

CHAPTER 5   **Effective Watering**   **46**

CHAPTER 6   **Insects and Diseases**   **56**
Prevention   57
Diseases   59
Insects   64

CHAPTER 7   **Controlling Weeds**   **68**
Annual and Vegetable Beds   72
Suppressing Weeds Around Young Trees   72

CHAPTER 8   **Furry and Feathered Pests**   **76**
Furry Animals   76
Feathered Pests   82

CHAPTER 9   **Planting and Care of Deciduous Trees**   **86**
Purchasing Trees   87
Planting Trees   90
Care of Trees   94
Pruning Trees   96
Moving Trees with a Tree Spade   100

CHAPTER 10 **Useful Trees for the Northern Prairie 102**
First Tier Trees   102
Second Tier Trees   115
Experimental Trees   124

CHAPTER 11 **Planting Shrubs Around the House   126**
The Plan   128
Planting and Care   131

CHAPTER 12 **Useful Shrubs for the Northern Prairie 136**

CHAPTER 13 **Evergreens   156**
Spruce   *157*
Arborvitae   *164*
Juniper   *169*
Pine   *171*

CHAPTER 14 **Hedges   176**
Formal Hedges   176
Informal Hedges   179
Purchasing, Planting, and Care 181

CHAPTER 15 **Windbreaks and Shelterbelts   184**
Quality Windbreak Trees   186
Trees to Avoid in Windbreaks   190
Windbreak Layouts   192

CHAPTER 16 **Vines   194**

CHAPTER 17 **Growing Fruit Trees in the North   198**

CHAPTER 18 **Small Fruits   216**

CHAPTER 19 **Roses   228**

CHAPTER 20 **Annuals   240**
Major Annuals   248
Novelty Annuals   264

CHAPTER 21 **Perennials   271**
Purchasing Perennials   273
Planting and Care of Perennials 274
Diseases and Insects on Perennials 276
Major Perennials for Our Area   277
Minor Perennials   291

CHAPTER 22 **Vegetables on the Prairie**   **302**
      Tomatoes   *309*
      Sweet Corn   *310*
      Salads and Greens   *311*
      Potatoes   *311*
      Root Crops   *311*
      Onions   *311*
      Cole Crops   *312*
      Melons   *312*
      Cucumbers   *312*
      Squash and Pumpkins   *313*
      Peas   *313*
      Beans   *313*
      Peppers   *313*
      Groundcherries   *313*

CHAPTER 23 **The Prairie Lawn**   **316**
    Controlling Weeds   320
    Creatures   323
    Lawn Maintenance   324

INDEX   326

ABOUT THE AUTHOR

Eric Bergeson has spent his entire life as a part of Bergeson Nursery, a business started by his grandfather Melvin Bergeson near Fertile, Minnesota in 1936. Eric owned Bergeson Nursery for seventeen years. He hosted cable television's *Little Garden on the Prairie*. Over the past twenty years, Eric has spoken to hundreds of groups about the joys and challenges of gardening on the northern prairie. *Successful Gardening* is Eric's seventh book, and his first about gardening.

CHAPTER 1

The Northern Prairie

This book is for amateur gardeners on the northern prairie, in USDA hardiness Zones 3a, 3b and 4a.

The northern prairie has the harshest winter climate of any inhabited area in the lower forty-eight states. In addition to the deep cold, our soils are predominantly alkaline, a characteristic of the prairie states which sets them apart from more populated areas.

Due to our sparse population and odd conditions, nationally-distributed gardening shows and books do not deal with our problems. Just as often, they address problems we *don't* have, often raising needless concerns in our area.

Despite the lack of appropriate instruction from national sources, there is plenty of information suited for our area available for those willing to search. Our hardy forbearers were eager to plant, and they wrote down their experiences. Since their founding, our land-grant universities have conducted research on plants and shared their results. Extension services continue to provide fully dependable information on their websites.

This book relies heavily upon relevant university research, as well as the practical experience gained from a career in the nursery and greenhouse business.

My grandfather, Melvin Bergeson, carried a wealth of information in his head. Had I been older and wiser before he passed away in 1992, I would have delved more deeply into his wisdom. Even so, we have benefitted from the knowledge he passed on before he left the scene.

The nursery trade has a long tradition of keeping no secrets. For example, what Bailey Nurseries in St. Paul, one of the premier wholesale nurseries in the world, learns from its customers is distributed by their knowledgeable sales people. Area nursery people love to share notes, and over the years, a body of knowledge has grown that combines hundreds of years of experience.

The wisdom of people who actually sell plants is important, as they have a feel for the struggles of the average gardener and know what knowledge is useful and what is too esoteric to be worth mentioning.

This book attempts to collect the information most valuable to the layperson and put it in a single volume accessible to all. It is not comprehensive. For deeper study of a particular plant variety or problem, the information is now readily available on the internet. Make sure the website originates from our area, however!

Advantages of living where we do

We should not forget that our location near the 49th parallel has its advantages, namely our fast and furious summers, filled with long days of sunlight and brief, cool nights.

•Annual flowers perform better the farther north you go. In our gardens, for instance, trailing petunias planted in the ground have grown almost twice as large as they have only two-hundred miles south. Because they usually don't experience as much heat as their counterparts to the south, blooming annuals last deeper into the season as well.

•Impatiens and begonias in particular grow larger in the north, sometimes by as much as double, and last longer through the season. In Iowa, Illinois and farther south, annual flower beds are often exhausted by late July. In our area, they can be spectacular well into October—and because the annual plants grow so large in our area, you only have to plant half as many!

•Scientists have concluded that the intensity of bloom color is deeper in regions with cool nights. Travelers to Europe, or Alaska, both well north of us, can attest to the spectacular nature of their summer flower displays.

•Some of the largest cabbage and broccoli heads you will ever see have been grown right here on the northern prairie. Cool nights help prevent cole crops from bolting, while the sunshine and rich soil increases yield.

•Because we have less rainfall and lower humidity than places south, disease problems on roses, flowering crab, and other plants are less pronounced. In fact, *most* of the very bad diseases don't make it up to our corner of the world. Same goes for many of the insects which have plagued trees in Michigan, Ohio and other warmer climes. As far as insects go, the cold keeps at least *some* of the riff raff out.

•Ornamental grasses seem to like the northern prairie better than points south. They are at home on the prairie!

•More summer sunshine means better sugar content and more intense flavor in our fruit. Nothing is richer than the flavor of northern-grown apples, plums or grapes.

Knowing our advantages, we can buck ourselves up to take on the challenges presented to gardeners by the northern prairie's climate and soils.

Soil is most important

Plants are only as good as their root and a plant's root is only as good as the soil in which it grows. Most northern plains soils lack a crucial ingredient necessary for root growth: organic matter. The addition of organic matter in the form of compost or peat will make everything grow much better. Money spent up front improving your soil *before planting* pays dividends later.

Trees are top priority

Nothing is more treasured and difficult to create than a large tree on the prairie. The northern prairie was originally virtually barren of trees, and for a reason. Trees are difficult to start here. But trees thrive here once established, and the more we plant, the more humane an environment we create for ourselves.

Mistakes in tree planting are costly. An appalling amount of money is wasted on unwise tree planting practices. More importantly, valuable years are squandered when non-hardy trees are planted, only to die in a tough winter ten years later. Even tough tree varieties can die from improper care, which often means too much care rather than too little.

Proper information on trees can save more money, effort, time and heartbreak than information in any other area of horticulture. We have included a detailed list of trees hardy for our area, along with instructions for their care.

Shrubs shouldn't be a drain

The planting of shrubs around houses and institutions should be neither difficult nor costly, but often ends up being both. This book advocates shrub plantings that are natural in appearance, long-lasting and low-maintenance. A shrub should last about fifteen years in the landscape. For that to happen, the shrub must be hardy, must be planted in a location where it will be both healthy and confine itself to the proper size, and must be given correct care, if any is required at all.

Raising fruit requires frequent reality checks

Fruit enthusiasts waste a lot of time and money stubbornly chasing impossible dreams. Skip blueberries, peaches and kiwi. They don't work. Plant fruits which have been proven here. On the prairie, the planting of large orchards has been a recipe for disappointment as well as physical and financial stress. Start slow, start small, start now. And start smart. Varieties highlighted in this book have earned their way here because they *work*.

Perennial common sense

Perennial books flood the market. There are thousands of varieties of perennials, even for cold climates. This book's chapter on perennials will outline some general principles of raising perennials in our area, and list some varieties which have performed particularly well, as well as some which should be approached with a sense of humor.

Annuals and vegetables

The information available to the gardener on annuals and vegetables is overwhelming. Seed catalogs fill the mailbox. Full-color plant encyclopedias flood the market. Information is easily found on the internet. Because annuals and vegetables are not affected by our cold winters, most of the information, with the exception of planting and harvesting dates, is solid and good and won't be repeated here.

However, there are unique problems of nutrition and climate that the annual and vegetable gardener should keep in mind, as well as some particular practices that will improve results for the northern prairie gardener.

For the hobbyist and new gardener

For those interested, gardening can be an endless study. You may pursue a PhD in garden mums, or join the Hosta Society, or study the several-thousand-year history of rose breeding, or memorize the Latin names of plant species.

Or, you may just want to have a handsome yard and a healthy, productive garden. If so, this book is for you. We have taken pains to omit needless detail which will likely only confuse and repel new gardeners. For those wishing to look into specific areas of gardening in greater detail, the information available on the internet is endless.

A northern prairie aesthetic

What is beautiful? The happy northern gardener has adjusted his or her notion of what is beautiful to conform to the realities of our climate, just as the Arizona gardener has learned to love cactus. Hardy shrub roses don't conform to the tea rose ideal presented by magazines, but a blooming shrub rose is a great joy, and much more beautiful than a dead tea rose—or even a live one!

The successful northern prairie yard is different from successful yards in other parts of the country. Prairie yards at their best are *handsome, dignified* and *stately.* They are less frequently *formal, cozy* or *cute.*

Names and categories

This book will use the names and categories that have developed within the nursery trade on the northern prairie. Latin names will be provided, but only for those who wish to do further research. To purchase a plant in this book, you should be able to use the common name given here at any local nursery or garden center.

Color pictures

To keep the price of this book moderate, this edition does not include pictures. Fortunately, horticulture enthusiasts have taken to the internet like a duck to water: simply type a plant's name in a search engine and dozens of pictures will pop up. Include the plant's Latin name to improve the accuracy of the results.

"First, do no harm."

The above phrase is often erroneously thought to be a part of the Hippocratic oath taken by doctors. The saying persists because it illustrates an important truth, one which applies to our yards as well:

• Remove a healthy, old tree only after much thought. It will not be replaced in our lifetime.

• Products which promise to make gardening easy usually don't.

• All things in moderation—except for peat.

•Plant hardy varieties.

•Plant them where they can succeed.

•Amend the soil, and do so *before* planting.

•Add fertilizers which work on the northern prairie.

•Keep chemical use to a bare minimum.

•Always seek out *local* instructions.

•The tried and true is nearly *always* better than the tempting and new.

•Weeding and watering can be made more efficient, but the two tasks will always remain *essential* to maintaining a beautiful yard.

Because it is assumed that readers will dip into portions of the book without reading others, there is some repetition of important points. If brevity is the soul of wit, perhaps repetition is the heart of learning!

CHAPTER 2

Getting Through Winter

Winter is a problem for outdoor plants, as well as indoor humans.

There are several ways our tough winters damage trees and plants. Knowing *how* winter kills can help us protect plants from harm. A summary first, with details later:

•*Plain old cold:* Every plant has a minimum temperature below which it will die. Even a couple of degrees below that point for *one night* can kill the plant by destroying its cell structure. The solution is to plant only hardy varieties.

•*Low humidity and high wind:* Trees and shrubs exposed to drying winds and the low humidity of our winter can simply dehydrate. Think freezer burn. The solution is to plant the more tender plants where they are protected from wind.

•*Cold fronts, warm fronts:* When a tree alternately warms to above freezing and then plunges to well below freezing, its tissue can be destroyed, particularly on the southwest side of the trunk. Evergreens suffer as well. Think of vegetables which freeze and thaw several times. They become mush. The problem, called *sun scald*, usually happens in February and March, when the days are longer but the temperatures are still cold. The solution is to wrap tender evergreens, and paint the trunks of tender trees white.

•*Deep snow before the ground freezes:* Perennial roots can rot when deep snow arrives before the ground freezes, particularly after a wet fall. It is actually possible for the ground to be *too warm* throughout the winter. Deep snow before freezeup happens only once in every couple of decades, but when it does, it is so destructive that it is worthwhile to take preventative measures. Most importantly, make sure perennial beds are slightly raised at planting so they are always properly drained.

•*No snow before deep cold:* Without snow cover, ground temperatures can sink to the point where the root is damaged or killed. Roots of woody plants do not tolerate deep cold as well as the tops, particularly the roots of very young trees. Grandpa used to keep bales of straw handy near the gardens in early winter. If a cold snap threatened before we had snow, out we went to spread the straw around the base of tender plants such as strawberries.

•*Danger to fruit buds:* Cold can kill the buds of more tender fruit varieties such as apricots and cherries, and in some cases plum. Because fruit tree blossom buds are more tender than their leaf buds, deep cold in the winter can result in less fruit in the summer. Leaving branches which hug the ground on the tender fruit trees such as plum can result in better fruiting on those branches covered with snow.

USDA hardiness zones

The United States Department of Agriculture has created a map of climates which has been adopted as a standard by the nursery trade. It is a simple system which divides the country into zones by typical minimum temperatures. The lower the number of zone, the colder the climate.

Plants are rated for particular zones—not by any official body, but by the nursery trade itself. Established nurseries have no interest in lying about the zone-hardiness of a plant. However, just because one nursery says a plant is hardy for a particular zone doesn't mean the next nursery will agree.

Plants rated for Zone 3 are usually well-tested on the northern prairie.

Zone 1 is for polar bears. Zone 2 is for tundra. Zone 3 is much of the northern prairies of western Minnesota and North Dakota. Zone 4a covers the remainder of North Dakota, the northern tier of South Dakota counties, and much of Montana.

This author remains skeptical of the northward creep of Zone 4 on recent maps. For most trees on the northern prairie, it is the *extremes* in temperature which kill. One solid night of -32 F can hurt trees otherwise solid for Zone 4.

Even if our temperatures have risen *on average*, the extremes still seem to be with us. A plant rated hardy to Zone 3 has been proven to survive temperatures as low as -40°F. If a nursery or mega-discount store cannot tell you the zone rating for a particular tree or shrub, don't buy it.

Avoid some late-season pruning

Pruning *young trees* late in the fall when the plant is dormant can result in the tree losing moisture through the unhealed wound to the dry winds of winter.

Grapes are most vulnerable to late-season pruning, which can cause them to dehydrate and die over winter.

Most deciduous *shrubs* will not be bothered by late pruning, and none will die of it.

Established trees can easily withstand fall pruning. If you have to use a chainsaw for your pruning, the tree is big enough for you to prune at any time of the year without harm—with the exception of oak, which should not be pruned *until* late in the season for reasons of disease.

Taper off watering when school starts

To discourage late growth on tender plants, growth which may not harden up before winter, do not water your plants the last weeks before they go dormant.

The exceptions are recently transplanted spruce trees, which stop growing in early August no matter what, and can truly benefit from watering right up to the time the ground freezes.

Low humidity and high winds

Low humidity and harsh winds hurt plants on the northern Great Plains as much as cold alone.

Winter's dry air, which sometimes makes humidifiers necessary in the house, has a drying effect on plants and trees outdoors as well. Strong winds make the problem worse.

Buds and branches dry out more quickly in a dry, cold wind than they do if it is merely cold and still. Young trees with a smooth bark, such as sugar maples and green ash, seem particularly vulnerable to drying winds. The bark simply snaps, revealing the white wood beneath.

For this reason, tender plants will do better where they are shielded from the northwest winds. Apples of borderline hardiness, pagoda dogwood, apricots, plums, and Japanese tree lilacs are a few of the plants which can survive in our cold as long as they are shielded from the worst of the north winds.

The plastic shield which is used to protect the bark of young trees from rodents and rabbits may also serve to protect the bark from the drying effects of the northwest wind. Make sure to remove the protectors in spring as they can trap moisture against the tree trunk and cause rot.

Sun scald on tree trunks

The bark of young apple and flowering crab trees, as well as faster-growing maples, is susceptible to what is called *sun scald*. Sun scald usually occurs in March when the southwest side of tree branches are repeatedly jolted in and out of dormancy by drastic changes in temperature.

Sun scald kills the bark on the sunny side of the tree, often for as much as one-third the circumference of the trunk. Sun scald rarely kills the tree, but it can take years for the wound to heal and the tree can be weakened for the long term.

The simplest way to prevent sun scald is to paint the southwest side of the tree's trunk in late fall with white latex paint. Once a tree matures enough to develop rough, corky bark, the problem of sun scald recedes.

After sun scald has happened

If a tree is already wounded from last winter, it is too late to paint. Simply clean the wound and allow it to heal without paint, tar or wrapping, all of which do more harm than good during the growing season.

Two popular recently-introduced trees are particularly susceptible to sun scald: The Honeycrisp apple and the Autumn Blaze maple (and other fast-growing hybrid maples which contain *Acer rubrum* genes). Unlike most trees in our area, Honeycrisp and Autumn Blaze can die from sun scald. Paint their trunks *every November* until they develop rougher bark. It can be a matter of life and death.

The danger of a large snowfall before the ground freezes

Much winter damage occurs in our area in the rare instance when deep snow falls before the ground is frozen. We had one such winter in 1996, during which many long-established tough perennials such as rhubarb, iris and peonies did not survive. Coincidentally, that winter featured a week of -40°F temperatures and most people attributed their loss of perennials to the extreme cold. However, the snow was too deep for the plants to feel the cold—in fact, they rotted in the warm, wet ground, as evidenced by the slimy goo gardeners found in the spring where their perennials once grew.

Perennial plants in our area prefer to winter in lightly frozen soil kept from deeper freezes by a generous snow cover. When the ground does not freeze, roots rot, especially if the ground is wet going into winter.

The problem of winter rot is made worse by heavy, poorly drained soils frequently found on the northern prairie.

Planting perennials in raised beds made up of peat can alleviate the problem by preventing water from sitting stagnant around the roots.

Deep snow also allows rodents to tunnel along the ground surface for the entire winter. Rodent damage is a big problem in winters with an early deep snow before the ground is frozen. If an early snow produces conditions ideal for voles and other rodents, stamp down a ridge of snow around your most prized plants and young trees. Rodents will not crawl over a ridge of hard-packed snow.

The danger of deep cold without snow

The best winter cover for plants is snow. When there is little or no snow before temperatures sink below zero, the ground becomes far colder than normal. Deep cold without snow can cause perennials of borderline hardiness to die.

My grandfather didn't cover such perennials *until* there was a threat of sub-zero cold without the benefit of snow cover. Shasta Daisies, mums, violas, primrose and other tender perennials can be damaged by deep cold without snow.

In severe cases, deep cold without snow can kill the roots of trees, particularly young trees with shallow roots.

The trees most susceptible to winter kill of the roots are *dwarf apples*. Apple trees are dwarfed by grafting them onto a special root. Dwarfing rootstock is not as hardy as the rootstock which produces standard size apple trees. If one plants dwarf apples, the root should be *mulched* in the winter. *Mulching* is a fancy word for covering the ground around the tree with about six inches of straw, or something similar.

The best winter cover of all for perennials

The ideal winter situation for most plants is provided by nature: leaves, blown in by the wind, coupled with snow cover, also blown in by the wind.

For this reason, do not cut the foliage off perennial plants until spring. The only exception are peonies, which should be cut back in September to prevent a disease called *botrytis* from working its way from the foliage to the root.

The standing dead foliage of perennials catches blowing leaves and snow without promoting rot. Piling leaves deeper than naturally occurs, or piling straw onto a perennial bed as one would pile blankets on a sleeping grandchild, creates the risk of rot, particularly if one is late in removing the cover in the spring.

Not all plants like warm climates

People who migrate from the Upper Midwest to warmer climates soon find out that many of their favorite Minnesota plants don't grow in warmer climates. Rhubarb, lilacs, even the popular flowering crabs, simply don't survive further south. Many plants, both woody plants and perennials, need a cold period in order to come out of dormancy in the spring.

Say what you will about our harsh winters, it is our climate which allows us to enjoy fresh rhubarb pie!

CHAPTER 3 ─────────────────────────────

Basic Yard Design

What is the goal?

To attain your dream yard, first bring your dreams into accord with our climate.

A beautiful yard on the northern prairie is usually more *handsome* than *cute* or *cozy.*

The beauty of a northern farmstead surrounded by healthy, tended windbreaks, accented with healthy shade tree specimens, softened by plantings of shrubs, and embellished with tasteful plantings of perennials and annuals, is something not seen everywhere, and a pleasure simply not available to the bulk of our population who lacks our ample space.

It is true that older homes surrounded by older shade trees in the middle of a prairie town can be made to look more *cozy* than *handsome*. But most of us can be thankful for a big sunny yard, and should take advantage of the sun and space to plant hardy roses, old-fashioned perennials, and a few hardy apple trees.

A realistic philosophy

Approach landscaping of one's yard the way you might approach long-term investing: start *slow*, start *small*, start *now*. Plant a few shrubs and a couple of shade trees every year as a constant practice.

If you just don't have the time

Many people feel an obligation to their neighbors and their own pride to have a nice yard, but they don't enjoy the work, or they just don't have the time.

However, if you are busy with career and kids, you can still have a handsome yard.

Simply plant a minimal number of low-maintenance trees, shrubs and perennials. Such plantings are easily done, cost very little, and can look very handsome. Planting bare root trees and shrubs substantially reduces the care needed to keep things alive.

Don't be intimidated by the task of planting shrubs and trees. With a few hours work on a Saturday in May, you can get a good start on beautifying your home for years to come.

Before building: have a little talk with the contractor

Developers and contractors are notorious for filling the yard in around new homes with terrible soil. Trees and shrubs need to grow in topsoil, not in clay or gravel. If the contractor has pushed clay or gravel up against your house, have them haul it out and bring in some nice topsoil before you plant shrubs or trees.

Make clear to your contractor the yard is to be covered with at least six inches of good topsoil right up to the house.

Before you pour the sidewalks

A common mistake is to pour sidewalks too close to the house, leaving three feet or less between the sidewalk and the foundation of the house.

Such an area is too small for most shrubs and allows for very little creativity in design. Ideally, the space between the house and any sidewalk should be at least six feet wide.

Don't leave little round holes in concrete for trees or flowers

Leaving small circular openings in the concrete for flowers or trees is usually a bad idea. Moveable planters placed atop the concrete look better.

Growing trees or shrubs in a three-foot wide opening in concrete is far from ideal. Trees fighting to live in concrete in urban areas tend to be short-lived due to the obviously unnatural circumstances around their root.

Should we build permanent planters?

Generally, permanent brick or concrete planters are a long-term curse.

Permanent planters look handsome *when maintained*. Trailing petunias cascading over the side of a brick planter make a spectacular show.

Then, one spring you have gall bladder surgery and you can't plant your planter. It grows up into weeds. Your home loses twenty-percent of its value.

Better to plant plants in the ground where they belong. If your health is good, or if you have a special event planned, load up on movable planters. If you want to take a year off, you can always stack the empty planters out back.

Permanent planters need to be planted each year anew with annuals. Shrubs and perennials seldom make it through winter in above-ground planters because the soil in planters gets about twenty degrees colder than the soil at ground level during the winter.

The bigger the planter, the better. Permanent planters should be at least 18 inches deep and just as wide, or they will dry out frequently in the heat of summer.

Brick planters absorb heat in summer. If you water daily, petunias can work, but if you sometimes forget to water, plant geraniums. They are tough, and there is something magical about the combination of bright red geranium blooms and brick.

Be thoughtful about using rows

Unless you are planning a hedge, it is best if the plantings in one's yard are random and natural-looking. Rows are for sugar beets, windbreaks, and soldiers. The whole idea behind planting trees and shrubs in one's yard is to soften the lines, to make the place look more *natural.*

Gardeners who attempt to establish a perfectly uniform row of trees, evergreens, or shrubs in their yard are usually frustrated. Soil and moisture conditions vary every few feet in most yards, which causes trees from one end of the row to the other to grow at different rates. When trees are planted randomly, the loss of one tree will not create an unsightly gap, and trees which grow more slowly won't stick out like a sore thumb.

Of course, if you have built a big house on the prairie, you want a shelter belt, and in that case rows are inevitable. Make the rows straight and, to ensure maximum uniformity, only plant vigorously growing varieties, such as those suggested in Chapter 15 on windbreaks.

Sometimes, a short hedge of five to ten shrubs can have a noble effect, such as a mass of hydrangeas planted along the shady north side of a lake home, a mass of William Baffin roses along a large, empty and hot garage wall, or a brief row of untrimmed dogwood long enough to screen out the propane tank. Such rows look best if the plants which form the row are maintained in an informal, lightly-trimmed state.

Use odd numbers of each kind of plant

Don't ask why, but a design rule-of-thumb when planting more than one of any kind of plant is to use an odd number. Groupings of twos, fours, sixes and eights tend to pair off in the eye of the beholder and can look like soldiers on parade. Odd numbers are more natural and pleasing to the eye.

Plant shade trees first

Because shade trees take a long time to mature, they should be planted as soon as possible after the house is built. A windbreak, if desired, should be planted as soon as you buy the lot or figure out which corner of the farm will eventually host your house.

Save what you have

If the lot has established trees, such as oak, think long and hard before bulldozing them to make room for the house. They will not be replaced.

If your lot is all woods, of course, you will have to take some trees down. It is best *not* to leave oak with branches overhanging the house, as oak often die from construction injury over the ten years after the home is built.

Most old trees have accumulated value that should not be taken lightly. A natural grove of aspen, for example, with its lovely parallel white trunks, is almost impossible to replicate by planting. If you have such a grove in the corner of your yard, *keep it.*

Foundation plantings: soften the corners

The first goal of planting shrubs should be to cover the corners of the house. The corners should have shrubs which are large and very hardy. Corners are tough spots for shrubs due to winds, as well as pet and children traffic. Tough, larger shrubs such as dogwood and Techny arborvitae are ideal. Avoid the tall, narrow pyramidal arborvitae unless you have a two-story house.

The shrub on the corner of the house should be planted diagonally from the corner, a minimum of four feet out. Alternately, a grouping of three large shrubs can be planted around the corner.

Avoid islands in the middle of the yard

As a rule, plantings should be concentrated around the house and the edges of the yard, where the plants can be tucked in most naturally. An island of shrubs planted in the middle of the front yard can make a house look more like the local branch of a bank than a home. Islands of annual or perennial flowers can be spectacular, but should only be resorted to after all other more natural places have been filled and you just have to have more flowers.

The place for stand-alone beds of flowers is off to the side or near the vegetable garden, where they don't look as if they are on stage. A flower bed can be attractive, but like a beautiful piece of furniture, it looks best if it fits into the broad scheme of things.

Don't draw attention to eyesores

A utility pole, a well, or an air conditioning unit is *not* going to look better with petunias planted around it. Don't attract attention to such eyesores, or even try to cover them, unless you completely screen the eyesore with big, informal, untrimmed shrubs. Usually it is better to simply draw attention away from the eyesore by planting a colorful flower bed somewhere else.

Look around your neighborhood

Before choosing shrubs and trees, look around your neighborhood. What is doing well? What is doing poorly? If you can find no examples of a type of tree that you desire, think again. It is very likely that the tree you are wanting was tried before by *somebody* in your neighborhood, and died. Dead trees and shrubs get pulled out long before they teach valuable lessons to the neighbors about what does and doesn't grow in the area.

Get local instructions

The tags on trees and shrubs are often full of instructions. Those instructions do not always apply to this part of the country.

Apparently, trees in some other parts of the country need to be hilled up around the base. On the northern prairie, however, trees and shrubs should be surrounded by a depression which collects water. That depression will collect water from rains and make it easier for the gardener to water by hand.

It is fine if the depression disappears as the roots of the tree mature and develop the ability to survive on what nature provides.

Instructions on the tags of roses often instruct the gardener to plant the graft at ground level. However, around this area, roses should be planted deeply, with the graft ending up about four or five inches below the surface.

Talk to local nurseries and local gardeners to find out what works where you live. Or, read the remainder of this book!

The importance of location

Determining the best plant for a certain location requires that one consider sunshine, available space, eventual size of the plant, moisture and soil, as well as the obvious question of appearance.

With annuals and perennials, one can experiment with various locations without risking much money. If an annual doesn't thrive in one place one year, try another area next year. Most perennials can easily be moved if they balk at one location.

Some gardeners plant annuals in pots and move them around their yard to discover where they do best before building a flower bed in that spot. Subtle changes in location can make a difference. Dedicated gardeners experiment with different flowers in different parts of the yard. If it works once, do it again next year!

Trees and shrubs are more permanent, and more expensive, than annuals and perennials. Before planting a tree or shrub, make sure to give thought to finding a good spot. Planting a tree or shrub in a bad location means losing time and money.

Plan for the future — plants grow larger!

Many professional landscapers concentrate upon producing a landscape that looks finished right away. Customers don't object, because often they want the landscape to look complete, whatever the cost. And graduation is next week!

To produce instant results, landscapers often crowd shrubs together, using far more plants than necessary or prudent.

Five years after such a planting, the front yard has turned into such a forest that it is often necessary to pull the shrubs out and start over.

Instead, it is wise to plant shrubs far enough apart, allowing them to grow more naturally to their intended height and breadth. Planting trees and shrubs where they can grow to their maximum size without constant trimming saves the homeowner work, hassle, and money, both now and later. In addition, the plants are allowed to look natural and healthy.

Although it may look odd at planting, foundation shrubs should be planted at least three-and-a-half feet from the house. At that distance, they get more rainfall and sunshine, and are free to grow naturally without rubbing against the wall.

Where not to plant trees

Trees are meant to *provide* shade, not live in shade. In our area, only two varieties of tree are meant to live underneath a canopy provided by other trees: pagoda dogwood and ironwood. All other trees, including smaller ornamental trees, do better if they have plenty of space and sunshine. If growing in partial sun, many trees will be sparse, and will lean towards the light.

Planting a tree in the shade of a big old tree which you believe is going to die in the next few years in hopes of getting a head start on replacing the big tree *does not work.* The younger tree will be stunted, both by the lack of sunshine and by competition for moisture with the larger tree's roots. And when the big tree finally comes down, it might well land on the smaller tree.

Look overhead for wires before planting. Imagine the tree at its final size. Will the power company need to hack the branches, thus ruining its shape? Save yourself trouble ten years down the road and only plant smaller trees beneath the power lines.

Consider your view from the house once the tree is mature. Put a stake in the ground where you want your new tree, then go inside and imagine your view from various windows when the tree grows to its projected height and width.

Where to plant shade trees

Trees provide the most shade to a home when planted on either the east or west side of the house. Trees planted south of the house do surprisingly little to protect a house from the hot mid-day sun, and they do nothing to stop the sunshine in the morning or evenings. A tree planted near a deck does most good if it is planted to the southeast or the southwest of the deck.

Boulevard plantings

Trees planted on the boulevard undergo more stress in the form of salt from the road, piles of snow, neighbor's kids and pets, than do trees in the back yard. For that reason, the boulevard is a place to plant hardy, tough shade trees such as disease-resistant elm, basswood, or perhaps a flowering crab. Hybrid poplars grow too large for the boulevard, as do silver maple. Evergreen branches are too low to the ground to be directly in front of a house unless you want to completely block your view, or the view of passersby.

An odd number of the same tree is usually the most dignified option for the boulevard.

Spacing of shade trees

Shade trees should be planted a minimum of thirty feet apart. In a row, or on a boulevard, spacing of less than thirty feet looks cramped.

Smaller ornamental trees, such as Mountain Ash, Red Leaf Chokecherry, and Flowering Plum can be planted twenty feet apart without harming each other or looking odd. Ornamental trees look best as single specimens.

Because ornamental trees bloom or show fall color at different times, planting different varieties helps create interest all year long.

Spruce trees should be kept at least fifteen feet apart unless one plans to trim and shape them regularly.

In general, people plant trees far too closely, forgetting that trees get big! And sometimes they get big a whole lot faster than we expect.

Before you dig

Before digging the hole, call the utility companies to check for underground cables. Oh, the bill you'll get if you cut a fiber optic line!

In addition, don't plant large-growing trees such as silver maple or cottonwood within twenty feet of a drain field or septic tank.

Shrub roots will not damage the foundation of a house, but a vigorous large tree, such as a cottonwood or silver maple, planted closer than fifteen feet to the house may cause future headache.

Watch for low spots

Avoid planting trees in spots where the soil stays saturated to the point of shininess for several days following a rain, or develops a white crust after the soil has dried. Even the slightest depression in the yard can produce stagnant soil. Grass may thrive in wet areas, but trees will not.

In a damp spot, Flame willow can work as a large shrub. A new option for wet soils could be the Prairie Horizon alder. Black ash were once ideal, but are now not suggested due to the emerald ash borer.

Planting where traffic once trod

Trees struggle where the soil has been compacted by traffic or machinery. The more difficult the digging, the more poorly a tree will grow. If you cannot penetrate the soil with a spade, it is certain that the tree will not easily penetrate the soil with its roots.

Where soil is packed, it is beneficial to bring in a backhoe and loosen the soil up to two feet deep and as wide as you can reasonably go.

Planting on former industrial land or farmland

Although the level of chemicals applied to farm fields today is a fraction of what it once was, fields are sometimes treated with chemicals which linger in the soil and can stunt or kill young trees planted there. On rare occasions, an entire new development has been cursed with toxic soil.

Land near a former filling station or farm shop can be saturated with motor oil and other chemicals toxic to trees.

If grass doesn't grow on a spot which has plenty of sunshine, don't expect a tree to grow there either.

Memorial trees

When we lose a loved one, or when we want to commemorate a birth or some other life event, we sometimes plant a tree. The impulse is noble.

But please remember: memorials are times to choose only the most dependable trees and make sure they are in a location which ensures their survival. A dead memorial tree is doubly sad.

Planting on the shoulders of ditches

Many people in the country are tempted to plant a row of trees right on the yard side of the road ditch. However, this "shoulder" of the ditch usually consists of clay and other poor soil excavated from the depths of the ditch. It has been packed hard by heavy machinery. Often, trees planted on the shoulders of the ditch simply do not put on much growth.

Again, it is not difficult to tell if a tree will do well in such a location: If the digging is easy, the tree will do fine. If the digging is difficult and you run into lots of hard-packed clay, the tree will struggle as surely as you struggle to dig the hole.

There is one plant which simply loves to grow on the shoulder of ditches: asparagus. Put a patch there and enjoy it for decades. Plant a big enough patch so larcenous neighbors and UPS drivers can help themselves without impacting your supply.

Planting where other trees once grew

There is nothing wrong with planting trees in the exact same spot where a former tree existed. However, make sure you do not plant the new tree in raw sawdust produced by grinding the stump of the old tree. Raw sawdust consumes nitrogen as it decays, and your new tree can suffer nitrogen deficiency and turn yellow. It is best to have the sawdust removed after the stump is ground.

Planting where there once was an old evergreen

Despite folk tales to the contrary, there is no evidence that the soil where an evergreen formerly existed is permanently damaged.

The ground beneath existing old evergreens is quite sterile, but not due to the effects of fallen needles on the soil.

Evergreen roots grow near the surface and suck up moisture and nutrients. The trees themselves create deep shade. The combination of the two makes it nearly impossible for anything to grow under an existing large evergreen.

When the evergreen is removed, however, it leaves no permanent and lasting effects on the soil.

Black walnut

The roots of black walnut, a tree once native in our area but now quite rare, deposit a chemical in the soil which makes the growing of other plants difficult for up to five years following the removal of the tree. Most black walnut on the northern prairie do not grow large enough to cause much of a problem, however.

Planting on the north side

The north foundation of a house, particularly if it is shaded by big trees, is a difficult place to grow plants, especially if the ground is wet. Hydrangea and alpine currant are the best shrubs for a shady north side. Hosta, astilbe, bleeding heart and lamium are the best perennials, and impatiens are the most useful annuals for a shady north side.

All plants which thrive on the north side prefer well-drained soil. You cannot go wrong using plenty of peat on the north side. Hydrangea thrive in peat, and all other plants will appreciate the good drainage. If we have a rainy, moist spell, the peat will keep the roots of plants on the north side from rotting.

Planting under older trees

The soil underneath older spruce trees, willow trees and silver maple trees is usually so shaded and filled with fibrous, hairy roots that it is difficult to get shrubs, annuals or perennials to grow there.

The best way to plant color underneath such trees is to use large pots and fill them with annuals—impatiens in particular.

Only the toughest plants, namely lamium and snow-on-the-mountain, grow reasonably well in deep shade beneath trees.

Consistent irrigation of the entire area can allow plants like hosta to flourish in such areas under trees, including evergreens. If you only water a small area, tree roots will zoom in to rob the moisture.

What does "full sun" mean?

When a plant needs full sun, it means *sun all day*. The east side of a house is not considered full sun, nor is the west side, despite the heat later in the day. Roses, for example, do best in full sun. They will not perform as well next to the east or west sides of the house.

Once you are ten to fifteen feet away from the house, the effect of the house on the sunshine a plant receives is minimal. The only consideration when farther away from the house is possible shade from surrounding large trees.

Consider the arc of the sun's path through the sky in summer. The sun rises in the northeast and sets in the northwest. That means that the north side of the house, if the sun is not blocked by trees or buildings, can receive many hours of sunshine, perhaps one-third of a day's worth.

However, a north side of a house in a deeply wooded area receives almost no direct sunshine. Select plants accordingly.

Sunlight is strongest between 11 a.m. and 4 p.m., so an hour of sun during those times is worth more than an hour at other times of day.

Most plants in our area thrive in the full sun

If plants made for the sun are planted in too much shade, they might survive, but will likely become leggy and weak. This holds true for most shrubs, trees, annuals and perennials.

Vegetable gardens are best planted in full sun. Full sun is required for fruit to ripen. And full sun, as well as the breezes of open spaces, cuts down on disease.

In fact, any plant that is used for food requires sunshine—except for mushrooms.

Where the wind blows

The northern prairie is one of the windiest places on earth. The summer winds are not a problem for most plants which grow here. However, tender plants straight out of a greenhouse can suffer, particularly if they are planted in a spot where the wind whips and whirls, such as the corner of the house. Winds accelerate around the corner of a house, and can twist the more tender plants right off at the base.

Consider the wind conditions before planting tender plants. Fast-growing, taller annuals and perennials are the most vulnerable to high winds, as are weak-stemmed plants such as tuberous begonias. Ferns and bleeding heart—some of the succulent, tender plants best suited for deep shade—also require the shelter from the wind that a shady area usually provides.

New transplants from the greenhouse sometimes lack the strength to withstand spring winds. It is important to purchase stocky, firm plants.

Growing garden seeds indoors often results in leggy, weak stalks due to too much warmth and too little wind. To harden off your plants for the garden, slow their growth and strengthen stems by using a small fan to keep your seedlings cool, particularly from sunrise until about 9 a.m. By mid-morning, most garden plants quit growing for the day. A small fan can create enough air movement to keep plants cool and strong, but that air movement has to start at sunrise.

The wind and the willows

Willow are notorious for dropping branches in windstorms. Silver maple and cottonwood are not far behind. But even the mighty bur oak can cover the yard with twigs during a summer thunderstorm.

Proper pruning (see Chapter 9) is important to avoid the loss of large limbs on shade trees to wind, or the worst-case scenario: a tree which splits in half.

However, the loss of small branches is harmless to the tree.

Plant trees which tend to lose branches in a spot where they will be protected from the north and west winds. Weeping willow are a messy tree, but they are too beautiful to give up on altogether just because they drop branches in the wind.

Today's mowers are so strong that you can just grind up fallen branches smaller than your thumb.

Plant for winter interest

Here are the best trees and shrubs to shorten the winter in years to come:

•Spruce and pine are a comfort in the winter. Scotch pine especially, with its orange bark and needles which whisper in the winter wind, can add memorable moments to the cold months.

•Willow, in particular Flame Willow, displays golden, even orange bark color which, in mass, can be seen over a mile away. The color seems to get more intense as spring approaches. One planted in the far corner of the yard, where the evening sun catches the branches in early spring, can brighten one's day in otherwise-grim March.

•Red Splendor Flowering Crab were given their name, not due to red bloom color (the blooms are pink), but due to the spectacular display of red berries in November and December. Other flowering crabs drop their berries, but the Red Splendor does not. Although the berry color dulls as January progresses, the cedar waxwings, even grouse, as well as other birds, will feast on them until they are gone.

•Red twig dogwood are a winter treat. To keep the branching bright red, frequently cut back the shrub close to the ground. The new shoots will be brighter in color and can add to indoor bouquets, or arrangements for the doorstep during winter.

•White birch are famous for their chalky white bark. Equally beautiful are the bronze outer branches of the birch tree.

•Ornamental grasses should be left to stand all winter. The grass stalks obligingly hold their seeds until spring arrives, and rustle in the wind as you walk by.

•Hydrangea blooms can be left on all winter to add interest. Sometimes they will maintain a little pink or green tint as they dry.

Plant trees for winter interest in your thirties and forties, even if you really don't see the point. As you grow older and appreciate the little things in life more—like the rustling of pine needles—you will thank your younger self.

CHAPTER 4

Soils and Fertilizer

This is the most important chapter of the book. If you take the advice in this chapter, the plants in your yard will be vigorous and healthy.

The information here is simplified, so much so that it may make scientists wince. But by making things simple, we increase the odds of people actually acting on this information. A scientifically perfect solution which sits on the shelf does nobody any good!

SOILS

The situation in our area

Soils on the northern prairie are predominantly alkaline. Most soils, with the exception of sand ridges, are finely textured and heavy. Almost all of our soils lack enough organic matter to allow roots to grow to their full potential.

The soils of the Upper Great Plains are very unlike soils in the more populated regions of our country. Advice on soil matters which work for 95% of our population is not advice for us.

The concept of pH, oversimplified

A little science is now in order:

Soil pH is measured with a scale developed by chemists: A pH of 7.0 is neutral. Below 7.0 is acid. Above 7.0 is alkaline.

Soil pH controls the availability of nutrients to the root. A high pH chemically locks up iron and other nutrients, preventing absorption by the plant.

Almost all trees and shrubs thrive in a pH of 6.2 or lower. As pH rises from 6.2, some trees struggle. Over 7.2, some trees such as apples and maple will show *chlorosis,* or iron deficiency.

Our soils are mostly just above 7, and in some areas of the northern prairie the pH can reach 8, which is extremely alkaline.

Every tree which grows in our area, even if it can endure pH levels of 7.0 or slightly higher, can benefit from a lower pH achieved through fertilization or soil amendment.

Over time, due to the alkalinity of our water, the pH of lower pH soils brought in from elsewhere tends to slowly rise. Therefore, constant applications of a mild acidifying fertilizer are *always* beneficial!

Organic matter

Both the heavy soils of the northern prairie and the sandy soils found on ridges and ancient beaches are sorely lacking in a vital ingredient: organic matter.

Organic matter is nothing more than decomposed plants. Soils with adequate organic matter contain millions of tiny air pockets which provide the root necessary oxygen.

Organic matter also loosens the soil so roots do not have to work so hard to penetrate outward from the plant. Most importantly, organic matter holds *just the right amount* of water near the roots so they can take what they need, but are neither drowned nor dried out.

Compost

Organic matter added to soil is often referred to as *compost*. Compost is a magic word to many people, and is a big priority on national gardening shows. Creating compost ("composting") is a favorite way for city people to feel they are protecting the environment by recycling their potato peels.

Compost is merely organic matter such as grass clippings, leaves, or vegetable peelings put in a pile and allowed to rot. By piling the raw waste deeply and adding moisture, the organic matter will decompose enough to become usable in the garden within a couple of years.

Many cities and towns have a compost heap made up of the decayed remains of leaves collected over the years, which they often give away for free. If it is available, it is usually good stuff. However, city compost can be high in salts. Watch for white stains on the soil after watering. Salts can be leached out of compost with heavy, sustained watering *with good drainage.*

Sometimes grass clippings put in a compost heap can be contaminated with broadleaf herbicides, which linger and can hurt annuals flowers and vegetables down the road.

Peat

Fortunately for those of us on the northern prairie, an elegant solution to many of our soil problems lies to the north and east, or sometimes in bogs in the back corner of our farm. Minnesota contains hundreds of thousands of acres of peat. Just to the north, Canada has tens of millions of acres more.

How does peat help?

•The pH level of peat is usually in the range of 5.9-6.2. Adding it will lower the pH slightly, which helps free up nutrients.

•Peat aerates heavy soil, thus invigorating the root, which can otherwise be water-logged, or even drown.

•In light, sandy soils, peat retains the correct amount of moisture around the root.

•Adding peat atop existing annual flower and vegetable gardens will increase drainage.

•Adding peat before planting perennials will raise the soil level enough to prevent root rot in the event of a wet, soggy winter.

Peat is nothing more than decomposed plant matter. It *is* compost, but peat has rotted for centuries, not years. It is a nascent form of coal, which eventually produces diamonds. Peat used in the garden produces satisfaction and beauty much more quickly than if you wait for the diamonds.

Peat moss is a different animal than our local peat. It consists of *sphagnum moss*. It is brown, and can be very dry and fibrous. Sphagnum peat is imported from other areas of the country, much of it from central Wisconsin. Sphagnum is the type of peat which large discount chains and urban garden centers tend to sell as peat. It is not decomposed to the extent of our local peat. It is decidedly inferior.

Sedge peat is the technical name for peat found in the swamps of northern Minnesota. It contains cattail and reed remains rotted for hundreds, probably thousands of years. Sedge peat retains water longer than sphagnum peat, is more finely textured, and is dark brown when dry, almost black when wet.

Not all sedge peat is good peat. It should be light and fluffy, not muck. It should be brownish when dry, black only when wet—and never gray.

In the rest of the country, *sphagnum* peat moss is preferred, possibly because most *sedge* peat found outside northern Minnesota is *too* decomposed. It can harden the soil rather than soften it. But in our area, sedge peat is so ideal that it can be used pure, or nearly so.

Indeed, professional landscapers across the nation are becoming aware of the superiority of northern Minnesota peat and are ordering it by the semi-load for use on golf courses as remote as California.

If Californians are ordering peat from northern Minnesota, certainly we should avail ourselves of this treasure.

How much peat should be used?

The use of good peat should only be limited by supply and budget. We spread six inches of it atop our flower beds each year. We use it pure in flower pots. This goes against advice from academics, most of whom have never had the pleasure of watching plants explode with growth in our northern sedge peat.

Peat is a joy to work with. A layer of peat on top of flower beds and around shrubs makes weeding a breeze. If you weed just as the weeds (which are few in peat, although there always will be some), germinate, you can simply run your hands through the peat and kill the little weeds before they are visible.

Does peat dry out plants?

In short, yes. However, local peat causes plants to dry out in just the right way. Sphagnum peat dries out too quickly. Our clay-like field soils dry out too slowly. Local sedge peat dries out at healthy intervals.

Some cautions

•Filling a hole for a new tree entirely with peat is a mistake, as the roots will enjoy the peat so much they will grow in circles just to stay in the stuff. The tree will not anchor properly, and will also dry out too quickly. The proper approach is to dig a much larger hole than necessary, and use a maximum of 50% peat to fill in around the roots. The tree will appreciate the head start, but will also send new roots out beyond the confines of the hole.

•Harrowing a thin layer of peat into the existing soil over the entire yard before planting grass will make for a healthier lawn. However, seeding a lawn on pure peat will make the yard so soft that it will track easily later, and not just when the propane truck backs in.

If I use peat, must I still fertilize?

Oddly, peat has almost no nutrients. It is simply the best *growing medium* for roots. So yes, fertilizing following the directions below remains a must.

Manure

Manure is rich in nutrients, particularly nitrogen. The more recent the manure, the higher the nitrogen levels. Fresh manure will burn the roots of plants.

Manure should be rotted to the point where it is nearly indistinguishable from black, loamy soil before use on the garden. It should have no smell. Ten-year-old manure is safe, any less is a risk. Also, remember that rotted manure is nearly *always* full of weed seeds!

Horse manure is higher in nitrogen than other manures, and should be fully decomposed before use in the yard or garden. Some people swear sheep manure is better than cow manure, but for no proven scientific reason.

Too much nitrogen of any sort, including that provided by manure, can result in lots of green growth but stunted flowering and fruiting. Indeed, apple trees planted in a former barn yard have been known to refuse to bear for ten years or more. They simply grow too fast to produce fruit. Potatoes can rot in high nitrogen, and tomatoes can vine without fruiting.

Due to the nitrogen levels of manure, moderation is far more important in the use of manure than it is in the use of peat. It is better to mix old manure with peat than to use manure pure.

Tilling the soil

Especially in heavy soils, it is not a good idea to till the ground when it is wet enough to form big clumps, no matter how eager you are to get out into the garden in the spring. Clumps formed when the soil is wet take a long time to break down, particularly in mucky clay soils. Tilling the ground when it is wet enough to form clumps is actually bad for the structure of the soil, as it reduces the number of necessary air pockets in the heavy soil. It can take the soil years to recover its "tilth" and "friability," (two lovely terms we should throw around more often).

Planting where the soil has been packed hard

If you are attempting to plant where the soil has been compacted by years of vehicle traffic, it is best to loosen the soil to a deep level before tilling. Compacted soil is virtually impossible to work with a spade, and breaking it up may not be easy for the homeowner.

If the soil is compacted, it would pay to have a backhoe come in to break up a good-sized area to two or three feet deep before attempting to plant trees or shrubs.

If you were lucky enough to get lighter, lower pH soil hauled in to your yard from outside the area, keep in mind that lower pH is not permanent: our water is alkaline as well, and tends to raise the pH over the years. For that reason, even better soils will benefit from fertilizers which lower the pH.

FERTILIZER

A primer on plant nutrition

There are two types of growth in plants: *vegetative growth*—the green tender growth which happens early in the plant's life—and *reproductive growth*, involving blooms, seeds and fruit, which occurs later in the life cycle.

Vegetative growth is fast and tender. *Reproductive growth* is slow and solid.

In annuals, the complete cycle from vegetative to reproductive growth happens in one season. In perennials, the cycle happens each season, but year after year. In trees and shrubs, the cycle plays out over the life of the plant.

Nitrogen encourages vegetative growth, and *phosphorus* nurtures reproductive growth. The two elements must be in balance for a plant to be well-rounded and healthy.

What do those numbers on fertilizer packages mean?

Fertilizers are usually labeled with three numbers, such as 8-15-10.

The above hypothetical fertilizer contains 8% nitrogen, 15% phosphate and 10% potash (alternatively called potassium). The remaining 66% of the fertilizer is inert matter designed to help spread the nutrients evenly to avoid the burning which can occur when a high concentration of fertilizer lands in one spot.

The three-number formula gives the false impression that the three elements act in a similar fashion. They do not.

Nitrogen

Of the three elements, the first, nitrogen, is the most needed, the most effective, the most volatile, and the most dangerous if applied in excess. Farm fertilizers, such as urea, with high nitrogen numbers *must not be used in the yard.* They will burn the plants.

Nitrogen spread on the soil surface and watered in penetrates the soil quickly and can give the plant a quick boost, visible in days.

Nitrogen is very soluble, so is effectively administered by water-soluble fertilizers.

Phosphorous (or phosphate)

Phosphorous, the middle number in the fertilizer analysis, helps plants mature and produce flowers and fruit. Phosphate fertilizers with a big middle number are sold as "bloom boosters."

However, phosphate *does not* work its way down through the soil very well. To do its best work, phosphate must be mixed with the soil before planting. Even then, it takes time for phosphate to become chemically available to the root.

Superphosphate is a form of phosphate which has been treated to be more immediately available to the plant. It does not flow down any better than phosphate's other forms, so it also should be mixed with the soil before planting.

Unlike nitrogen, the phosphate in water-soluble fertilizers tends to filter out on the top layer of soil.

Bone meal is a natural form of phosphate, and is quite mild. Like other forms of phosphate, bone meal is best tilled into the soil before planting, particularly in perennial beds. If you merely sprinkle bone meal on the surface around existing plants, the phosphate will likely never reach the root.

Luckily, phosphate, once tilled into the soil where the roots can get at it, doesn't disappear. Repeat applications are not needed.

What if you do keep putting on small amounts of phosphate in the form of a 10-10-10 fertilizer each spring?

Fortunately, the amount of phosphate needed to *hurt* a plant is very high. Unlike nitrogen, there is almost no risk of hurting plants by giving them too much phosphate in the form of a garden fertilizer. The plant grabs what it needs and leaves the rest.

But do not go hog wild and dump on mounds of phosphate fertilizer, particularly in pots, where it can become toxic more quickly than the ground.

Minnesota restricts the application of phosphate to lawns out of concern for run-off into lakes, which can cause an explosion of algae growth.

Fortunately, the amount of phosphate applied to the vegetable and flower garden, if used according to directions, is negligible compared to the amounts once used on lawns. If the phosphate is mixed in deeply, as it should be, run-off should be minimal or non-existent.

Potassium (potash)

Potassium, the third number in the fertilizer analysis, is essential for the development of roots and stems. It is seldom missing from our existing soil. If you grow plants in pure organic matter, such as peat, adding potassium is a good idea, but sufficient potassium exists in all balanced fertilizers, such as 10-10-10, to do the job.

Micro-nutrients

Other elements such as iron, calcium and magnesium are essential to plants but are usually present in the soil. If plants suffer from a deficiency of micro-nutrients, lowering the pH is usually all that is needed to free up the nutrients which already exist in the soil.

Fertilizer confusion

Garden fertilizer companies prefer to keep the public confused enough to think that they need to buy a separate form of fertilizer for every type of plant in the garden. In fact, gardeners can usually get by using a simple, balanced garden fertilizer such as 10-10-10 for nearly everything. Such a mild and balanced fertilizer is the safest and most economical way to go.

Do not be deceived: there are no magical formulas for any one particular plant. Inexpensive general-purpose garden fertilizers help everything.

So what is one to do?

There are two fertilizers which cover almost every plant's needs in yards in our area.

First, there is 10-10-10 (or 8-10-8, or 12-10-12, or any set of three numbers which are balanced and below 20) which you can find in any general store, preferably for cheap. 10-10-10 is best applied and tilled into flower beds, vegetable gardens and berry patches *before* planting. Tilling the fertilizer in increases the odds that the last two elements, phosphate and potash, will reach the roots. Fall fertilizing, followed by tilling, seems to work even better than early spring application.

The addition of peat should always be accompanied by the application of 10-10-10 fertilizer.

Additional yearly applications of 10-10-10 are beneficial to everything. However, to give plants a boost later in the season and later in their lives, there is a more efficient fertilizer which is *not* as generally available, but should be. Indeed, if we had only this fertilizer to use, things would be just fine:

The miracle fertilizer for our area

Ammonium sulfate is commonly labeled 20-0-0. However, when the fertilizer formula is extended to include a fourth ingredient, sulfur, the result is 20-0-0-20, which shows that the bag contains 20% sulfur, the vital ingredient in a fertilizer which produces spectacular results.

Ammonium sulfate is too mild for efficient use on farm fields. However, farmers mix ammonium sulfate with other chemical sprays to hasten the effect. Therefore, ammonium sulfate is not only available at the garden center in five pound bags, but is stocked by many farm supply stores in very affordable 50 lb. bags.

You will hear nothing of ammonium sulfate in books and television shows aimed at a national audience, as soils in most of the country require *lime* to raise pH rather than *sulfur* to lower the pH.

Ammonium sulfate comes in granular form, and can also be used mixed with water in its water soluble form. One great advantage to ammonium sulfate: it can be spread on the top of the soil and will not lose potency if it sits there awhile before a rain, or before it is watered in.

Ammonium sulfate is ideal for lawns. It does not contain phosphate, so one can apply it without worry about polluting the lakes. The nitrogen gives the grass an immediate boost, while the sulfur lowers the pH to make other nutrients available.

But the real value of ammonium sulfate for the gardener is to boost every plant in the garden after planting. A dose of ammonium sulfate watered in can change the entire cast of a yard within a week. If young plant leaves are slightly yellow, whether from lack of nitrogen or from iron deficiency caused by high pH, ammonium sulfate will bring back a healthy dark green.

Although ammonium sulfate lacks phosphate and potassium, the sulfur acts to make those two elements, which are likely present in the soil, more accessible to plant roots.

One-quarter cup of ammonium sulfate should be added to every new tree or shrub. Apply ammonium sulfate to the top of the soil after planting. Do not pour ammonium sulfate in the hole during planting, as it may burn the roots.

Yes, it is possible to overdo ammonium sulfate. However, ammonium sulfate is milder than other forms of nitrogen, so it is likely you will not burn your plants by accident.

Make sure the bag you buy is ammonium sulfate, *not* ammonium *nitrate*, nor *aluminum* sulfate, which you will also find on the market.

Spread ammonium sulfate at the rate prescribed on the bag, which amounts to covering the ground with granules at about the rate you would put pepper on an egg.

Fertilizer summary

Two fertilizers are all you need: The all-purpose 10-10-10 should be used for tilling in to the soil before planting, particularly if you add peat, which can benefit from an addition of the last two elements, phosphate and potash.

However, *ammonium sulfate* should be used to give a boost to plants in late June, and it can be used on trees and shrubs to give a boost at any time. It also is ideal for lawns.

Many books say do not fertilize trees or shrubs late in the season in order to prevent late growth which may not withstand the winter.

In heavy soils, however, the ammonium sulfate moves more slowly through the soil down to the root. The moderate nature of ammonium sulfate makes it unlikely that it will cause a burst of late growth. Spread ammonium sulfate when you feel like it. Do it once per year and your yard will be healthier for it.

Fertilizer spikes

Fertilizer spikes are simply regular garden fertilizer pressed into sticks, which the gardener then presses into the ground. Spikes work, but they are not necessary or economical. You had just as well purchase granular fertilizer, spread it on the surface and water it in. If you are in a hurry to get fertilizer to a tree's roots, make a several holes around the tree with a crowbar, just within the perimeter of the branches, and pour moderate amounts of fertilizer (measured in teaspoons) in each hole.

Grass robs nutrients

Before fertilizing, make sure nothing else is robbing the plants of nutrients. Is the grass kept a healthy distance away from all young trees and shrubs? Grass steals nutrients before they reach the roots of trees or shrubs. Get rid of grass around your trees and shrubs with glyphosate (Roundup) to make certain that the grass doesn't consume the fertilizer before it gets to the roots that need it.

Where to spread the fertilizer

Fertilizing the entire area within the perimeter the branches is the best way to ensure that fertilizer gets into the system of the tree. Fertilizing right near the trunks of older trees misses most of the roots. The most vital roots are found beneath the outer perimeter of the branching.

Plants with special fertilizer needs in our area

Sugar maple can become a sickly yellow (chlorotic) in alkaline soils, and may even die. *Silver maple* will likely survive, but the leaves can turn yellow. Both trees will benefit from ammonium sulfate, which will release the iron in the soil. The nuclear option is to add *iron chelate*, a treated (but expensive) form of iron which is immediately available to the roots.

Because trees develop such large root systems it is unlikely that fertilizer will provide a permanent solution to iron deficiency.

Hydrangea prefer acid soils. Because they are a shrub and have relatively small root systems, it is a good idea to dig out some of the existing soil and replace it with peat, which is naturally acid, before planting. After planting, regular treatments of an acidifying fertilizer such as ammonium sulfate will make for a more vigorous plant. *Blue hydrangea will not be blue in our area, and they are not hardy anyway.*

All *evergreens* can benefit from ammonium sulfate or other acidifying fertilizers. Evergreens are native in areas with acid soils. As one moves east across Minnesota away from prairie, evergreens begin to appear in the wild, a sure sign that the soil is becoming more acid.

Although most evergreens are not native to the northern prairie, many varieties can grow healthily there. They will be even more healthy if given regular doses of ammonium sulfate.

CHAPTER 5

Effective Watering

The ability to water plants properly requires a strong character. In that regard, your author is a failed waterer and is giving advice from a position of complete hypocrisy.

•Watering requires patience. Water soaks in slowly. Rushing the process ruins the result.

•Watering requires vigilance. Plants need water at irregular intervals, and only then. You must frequently check the soil for moisture and only water when the topsoil has begun to dry out.

•Watering requires depth. To promote deep roots, the water must soak through. For water to soak through, it must be administered slowly. Letting a hose run at a slow trickle for hours is truly effective.

•Watering overhead requires that you get up early in the morning. Evening overhead watering leaves droplets on the leaves of plants which promote disease. It is not fussy when you water with the trickle method, or with soaker hoses.

•Watering requires empathy. Understanding the needs of plant roots and working to fulfill them is essential to becoming a good waterer.

•Watering requires good equipment. Cheap hoses, flimsy nozzles, plastic sprinkler heads will come back to haunt the bargain hunter sooner rather than later. Expense up front pays rewards for years.

What do roots need?

Roots prefer to have water occasionally flow through to moisten their surroundings. To function, most roots also need air back in within minutes of the water gurgling past.

The roots of some trees, like those of a cottonwood along a river, can withstand a week or two of saturation during a summer wet spell. More sensitive roots of maple, birch, or a raspberry plant, will drown after a few hours without air, killing the plant above.

How often do I need to water?

It is impossible to set a specific interval of time between waterings. To the question, "How often do I need to water?" there is no answer other than "water when needed." That means waiting until the soil surface has started to dry out.

In general, it is better to water deeply and less often.

Is there such a thing as too much water?

In heavy soils, heavy watering can do more harm than good. Too much water can kill the plant in a matter of days by saturating the soil and depriving the roots of oxygen.

In the light soils one finds on the sand and gravel ridge shorelines of old Lake Agassiz, gardeners need not worry about overwatering. Water sinks right past the roots. In sandy soils, watering every day may not be necessary, but it will do no harm.

How do I know when plants need water?

The basic rule: Water *only* when the plant needs it. A plant needs water if the soil around the plant is dry to the touch about a quarter-of-an-inch below the surface. If the surface of the soil is still visibly wet, pouring on more water is not only unnecessary, but it can harm the plant.

How not to water…

It is impossible to water a plant properly by holding one's thumb over the end of the hose and waving the stream of water back and forth. Your thumb will fall off before you do the plant or lawn any good.

Wagging the hose towards the plant in hopes that the water will sink down faster is akin to shoving the remote control towards the TV in hopes that the rays will concentrate and finally change the channel.

How to test your watering effectiveness…

To check the thoroughness of your watering, dig down in the soil several inches after you are finished. See how deeply the water has penetrated. Even though the surface of the soil might look slimy and wet after a few minutes of standing with one's thumb over the end of the hose, the water has likely penetrated no more than a half-an-inch below the surface.

Shallow watering of lawns encourages roots to grow towards the surface, where they become dependent upon the frequent watering and are less able to withstand drought or a weekend of neglect.

The best watering happens when a hose is left on at a slow trickle next to a tree, shrub, or flower bed, for several hours, and then moved to the next tree.

Are sprinklers a good option?

Sprinklers, if used properly, are a good way to water thoroughly and deeply. They are really the only way to water a lawn.

Many sprinkler systems are timed to turn on every day or night for only a short time. A healthier practice would be to turn on the sprinkler for several hours, and no more than two times per week. Dig down to see how deeply the water has penetrated, or set out a coffee can to measure and don't turn the sprinkler off until at least an inch has accumulated. It will take hours.

When is the best time of day to water?

When one waters *beneath* all of the foliage of plants, shrubs and trees, it doesn't really matter what time of day you water. But if one waters *overhead*, with a sprinkler, or with a hose—and it is impossible to avoid wetting the foliage—it is best to water early in the morning. Watering plants overhead at sundown leaves droplets of water on foliage all night. Fungal diseases often require just that: a droplet of water sitting still for a number of hours.

Droplets on blooms and leaves in the hot afternoon sun can act as tiny magnifying glasses and burn holes in the plants, particularly tender petunia blossoms and impatiens leaves.

Should I spray a plant's foliage?

There is seldom any virtue in hosing down the foliage of a plant, unless one wishes to use water pressure as a natural way to spray worms and insects off of plants.

Some instructions for water-soluble fertilizers suggest spraying the foliage of plants and trees with fertilized water. This is not a good practice in our area. Although a few plants are able ingest a small amount of nutrients through their leaves, the better way to improve the health of the plant is to fertilize and water deeply around the roots.

Leave a depression to hold water around all plants

To make proper, deep watering possible, make sure *all* plants end up with a saucer-like depression around their base after planting. The saucer should be three inches deep. Maintain that depression for the first year or two of the plant's life. With a depression, water will run towards the base of the plant and sink down deeply. With a depression three inches in depth, stretching out two feet from the base of a newly planted tree, it is possible to water the tree thoroughly by merely filling the depression a couple of times, letting the water soak down in between.

In much of the country, it seems the fashion to pile mulch up around the trunk of trees. In light soils, the mulch is meant to preserve moisture.

Researchers at the University of Minnesota have found that the practice of hilling up soil around tree trunks can have disastrous long-term effects on the health of the tree trunk and root system.

Well-drained soil

Instructions for nearly every plant include the statement: "prefers well-drained soil." Very few plants can stand constant saturation, and almost no plants actually thrive in saturated soil.

To avoid constant saturation, add peat, compost or other organic matter before planting. Raised beds never suffer from lack of drainage.

As noted, peat does cause the soil to dry out more frequently. That is what plants love: frequent water infusions which pass through, leaving the soil moist, not saturated.

Watering potted plants

Potted plants need very frequent watering. Because pots are above the ground and subject to more heat and wind, their soil dries out quickly. There is little danger of saturation in pots, *unless* the container does not have drainage. A pot without drainage which fills up with water to near the surface of the soil will kill a plant within hours.

Always make sure your pots and planters have a drain hole. If you are unable to drill a hole in the container, put rocks in the bottom of the pot and be very careful that you do not water until the soil up top has dried.

A pot is well-drained when water flows out of the bottom of the pot before you finish pouring the water in the top. If you don't want the mess of water running all over your deck, use saucers, but make sure that water does not sit stagnant in the saucers for days on end.

It is best to pass over pots twice when watering, with a few minutes in between to allow the first watering to soak in. The first watering of a potted plant serves to swell the soil enough to make the second watering a few minutes later much more effective.

Most pots can stand to be watered every day or two. If pots stay wet for any longer than three or four days, the plants may suffer from the excess moisture. Containers which breathe, such as clay pots, will need more frequent watering than solid containers made of ceramic.

Most people use containers which are too small for the plants put in them. A trailing petunia will outgrow a ten-inch pot by mid-July. The plant will go into severe decline, even with frequent watering. Fourteen-inch baskets are best for trailing petunias, and will result in the plants thriving late into the fall if they are watered daily.

The ratio of foliage to soils makes a big difference in choosing how to water containers. In the spring when plants are small, care must be taken not to overwater. Later in the summer, when temperatures are high and the plants have filled out the pot, there is less risk of overwatering and it becomes more important not to let the plants wilt.

Should I water with water-soluble fertilizer?

Potted plants can stand a half-strength dose of water soluble fertilizer nearly every watering, or a full strength dose once per week.

For flower beds and for trees and shrubs, water soluble fertilizer is expensive and difficult to mix in large enough amounts. Better to buy granular fertilizer (ammonium sulfate), apply it according to the instructions, and water it in after application.

Watering trees and shrubs purchased bare root

Bare root trees and shrubs need a good watering right after planting—at least a few gallons per plant. The first watering packs the soil around the tree's roots better than you can do with your hands, and it eliminates large air pockets which will dry out sections of the root.

Do not put water in the hole before planting the tree, as some instructions indicate. It is a waste of water and makes for muddy planting.

If the season becomes quite dry, bare root trees and shrubs can *benefit* from water, but if planted properly, they should not *require* more water

51

to survive. Use the same test as for any other plant: Stick your finger down a half an inch. If the soil is dry, a thorough watering is in order.

In sandy soil, all plants, even those planted bare root, will need additional water during dry spells.

Watering trees and shrubs purchased in a pot

Trees and shrubs purchased in pots need watering *every day* until they are planted. A potted tree can die in a matter of hours if left to dry out. Root-bound potted plants from the big box stores, which people tend to buy because they look good right away and aren't that heavy, are dependent upon humans for a constant replenishment of water. They have been fertilized immoderately to promote a flush of green growth. That tender new growth will wilt within hours on a hot day without water.

Once in the ground, plants purchased in a pot require more frequent watering than those planted bare root. However, because the potted plant is now in the cooler ground means watering need not be daily. Test for moisture by inserting your finger into the root ball itself. *Even if the soil around the base of the tree is damp, the root ball may be dried out underneath due to the high concentration of roots.*

With plants long-established in a pot, one should break apart the root ball and pull the roots out from the plug at planting so they are established in the new soil where they are planted.

Breaking up an established root ball requires some violence and is not for the faint of heart. To loosen the roots of a container-grown arborvitae, for example, one must stomp on the root ball with great vigor and then pull the roots apart with the help of a screwdriver (Phillips or standard) or similar weapon.

In the rare instance where the purchased plant is *newly* potted, the very opposite is true: You must take care *not* to allow the root ball fall apart. Cut the pot off with a carpet knife and gently slide the ball of soil into the hole. Newly potted roses, as well as newly potted spruce and pine, will not survive if their root ball falls apart at planting.

Potted trees and shrubs should be watered as needed for up to two years after they are planted.

Taper off in fall

Most trees and shrubs finish growing by early September. A dry fall is beneficial to winter survival as late growth spurred by wet fall conditions is not as hardened before winter. Water shrubs and trees after Labor Day only if they are parched.

The lone exception to this rule are newly planted evergreens, which should be kept good and wet right up to freeze-up.

Do trees moved in with a tree spade require watering?

Oh boy, do they ever. The bigger the tree, the more roots were cut off by the spade, and the more water the tree needs as the roots struggle to regrow at the same time they support an inordinate amount of foliage above.

Tree-spaded larger trees should be watered frequently by leaving a hose running at a slow dribble for hours at a time into the crevice created by the spade.

Watering perennial and annual flower beds

In the heat of the summer, perennials and annuals can use frequent deep watering. Annuals in particular suffer if allowed to dry out completely. Water underneath if possible. Soaker hoses are ideal. If sprinklers must be used, water early in the morning. In hot weather, if you have used peat to lighten the soil, or you have sandy ground, you can water every morning without fear of overdoing it.

Watering practices are probably the number one difference between a flower bed looking great at the end of the summer or looking scraggly. When many annuals and perennials are allowed to wilt even once, they often look bedraggled for the rest of the season even after they've been watered. Wilting is stressful for plants, and can make them more susceptible to disease.

Watering vegetable gardens

To minimize disease, water vegetable gardens underneath the foliage. If that is not possible, and you must use a sprinkler, water early in the morning. Early watering means that the droplets of water left by the overhead watering will dry more quickly and won't be allowed to play host for fungal disease, particularly on tomatoes.

Watering lawns

A sprinkler system is best. It is better to set the sprinklers to run a couple of times per week for many hours than for a half-hour each night.

If you have young trees within the range of the sprinklers, make sure water does not sit in the depression around the tree for more than a few minutes after the sprinklers have quit. In general, avoid having young trees within the range of a sprinkler. If that is impossible, you may need to fill in the depression around the tree, taking care not to raise the soil level right against the trunk.

Grass, like all other plants, is best watered in the early morning for purposes of disease prevention.

Get good equipment

High quality brass sprinklers and nozzles, as well as heavy-duty, flexible hoses that do not kink are always worth the extra money.

To soften the stream of water when watering with a hose, a rain-nozzle should be used. The stream of water should not be violent enough to disrupt the soil or harm a plant's foliage. Save the high-pressure nozzle for the sidewalks.

A caution to farmers

It seems that no matter how many times you rinse out a chemical tank, enough residue remains to kill trees, shrubs and other plants if you use that tank to haul water. The use of agricultural equipment, sprays, and fertilizers has caused the heartbreaking loss of many yard plantings.

Is city water hard on plants?

Some people claim collected rainwater is better than water from a well. Others swear by water taken from a pond or river. Some think the water shouldn't be cold.

One thing is certain: city water can be very high in alkalinity. Collected rainwater is much better, especially for plants in pots. If your potted plants start turning yellow, add a few tablespoons of vinegar to each five-gallon pail of water to lower the pH. Citric acid accomplishes the same goal.

CHAPTER 6

Insects and Diseases

The first thing to remember about disease and insects on plants is that, in most cases, both can be ignored without long-term damage to the plant.

Insects and diseases seldom kill vigorous, healthy plants.

We tend to believe that for every ache and pain we suffer, there is a pill which will cure it. Some gardeners assume the same is true for plants: for every problem their plants suffer, there should be a spray which will take care of it.

Chemical companies understand this market, and have come up with a product for nearly every problem. For every leaf-spot, there is a spray. For every insect, there is an insecticide.

However, by the time gardeners discover the symptoms of the problem, whether the damage is caused by insects or disease, the problem has usually run its course. *A vast majority of the spraying done for insects or disease by home gardeners is unnecessary or wasted.*

There are, however, a few insect and disease problems which are potentially fatal to plants in our area. Other problems are unsightly and so easily treated that it is worthwhile to do so.

But first is the far more important and relevant matter of *prevention.*

PREVENTION

Preventing disease and insect problems

The spores and bacteria of plant diseases are present almost everywhere. So are the eggs of insects. One never will be completely rid of them. However, gardeners can prevent the *conditions* which encourage insects and disease.

Prevention is usually not difficult.

The importance of weeding

Keeping weeds down is a must in order to control insects and diseases. Not only do weeds steal nutrients and light from the good plants, thus weakening them, but weeds act as hosts for diseases and insects which then spread to the good plants.

Weeds also make the air stagnant around the base of shrubs and plants, increasing the likelihood that fungal disease will develop and spread.

A well-weeded garden goes a long way towards keeping insects and diseases at bay.

The importance of watering

Plants allowed to dry out enough to wilt are more susceptible to disease and insects, particularly annuals and vegetables. Proper watering is essential to the prevention of insects and disease.

Do not plant too closely

From tiny annuals and vegetables to large trees, plants which are planted too closely are more subject to disease. Not only does disease travel more easily from plant to plant, but tight plantings do not permit the air and sunshine to dry the dew off the leaves and needles in the morning.

Fungal diseases need moisture to multiply. In fact, they need a droplet of water to remain on a leaf or branch for a certain number of hours before they are able to reproduce their spores. Once they reproduce, the spores can multiply into the billions in very little time at all.

Where sunshine or wind dries the leaves or needles of trees early in the morning, disease is reduced.

Fall cleaning

Much can be done in the fall to prevent insect problems the next summer. Remove the dead plants from the vegetable and flower gardens before tilling.

Tilling the former vegetable garden and annual flower beds in late fall can expose insect eggs to the cold. Cleaning up all fallen apples before they rot will keep apple maggots from laying their eggs in the soil.

An exception: Perennial plants are best left standing to improve winter protection. Only peonies and iris should be cut back to reduce disease.

Rotate crops

Changing the location of the garden plot, or simply not planting the same thing in the same place year after year, can lessen insect and disease problems a great deal.

Note changes in sunshine

Many people plant tomatoes in the same place each year even though the shade created by nearby shrubs and trees has increased. Any decrease in sunshine and breeze will increase the chances of disease. Keep the vegetable garden in open sunshine, where the breezes blow.

Remove diseased plants

In our experience, plants which get completely overtaken by disease had other problems to begin with. Spraying addresses disease, but not the problems which originally allowed the disease to take hold. If a plant looks sick, it is best to pull it out. Quickly.

When it pays to spray

There are a few instances where it pays to spray as a matter of habit, even if one has not yet seen any symptoms of disease.

Roses are so prone to leaf disease that it is just as well to spray them every couple of weeks throughout the season with a fungicide, or an all-purpose rose spray. During most seasons in the north, we have found that our roses look better come August if we spray.

During bad disease years, if we do not spray the roses, they may lose all their foliage by late August and look just plain dead. Although they will likely come back the next spring, spraying can earn you a full month to six weeks of extra enjoyment out of your rose bushes per season. Consecutive years of leaf disease can slowly weaken the plant.

If your *tomatoes* have problems with blight year after year, it might be wise to spray them with a fungicide in June, even if there are no signs of blight. Once the blight starts, spraying will only stop it from advancing. It will not reverse the damage.

DISEASES

Common pestilences suffered by plants in our area

What follows is a list of troublesome diseases which frequently afflict trees and plants in our area. We start with the most dangerous, and proceed to those which merely annoy.

Fire blight

Fire blight attacks several forms of trees, especially those in the apple family. The affliction is called *fire blight* because it causes the leaves of the tree to turn a dark brown, as if burned by fire. The stem of the infected area turns tarry and black.

Fire blight is a bacterial infection which attacks the fresh, new growth of apple trees, flowering crab, mountain ash and cotoneaster. It can spread like wild-fire in moist conditions. It may merely damage the tips of the branches, or, in the worst case, can kill the tree. Fire blight is at its worst in late-June and early-July, when the growth on young trees is fresh, and when hot, moist conditions are common.

If one notices fire blight on a young tree, one should clip off the infected branch about four or five inches below where the infection is visible. *Disinfect the clippers in a solution of bleach or alcohol in between each cut, as the disease can be spread by the clippers.* Burn the clippings, or at least take them far away from any trees. Watch the tree over the next weeks for further evidence of infection, and take the same steps again. If a tree looks as if it is turning completely brown from fire blight, *pull it out.*

Fire blight prevention

Although fire blight is bacteria, there is some evidence that copper sulfate based fungicidal sprays such as the old-fashioned Bordeaux mix can prevent the disease if sprayed on the leaves and branches when the buds are just emerging in May. This is not a practical solution for the home gardener, as the timing must be exactly right.

Fire blight may be prevented in the same ways one can prevent other diseases: trees should be planted far enough apart. Fresh, young vertical growth in apple trees, known as *water sprouts,* should be pruned out as soon as they appear. The tree should be regularly pruned to thin the branches, which increases air flow.

Fire blight can kill trees, and has been particularly hard on mountain ash in recent years. Fire blight can be more of a problem after bark on the branches and trunk of young trees is damaged by hail. Hail-damaged trees of the apple family could benefit from the Bordeaux mix spray treatment.

Because older trees grow more slowly, the incidence and seriousness of fire blight tends to decrease as the tree becomes established.

Emerald ash borer

This pernicious insect has removed green ash from the list of trees useful in our area. Although at this writing in 2017, the emerald ash borer has not been found in most areas of the northern prairie, it is generally agreed that its arrival is imminent. That arrival, however, could happen months, years, or decades from now. Do not plant new ash trees, but also, do not preventatively cut down existing, healthy trees. We cannot predict how fast the insect will move, even once it arrives in our area.

Ash trees suffer from other maladies which cause people to think, erroneously, that the borer has arrived. The test: if your ash tree looks healthy, let it be; if it looks sick, rip it out.

At this time, there are no preventative measures worth taking. As the situation changes, it is important to respond only to *local* expertise, and to use remedies specifically endorsed by the extension services.

Dutch Elm disease

It appears that the American elm trees which have survived to this point are dying at a slower rate than when the disease first appeared in our area in the early 1970s. As for the treatment of existing old elm, it is expensive, but research indicates it may work.

In any case, it is important to saw down and get rid of dead elm. The dead trees host the beetle that spreads the virus.

Recently-introduced disease resistant elm varieties such as the Princeton are thus far doing well.

Leaf-drop on green ash early in the season

During some springs, a fungus called *anthracnose* attacks the tender young leaves on ash trees, and they may drop to the ground at alarming rates. The culprit is anthracnose, a fungus which can cause spots on the leaf. If that spot happens to be at the base of the leaf, or on the stem, the leaf will drop. The dropping of tender green ash leaves in May causes great alarm, and may inspire a few panicked front-page articles in area newspapers, but it does no long-term harm to the tree. There is nothing which can or should be done to prevent the problem.

Oak wilt

Oak wilt is a frightening disease which, according to scientists in the know, is not yet present in our area. It thrives where there are greater concentrations of red oak, and we have only a few amongst the more prevalent bur oak. If and when oak wilt disease arrives, and it is fully possible that it won't, you will hear about it in the news.

Even then, don't panic. It is very possible that news articles from southeastern Minnesota, where oak wilt is a problem, will filter north before the disease does.

Just in case, the biggest thing you can do to prevent the spread of the disease is *do not prune oak branches before July.*

Other known preventative measures (such as cutting the roots between trees) will probably kill more oak than they save, and should not be taken unless presence of the disease is confirmed beyond the shadow of a doubt by local authorities.

Powdery mildew

Powdery mildew affects the foliage of plants of the currant family including gooseberry, Red Lake currant, and ninebark, as well as alpine currant, a common ornamental shrub. Powdery mildew also affects roses, lilacs, tomatoes, phlox, monarda, zinnias, clematis and several other varieties. Mildew appears as a white powder on the leaves. The entire plant can eventually look gray.

Powdery mildew can be prevented by spraying a fungicide as soon as summer's high humidity hits, and before symptoms appear. Spraying a solution of baking soda (one tablespoon per gallon of water, with a drop of dish soap added to make the spray stick to the leaves) can help prevent powdery mildew by changing the pH of the leaf surface. Baking soda should only be relied upon as a preventative, not as a cure.

Powdery mildew is unsightly, but rarely inflicts long term damage on plants. It can cause the leaves of the currant family and of monarda to dry up and disappear altogether, although those plants will put on new leaves the next season. Powdery mildew thrives in rainy, humid weather, particularly when there are cool nights followed by hot days.

Prevent powdery mildew by spacing plants adequately, planting gardens in full sun, raking away leaves from beneath plants which have had the problem, and by avoiding overhead watering. If you just can't stand it, mark your calendar to spray the plants with fungicide next year *before* the powdery stuff appears.

Black knot

Black knot appears on chokecherries, including the ornamental Canadian Red Chokecherry, and less frequently on plums. It is ugly. The fungus develops into a black, tar-like growth on the branch. Eventually, the knot will weaken and kill the branch. Black knot is a particular problem on trees that have been damaged by hail.

Prune out all knots and even areas where the branch is beginning to swell in late winter. Trim four inches below the knot, as the fungus may have gone further than it appears. Watch for new swelling as spring proceeds, and trim out those swellings immediately.

Black knot spores spread from the older knot in spring. Although pruning out black knots is the best method, in severe cases, the branches of the tree can be sprayed with a lime sulfur fungicide after pruning and *before* the tree puts on leaves.

The best solution is not to plant Red Leaf Chokecherry.

Aster Yellows

Many annuals, some perennials, and several vegetable varieties are susceptible to aster yellows, for which there is no cure. Yes, asters get the disease, but the disease seems almost a worse problem on marigolds and petunias, if only because those varieties are planted more frequently.

Symptoms of aster yellows include: stunted blooms which emerge white; whitish-yellow and stunted leaves; leaves growing in tight, deformed bunches; spindly, yellowed stems. *When a plant is discovered with Aster Yellows, remove it immediately.*

Aster yellows is caused by a phytoplasma, a microorganism similar to bacteria, spread by leafhoppers, tiny insects which blow in from the south in the spring. If there are no leafhoppers, there will likely be no aster yellows.

Regular sprays of systemic insecticides on flowers early in the season may control leafhoppers, but in general, spraying to control leafhoppers is not practical for the home gardener. The best bet is to simply get rid of any plants infected with aster yellows, and hope for a better season next year. Some years aster yellows is a big problem, most years the disease does not appear at all.

Damping off

The problem of plants rotting at the base early in the season is called *damping off.* Cool, wet weather makes the problem worse. It affects mainly tuberous begonias, melons, and New Guinea impatiens.

Damping off causes the plant to snap off at the base and virtually disappear overnight. To prevent damping off, do not water susceptible plants until the soil is dry on the surface, particularly in cool weather early in the season. Do not plant melons before Memorial Day, particularly during a cool spring.

INSECTS

Aphids

Aphids are more a problem indoors than out. They are the scourge of greenhouse owners. Once a plant is in the ground outdoors, however, aphids seldom cause damage.

For your indoor plants, a systemic insecticide, preferably in granular form placed in the soil, will prevent most aphids.

Aphids attack fresh, new growth. They attack nearly every sort of tree, shrub, annual or vegetable. There are *thousands* of kinds of aphids, and

new ones appear each year. If a plant you purchase turns out to be covered with aphids, gently let the greenhouse owner know of the problem. Wash the aphids off the foliage with soapy water and you can plant the plant without further worry.

Aphids on large, established trees

Large, established trees can become completely infested with aphids. The aphids are usually not visible, but their droppings, called *honeydew,* a clear, syrupy liquid, can make a mess on cars. The same droppings make the leaves of large trees, in particular bur oak, look glossy. Subsequently, black, soot-like fungus will grow on the honeydew, producing the black soot which appears on the roofs of old cars which are parked in the woods.

It is not a good idea to spray the aphids. They will quickly come back, and whatever spray gets the aphids will get their natural enemies as well. Spraying large trees for aphids might well have the effect of making the aphid problem worse later on.

Aphids on young, newly-planted trees

On newly planted trees, aphids can do more damage than they do on established trees. Aphids can sometimes stunt the growth at the tips of the young tree. A good, stiff spray of water can remove the aphids, and systemic insecticides can do the job as well.

Honeysuckle aphid

The common honeysuckle, once prevalent in hedge rows and windbreaks, are no longer recommended for use in our area due to the arrival of the honeysuckle aphid. The aphid attacks the tips of the honeysuckle branches causing the formation of a grouping of fine, stunted branches called *witch's broom.* The witch's broom dies over winter. Cutting the honeysuckle back can allow it to regrow, but inevitably the aphid will return. The honeysuckle vine is not susceptible to the aphid.

Leaf warts on the leaves of maples, willows, hackberry

Leaf warts, or *leaf-gall,* as the problem is more properly called, are caused by tiny mites which damage the leaf while it is still in the bud stage. The warts grow like tumors on the leaves in response to the venomous bite of the mite, which happened long before. The warts do no long-term damage to the tree. There is nothing which can or should be done about this admittedly creepy problem.

Gall on branches of oak and ash

Mites can cause some oak and ash trees to form clusters of round little balls of a woody texture along their stems, or at the tips of the branches. This problem is called *gall*, and it is caused by mites in much the same way as mites cause leaf warts. There is nothing which can or should be done about this problem but to pick off the little round things within your reach.

Slugs

Slugs are snails without the shell. They love hosta, but also go after vegetables. They destroy the plant's foliage. Slugs are worse in smooth-textured soils such as the gumbo of the Red River Valley. They do not like sand, and they do not like crawling over rough mulches, egg shells or wood ash.

Commercially available slug bait is the easiest way to combat slugs. Make sure it is a type which specifically states that it is not harmful to pets. The most common active ingredient in these slug baits is iron phosphate, which is non-toxic and breaks down into fertilizer. The treatment is most effective if started early in the season, since slugs multiply exponentially throughout the summer.

Spider Mites

These tiny insects infect many trees and plants, but reserve their most pernicious damage for spruce, arborvitae, strawberries, and in hot, dry years, potentilla. If any of these plants start turning a dull color in the heat of the summer, tap a branch over a white 3x5 card. The mites will appear as red specks of dust crawling around on the card.

Conventional insecticides are not effective against spider mites. A "miticide" is necessary. However, a stiff spray of water once per week can wash mites off the plant and minimize the damage without sprays.

Cutworms

Nothing is more discouraging in the early season than to find your newly-planted vegetable plants toppled by cutworms. Cutworms are ugly fat grubs of a whitish color which are found curled up in the soil.

If cutworms are a problem, they can be kept away from the plant with milk cartons or tin cans placed around the stem.

Spotted Wing Drosophila

This relative of the fruit fly attacks a variety of soft fruit including cherries and strawberries, but will probably be most reviled for its attack on raspberries. Infected fruit will have a soft spot, and if you look closely you might find tiny white larvae. Since it attacks just as the fruit is getting ripe, it seems unwise to spray insecticides. The best strategy is to eat or process the fruit quickly without looking too closely at it.

As new diseases arise, and if new insects arrive

University extension services are usually on top of the most recent disease and insect issues, and new ones arrive all the time. Do not hesitate to call them, as they rely on home gardeners to give them a picture of what the disease is doing out in the field.

CHAPTER 7

Controlling Weeds

As a child, the most dreaded task in the garden was weeding. However, many gardeners learn to love pulling weeds. My grandfather once left intensive care after a heart attack and was in the garden weeding within one hour. Weeding was his best medication.

What is a weed?

A weed is a plant growing where it does more harm than good. Any plant can become a weed. Weeds do harm by choking out desired plants.

Many desirable and beautiful plants produce seeds by the million which become next year's weeds. Amaranthus are a prime example. Buckthorn, once sold as a cultivated tree, have become a weed and are taking over our woods.

Kill weeds when they are young

The difficulty of weeding increases exponentially the longer you delay. If you begin with a well-tilled garden, weeding can be as simple as disturbing the soil once it has formed a crust following a rain. Such disruption will kill the tiny, barely visible weeds and make it more difficult for others to germinate.

Disturbing the soil can be done very quickly, with long sweeps of a hoe. Once the weeds become visible, killing them becomes a much larger task.

Another reason to add peat

A layer of well-ground peat spread on the surface of the garden makes weeding a breeze. The more organic matter in the soil, the easier it is to weed. An exception to this rule is manure: old manure piles contain weed seeds galore.

Remove weeds by the root

Pulling the top of a weed off and leaving the root does little good. The weed will return. Weeds must be removed by the root. Weeding early, before the roots go deep, is of utmost importance. Pulling up weeds once they are large can disturb your desirable plants.

Use a sharp hoe

Don't mess with dull tools. Grandpa used to sharpen his hoes on the emery wheel almost daily. Consider using a very sharp triangular sickle hoe for larger weeds.

A sharp gardening spade can be a good tool to slice out large patches of big weeds.

The most vicious weed of them all

No plant can compete with grass. If grass is allowed to creep in on young trees and shrubs, they will likely quit growing and possibly die. Merely mowing the grass right to the trunk does no good. Young trees and shrubs will do their best if surrounded by a circle of cultivated soil.

Turf and trees are fundamentally incompatible, which is one reason why trees planted in urban and suburban landscapes have half the life-expectancy of their rural cousins.

Glyphosate, the wonder chemical

Glyphosate (commercially known as Roundup) is the most effective way to kill the grass around young trees. Glyphosate only enters plants through the leaves, therefore you will not kill a tree by spraying Roundup around its base.

Here are some ways glyphosate can be used to ease the lives of area gardeners:

•Rather than fighting the incursion of grass into flower beds with a spade, carefully spray with glyphosate to define the bed's perimeter.

•To best way to get rid of grass before tilling a new area for planting: spray glyphosate on the area when the temperatures are high enough for the chemical to take effect. In three days, however lively the grass or weeds still appear, the chemical will have spread throughout the plants, insuring their death.

•Spray glyphosate early in spring to clear grass away from young shrubs and trees. Spraying low, and spraying *before the shrubs have leafed out*, but after the grass has started to grow, prevents harm from overspray and can eliminate hand weeding for much of the summer.

•The difficult task of getting rid of quack grass from established perennial beds, such as iris, is made easier with glyphosate. Wearing rubber gloves, wet a cloth with glyphosate concentrate. Brush the individual strands of quack with the cloth, taking care not to touch the desired plant. This sounds tedious, and it is, but there is no better way to kill quack *by the root*. You need not hit every leaf with chemical. Simply get most of them, and the others will die when the entire plant dies. This process is well known to farmers, and is called *wicking*.

•Thistle, once established, requires a real harsh dose of glyphosate, perhaps two or three. Even so, glyphosate will do a more thorough job of eliminating the weed than pulling the thistle, which inevitably leaves enough root fragments in the ground for the plant to regenerate.

Caution with lawn weed killers

It is tempting to use broadleaf weed killer to eliminate dandelions and other weeds from the lawn without hurting the grass.

We urge caution.

The chemicals in lawn weed killers, usually a version of the broadleaf herbicide 2-4D, are dangerous to all plants and trees in the yard.

Broadleaf herbicides are quite volatile, and seem to move around to other plants even after the actual spray has settled and dried. Instances of trees and shrubs dying due to lawn weed spray are common. We have even seen instances where we suspect the herbicide has killed annuals planted within a day *after* lawn weed killer has been sprayed.

Keep in mind that regular mowing is the best way to keep lawn weeds down. Dandelions disappear later in the summer, and their yellow blooms could just as well be enjoyed as reviled. Consider avoiding lawn weed killers altogether and concentrate upon creating a healthy lawn through fertilizing and mowing. With good care, grass will win out over most any weed.

We do not suggest using "weed and feed" mixtures of chemical and fertilizer. The mix is volatile, and having it around the garage for a long time is not a good idea. In addition, it is cheaper and safer to use a simple lawn fertilizer like ammonium sulfate to give nutrition. That nutrition alone will encourage grass to crowd out weeds. If you must use chemical weed killers, use them alone, and in moderation.

The amount of chemicals spread on lawns in this country exceeds that put on farm fields, and the tons of chemical are spread over far less area. That acreage, unlike farm fields, is where we play. Let's be smart.

Caution with pre-emergent herbicides

There are very popular products on the market which claim to prevent weeds from growing in the flower garden for the entire season. Spread these granules over the ground after planting, and your weeding time will be cut to a fraction. These pre-emergent herbicides work like a charm. *And we don't use them.*

There is some evidence, both anecdotal and scientific, to indicate that pre-emergent herbicides *stay in the soil for years* and can make it difficult to grow particular varieties on that spot of ground. Their use should be limited to public-space flower beds reliant on sporadic volunteer labor.

CONTROLLING WEEDS: ANNUAL AND VEGETABLE BEDS

•*Start with clean soil:* Prepare the spot for new beds a year in advance to eliminate many weed problems. Allow the weeds and grass to grow up again and spray the area with Roundup. Do this a couple of times, either before tilling the soil or while keeping the soil cultivated.

•*Add peat:* Adding fresh peat to the surface of the garden each year before planting reduces weeds and makes killing the weeds which do grow easy and enjoyable. The peat can be worked into the ground that fall, providing the soil with much needed organic matter.

•*Hoe soon after rains:* As soon as a dry crust forms on the soil after a rain, weed seeds begin to germinate. Merely disrupting this crust kills weeds by the thousands and requires a fraction of the work of weeding visible weeds.

After a crust forms on the soil, one can better see the millions of freshly germinated weeds by getting down on your hands and knees and looking across the soil from a few inches above ground level. When you see pink, which is the initial color of many weeds as they emerge from the seed, you are seeing the new weeds and it is time to break up the crust.

SUPPRESSING WEEDS AND GRASS AROUND YOUNG TREES

•*Fabric:* If you have a young windbreak containing hundreds of trees, keeping the weeds down can be a daunting task. It may be worthwhile to lay a strip of landscape fabric down and plant the trees in slits in the fabric. The edges of the fabric would have to be buried in the soil. Fabric is expensive, but it is far better than allowing young windbreak trees to die due to weeds as they often do otherwise. Although shrub plantings seem to balk at the use of fabric, the vigorous trees used in windbreaks would rather have the fabric than try to survive growing amongst tall weeds.

•*Old newspaper:* In the yard, a matting of thirty pages of newspaper covered by cedar mulch will keep weeds down for the first couple of years, and will degenerate naturally, leaving no unsightly rocks or frayed edges of plastic to get in the mower.

•*Glyphosate:* Spray glyphosate (Roundup) around the base of young trees, taking care not to hit any leaves of the tree, to a width of at least three feet. It does not matter if glyphosate hits the trunk of the tree as long as there are no suckers with leaves on coming from the bottom. *Never spray suckers as they are connected to the larger tree.*

•*Hoeing:* If you create a three foot wide circle by removing the sod when you plant a new tree, keeping that area clean with a hoe is not that difficult, particularly if you add compost or peat to the surface.

Landscape fabric and rock

It has become a universal practice to put down plastic or landscape fabric and rock around shrub plantings, particularly in a commercial setting. In theory, rocks and fabric eliminate the problem of weeds and grass. If done properly, it is true that fabric covered by rock can work to suppress weeds for several years.

However, it is becoming clear that roots of shrubs do not like to grow under fabric or plastic. Although evergreens such as arborvitae or juniper don't seem to mind, most deciduous shrubs seem less vigorous when surrounded by plastic and rock. This only makes sense, as roots need oxygen to thrive. Some shrubs have been discovered to send their most vigorous roots up and out through the plastic into the rock.

More troubling is the inescapable fact that rock and plastic inevitably deteriorate. Rocks migrate into the lawn and can be thrown by the mower. Plastic or fabric can creep up, become exposed or ripped, and create a true eyesore.

The best ongoing weed prevention

One can eliminate the plastic and simply use rock, cedar mulch or some other form of mulch applied to a depth of five or six inches. Using that much mulch can be expensive, but it is necessary if the weeds are going to be kept down.

73

The best option is a thick layer of cedar mulch, finely textured so it meshes into a mat and does not blow away. What weeds come through will pull easily. Add several bags each year to freshen things up.

Avoid using fresh sawdust, or anything similarly white, as a mulch. Sawdust uses large amounts of nitrogen as it breaks down, and can actually make the leaves of the shrubs they surround turn yellow.

Only plant what you plan to weed

New gardeners often overreach early in their gardening careers and plant more than they are able to maintain. Plain old mowed grass is far preferable to a flower or shrub bed that is poorly maintained. Think about weeding before planting.

There is no permanent solution to weeds

There few things sadder than when a formal island of shrubs around the "Welcome" sign outside a town begins to deteriorate only a couple of years after the Welcome sign committee decided to just take care of it and plant something "permanent." The plastic emerges from the ground. Weeds come through. The rock gets gray. You can't hoe because the hoe clanks against the rocks and gets caught in the plastic. And nobody has time. A nightmare. And the town's reputation goes to pot.

Think long and hard before attempting a "low maintenance" planting which features rock and plastic. The person who has to tear it all out ten years down the road will curse you, or your memory. Better to only plant what can be realistically maintained. Committees should be banned from putting down plastic and rock, as you can be sure nobody will step up to take care of it once things go to seed.

The logical way to eliminate weeds completely is to put in a parking lot. Stop to think of it, even that won't work over the long-term.

So, we must accept that weeding is part of the human condition.

Consider eating the weeds

Several weeds common in our area are edible. The two very most nutritious (and delicious) are *lamb's quarters* and *purslane.* Lamb's quarter foliage is sold for very high prices in farmer's markets in other parts of the nation. Here, we grow it by the bushel with no problem!

Google the two plants to 1) find pictures which help you properly identify the plants and 2) get instructions for their culinary use.

CHAPTER 8

Furry and Feathered Pests

The most destructive enemies of the gardener on the northern prairie are furry animals, big and small. Nibbling deer, rabbits and rodents stunt a plant's growth. At their worst, furry animals can destroy entire plantings in one night. It is safe to say that more frustration is caused by deer, rabbits and rodents in our area than by disease or insects.

FURRY ANIMALS

Whitetail deer

Deer are the worst offenders of all. A newly planted apple tree can flourish out of the gate, and in one night the deer can strip the tree of leaves and new growth, and even break the tree down. Infuriating!

Arbor vitae look beautiful and green in the summer, but come winter, deer eat the foliage as a source for Vitamin C. Hostas are at their lush peak in June, but in one night deer can mow the glade to the ground.

Although deer have their favorites, they will eat most any plant if they are hungry enough, especially as winter wears on and the snow deepens.

With annuals and perennials, one can gamble that deer won't find them and only take protective steps after they do. However, with newly-planted shade trees and fruit trees, gardeners should take steps ahead of time to protect their investment from the deer.

Where deer are a problem, it is unwise to plant young trees, especially those from the apple family, unless one surrounds them with chicken netting or a cage made of similar materiel. One can simply hang a cylinder of chicken netting on the branches of the tree, or one can put three rebar rods in the ground around the tree and wrap netting around the bars.

Specific ways deer make our lives difficult

•Deer love the fresh new foliage of plants in the spring and early summer. Some domestic plants emerge more quickly from dormancy than those in the wild, and the deer go for what is softest and sweetest.

•Deer love the new branching of apple trees, flowering crab, roses, and, to a lesser extent other trees and shrubs.

•Bucks do enormous damage to younger trees in November by rubbing their horns against the trunks and skinning the outer bark to the point where it can kill the tree. Once a tree's trunk firms up and develops corky bark, bucks leave them alone.

•Deer prefer the soft green foliage of arborvitae and juniper in the winter. Once the arborvitae foliage within reach is stripped, deer move on to pine, and, as a last resort, spruce.

•As the winter progresses, deer will eat the branches of almost any deciduous shrub, or the lower branches of trees. Sometimes the damage amounts to nothing more than a good trimming. Deciduous shrubs will come back. Small trees, however, can be destroyed.

Ways to keep deer at bay

The most fool-proof solution to a deer problem is an outdoor dog. There is simply no better way to keep a farmstead free of deer than a vigilant canine. Dogs are even more effective than a fence.

Lacking a dog, a barrier is the next best solution.

A high, impenetrable fence (10-12 feet) around the garden or orchard may seem extreme, but it works.

Electric fences work *for a while*. When a deer approaches an electric fence while on the run, it will jump it—and then discover the goodies inside. Once the electric fence has been breached, the deer *will* return.

Small evergreens can benefit from cover by a burlap sack. Make sure it is fastened tightly, or the deer will pull it off! The sack doubles as protection against sun scald, another enemy of small evergreens in winter.

Ammonia-based repellant sprays can keep deer away from big hosta beds, masses of impatiens, or even individual apple trees during the summer. However, commercially-available deer repellants must be applied at least every two weeks, and after every rain, throughout the summer.

In urban areas deer and rabbits are hungrier and more determined, which makes sprays less effective. Spray more often.

We have found that a good, solid application of deer repellent applied in early winter can prevent deer from touching arborvitae for the remainder of the season.

There are dozens of folk recipes for deer repellant, all of which work—to an extent. Ivory soap bars hung from the branches; human hair collected from beauty shops, stuffed into old nylon stockings and hung from tree branches; a spray of ammonia and raw eggs—these and many other home-made concoctions can work *for a while*. But if the deer get hungry, they will get over their aversion to any scent and nibble away. And once they know where to find food, deer are less repelled by the repellent and will return out of habit.

Are some trees deer-proof?

No plant is completely out of the woods when it comes to deer. However, we have found that deer almost never eat maples, hackberry, large spruce, or buckeye.

Deer will nibble on fast-growing poplar. However, poplar usually outrun the deer by growing faster than the deer eat them! Same for compact willow and dogwood: Deer eat the branches, yes, but it doesn't really matter.

Protecting the bark of young trees for winter

All young trees should have their trunk protected by hard plastic tree guard during the winters. Rodent and rabbit damage is particularly infuriating because it is so easy to prevent.

Rabbits and mice love to eat the smooth bark of young trees, and bucks often rub their antlers against the trunk of young trees, doing terrific damage. Because the most vital living tissue of trees, the *cambium layer*, lies only a fraction of an inch beneath the bark's surface, an animal does not have to penetrate very deeply into the young tree's bark to damage a tree. If the tree is *girdled*, that is, if a gap in the cambium layer completely circles the trunk, the tree will die above that point.

Once a tree has developed rough, deeply grooved bark, the rodents and rabbits generally stay away. In the rare winter where the rodents go after a larger tree trunk, they often don't go deeply enough to kill the tree.

Protecting against rabbits

Rabbits are more creative and tenacious than rodents. They work above the snow level and use the deepening snow to get at the higher branches of the tree.

If you know you have rabbits, and the snow becomes deeper than the plastic protector around the trunk, add protection to the higher parts of the tree. Once again, chicken netting is a sure and certain solution.

Rabbit damage is often worse in urban areas where the rabbits don't have wild plants to eat. City folks' obsession with not having dandelions in their lawn makes the problem worse by taking away a food that rabbits would probably prefer over shrubs and perennials.

Preventing vole and mice damage

Voles are a lesser-known rodent that is half mouse and half mole. Voles are nearly blind, but not entirely blind, as are moles. In winters in which the ground does not freeze before there is a deep snow cover, voles tunnel along in the grass beneath the snow until they find a tree, and then they nibble on the bark. Voles seem to reproduce throughout winters favorable to them. When the snow recedes in the spring, entire neighborhoods can find that the base of their young trees has been stripped of bark down to the bare, white wood.

A circular column of metal window screen, or the more traditional plastic guard, placed around the base of the trunk will protect from voles.

Alternately, we have found it effective to stamp down a circle of snow around each of your young trees, even if you have protected the tree with tree guard. Mice and voles will not crawl over a pack of ice to get to a tree. They crawl right against the ground. When confronted with a ridge of hard-packed snow, they will turn around and tunnel somewhere else instead.

To protect a larger grouping of trees, drive in a circle around the grove with an ATV after the first snow to create a snowpack which will likely keep voles out of that area.

Putting out poison (make sure it is designed for outdoor use) can work as well. Buy individual packets and put one at the base of each tree, and several in the shrub and perennial beds around the house.

We can go several winters without vole problems, and then one winter the population explodes for whatever reason and we are caught unawares. It is a wise insurance policy to protect against voles every winter, particularly plantings of young trees. Make protecting against voles an annual habit even if they do not appear each winter.

Beaver deterrent

Trees of any size near water can be felled by beaver. They aren't fussy what kind of tree they fell. Chicken netting around each trunk is an effective deterrent.

Once the damage is done

If a mouse eats the bark off the trunk of the tree, or if rabbits eat the bark, or if deer have stripped the bark with their antlers, the best one can do is to clean up the wound and allow the tree to heal itself.

It is never necessary or desirable to put paint or tar on wounds, or to wrap the wounds of trees. It is a great misconception that trees need bandages to heal their wounds.

It is better for the wound to have contact with the air, just as one would allow a skin wound to form a scab by removing the bandage. Tree wrap, paint and pruning tar can trap moisture against the wound and delay healing.

Identifying the culprit

Mice and voles leave a very clean scar on the bark. If you look closely, you can see almost microscopic little teeth marks in the wood. Rabbits are more sloppy, leaving strands of bark hanging from the trunk.

Injury caused by deer antlers is sloppy in the extreme.

Even if it *appears* that the animals have eaten all the way around the bark at the bottom of the tree, don't dig the tree out right away. Wait until June. There have been instances where the rabbit or rodent damage has looked fatal, but where the vermin didn't actually eat deeply enough to kill the tree. That doesn't mean that the tree is without long-term damage. It simply means that it has survived for the time being.

If the animals scraped deeply into the bark, and the tree is fully girdled, it may still put out thumb-sized leaves in May before they stop growing, droop, and die in June. The bark above the base of the tree sometimes contains enough nutrients to push out dime size leaves without any support from the root.

If the tree has vigorous, normal leaves in mid-June, it is out of the woods! Make sure to protect better *next* winter.

If the animals leave even the smallest gap of bark connecting the bottom of the tree with the top, it is likely that the tree will live. Trees are amazingly resilient. Apple trees which are partially girdled can actually bear *more* fruit after the mouse damage than before, due to the slowing of growth on the upper branches from the wound.

FEATHERED PESTS

Most of the time, we hope to attract the birds by planting shrubs and trees with edible berries.

However, when the birds eat fruit we want ourselves, they become a pest. Fortunately, there are wonderful nettings on the market which one can drape over most small fruits with ease.

Birds are not that smart about finding a way to get past netting. Sometimes an overhead netting is all that is needed, which allows humans to pick fruit unimpeded beneath.

Or, rip a little hole in the net so you can reach through and pick some fruit.

Sapsuckers

The most destructive feathered pest is the sapsucker, a small woodpecker which drills holes in unsightly rows on the trunks and sometimes the larger branches of trees. Sapsuckers love trees with smooth bark.

Sapsuckers primarily love Mountain Ash, birch, Amur chokecherry and basswood. However, they can prey upon any young tree with sap, which is all of them as far as we can tell.

Only one remedy to sapsuckers has proven foolproof (other than birdshot): old Conway Twitty CDs. Recordings from other artists work as well. Hang them with fishline in the tree, making sure the discs are free to twist in the breeze. The brilliant flicker of light they produce is enough to keep sapsuckers away for good.

If damage has already been done and you have some ugly rows of holes, once again, *do not* wrap the damaged area of bark in any way. Let it heal in the open air. The danger of wrapping is that rot will settle into the wounds, which eventually can kill the tree.

Do not rub Vick's Vapo-rub on the tree holes, however appealing it is to imagine a sapsucker with a beak full of the stuff. The petroleum-based goo can kill the tree.

Furry animals who eat healthy vegetables

Deer can be safely discouraged from nibbling in the vegetable patch and the flower garden with an ammonia-based spray. Household ammonia, mixed with water in the same proportion as you would for cleaning, sprayed on and around the perimeter of a garden on a weekly basis, and after every rain, has been successful. Commercial sprays containing ammonia do not harm vegetables. Wash them well before eating.

Rabbits are notorious for eating fresh radish shoots, lettuce, beet tops, and other garden plants. They can go after flowering annuals as well. Ammonia sprays can work just as well against rabbits as deer.

A natural remedy which works for rabbits: Spreading a ring of *blood meal* around the perimeter of a garden can keep rabbits out—that is, if you spread the blood meal *before* rabbits discover the feast available inside the ring.

Raccoons are famous for eating sweet corn. Loud radios, chicken netting fences, sprays—people have tried most anything to keep raccoons out of their sweet corn patch.

A single wire electric fence, six inches off the ground, works wonders to ward off the masked marauders. Sprinkling powdered cayenne pepper on each of the tassels is a lot of work, but has proven to be nearly foolproof.

When dogs and cats go bad

Male dogs damage arborvitae and junipers by urinating on them. Dog urine is so high in nitrogen that it burns what it touches. If Fido douses the entire arborvitae plant, it may die. Placing a small fence around the base of the tree can make it inconvenient enough for Fido so he goes somewhere else.

Once the shrub is large enough so the bulk of the foliage is out of harm's way, the problem diminishes, although the lower evergreen foliage dog urine does touch is likely to burn and not recover.

Dog urine can burn spots in the lawn, or create green patches of vigorous grass. Irrigating heavily can lessen, but not cure, this problem. Fertilizing can equal out the disparity between the green spots and the rest of the lawn.

There is no easy way to change the habits of a dog or a cat. If you plant where they are used to sleeping, or digging, they will not change. There is no foolproof chemical spray to use to keep dogs and cats at bay. Consult an animal behaviorist.

Some people have kept cats off their window boxes by hanging plastic grocery bags nearby. The grocery bags, unfortunately, are ugly enough to cancel out the good done by the flowers.

Squirrels

Squirrels are too smart for any of us. Once they set their mind to destroying something, there is no remedy. Luckily, squirrels seldom attack plants.

CHAPTER 9

Planting and Care of Deciduous Trees

Shade trees vs. ornamental trees

Shade trees grow large and are long-lived, providing more and more shade as they age. Oak, cottonwood, elm, ash, silver maple, hackberry and American linden (basswood) are the primary shade trees in our area.

Ornamental trees are smaller, shorter lived, and are used merely as an accent in the yard. Flowering crab are the most common. Mountain ash, birch, Red Leaf Chokecherry are also favored as ornamental trees. The hard sugar maple acts more as an ornamental than a shade tree in our area.

Shade trees should outlive those who plant them

Shade trees are passed from generation to generation. They occupy an honored place in the yard. In such important matters as leaving a legacy, you don't want to plant an odd, semi-hardy tree as an experiment. In those cases, a tree that dies fifteen years down the road is worse than no tree at all. Choose trees which are certain to outlive you, and put them in a location where they will be allowed to outlive you. Catalpa, Honeylocust, and Gingko are only dependable in Zone 4a on the northern prairie. In Zone 3, they are experimental. Try one out back, if you have the room.

Ornamental trees are for fun

It is good to separate in one's mind the trees which one wants to last forever from the trees which one merely wishes to enjoy for as long as they thrive. A catalpa is not hardy enough to count on as a shade tree, but some may wish to experiment with it in an odd corner of the yard due to its oversized leaves and unique seed pods.

PURCHASING TREES

Choose only hardy varieties

The best trees for the northern prairie are listed in the next chapter. However, new varieties come out each year. Make sure they are rated for Zone 3.

When is the best time to plant trees?

Fall planting was favored in the old days on the northern prairie. Today, planting in April or May is preferred. Nurseries have fresh stock in the spring, and peak selection. The newly planted tree will have a few months to establish before going into its first winter. As one moves into the heat of summer, planting trees simply becomes unwise.

Grafted trees vs. seedling trees

The term *grafting* tends to bring to mind novelties such as an apple tree which bears several different varieties. In fact, grafting is an ancient form of cloning which is the primary way to reproduce most types of shade trees, as well as all named varieties of fruit trees.

Why is grafting necessary?

Trees grown from seed are not genetically identical to their parent. In some cases, such as with windbreak trees, the genetic variation in the seedlings is unimportant. But with apple trees, for example, the seeds of a large, tasty apple will not come true and will instead produce a tree that is completely different, and almost always inferior.

To recreate a wonderful variety of tree exactly, it must be *cloned*—reproduced *asexually*—without the genetic compromises which occur in pollination.

The most common method of grafting places the actual splice at or near ground level when the tree is a sapling. By the time of purchase, the graft is visible only as a lump at the base of the tree. The entire tree above the graft is of one variety—that is, the tasty apple—while the root is a wild, seedling-raised variety, usually a variety which is known to be hardy. The desired tree is called the *scion*. The tree which provides the root is called the *rootstock*.

Named varieties of shade trees are nearly always grafted, particularly if they are seedless. Bergeson Ash, for example, is a form of green ash which was discovered by Melvin Bergeson growing in a row of thousands of seedling green ash. It stood twice as high as the other green ash, with a better shape and a darker leaf, and it turned out to be seedless. To reproduce the Bergeson Ash, tiny buds from the original trees were spliced into the trunks of green ash seedlings. As those buds grew into a vertical trunk, the original tree was cut to the ground and a new tree, bottom half seedling, top half Bergeson Ash, was born.

The home gardener may or may not be interested in grafting, but should know that the lump at the base of their new trees is not a defect.

Grafted trees are more expensive, but well worth the cost. The difference between the bundles of small trees purchased from the Soil Conservation District for windbreak and the large trees purchased at a nursery has to do with more than size. The small trees are seedlings suitable for a long row out on the back forty. The large trees are named, selected, grafted varieties with characteristics that make them desirable as a specimen.

Bare root or potted?

Deciduous trees can be purchased either potted or bare root. Large trees may have their root ball wrapped in burlap, or in wire mesh. More nurseries are selling trees bare root all the time. Bare root trees are much easier to transport and plant. They are dormant and leafless at planting, but take off right away with the warming weather. They are best planted in spring.

Purchase medium-sized trees for best results

Avoid extremes of size. Purchasing single-stem trees under two feet in height saves money, but such tiny trees are more easily mowed, weed-trimmed to death, driven over by snowmobiles, or eaten by furry pests than are trees with more substance.

On the opposite end of the spectrum, shade trees which exceed ten feet in height, or have grown beyond one-and-a-half inches of caliper at the base, often frustrate those who purchase them by not growing any further for many years. *The larger the tree, the more traumatized the root is by moving.* The more traumatized the root, the longer the tree takes to recover enough to resume its task of growing.

The *ideal size* of shade tree to purchase is about six to eight feet in height. Such moderately sized trees tend to take off and *surpass the trees planted at twice their size.*

Roots are more important than top

Planting time is usually the only time one gets a chance to see the roots of the plant. The importance of the root should not be overlooked. Not only does the root draw up the moisture and nutrients to the branches, it anchors the tree in place.

The little, fine, furry roots, those with healthy looking white tips, do much of the work for a tree. If you purchase a tree without those roots, it will likely not do much until it has developed such roots. Hairy roots absorb moisture and nutrients better than thicker roots.

A tree which needs staking is a bad tree

Trees which need staking are trees purchased with too much top and too little root. The practice of staking is so universal because so many trees are sold in that condition, particularly at discount chains. Trees with proper root systems will seldom lean or tip after planting, and if they do lean after a storm they can be righted by merely pulling them back in position.

There may be an occasional need to use a single bamboo stake or smooth steel rod to encourage a tree's lead branch to grow straight—particularly with young basswood.

PLANTING TREES

How big a hole do I have to dig?

Grandpa used to say, "dig a fifty-dollar hole for a ten-dollar tree." Adjusted for inflation, that means dig a hundred-dollar hole for a thirty-dollar tree.

Digging a large hole serves two purposes: First, it loosens the soil, which can benefit the roots of the tree for years. Ironically, *the harder the ground, the bigger the hole you should dig*. If the digging is tough due to hard, compacted soil, it is going to be very difficult for the tree to penetrate the ground with its roots.

Secondly, a large hole allows one to *spread out the roots* from the trunk right away. Roots which are curled, or which remain in the original root ball, never straighten out. They just get bigger and bigger in that same configuration, and as the tree gets older, that mass of curled up roots can either choke off the trunk of the tree, or make the tree more likely to fall over in a wind, according to recent University of Minnesota research.

The time and effort spent digging a big enough hole for a new tree, which usually means digging a hole wider than it is deep, will pay dividends for years in added growth, as well as the long-term health and strength of the tree.

For most six foot trees, a hole three to four feet wide and two feet deep is sufficient. *Skim the sod away first and set it aside*, then dig out the remaining dirt. If you have no use for the sod elsewhere, throw it in the bottom of the hole before planting the tree to provide humus.

Add good soil if needed

If, as you dig, you find mostly clay or gravel, get rid of it. Dig the hole larger than necessary and fill it with black dirt, perhaps mixed with peat. About fifteen pounds of black peat mixed in with the soil will help the root a great deal. Putting a handful of 10-10-10 fertilizer in the hole is a good idea as long as it is evenly distributed and does not fall into a single pocket.

Make sure the roots are spread out at planting

When planting a tree, whether it is purchased bare root or in a pot, it is important to spread the roots out as much as possible. Avoid curling roots around in a circle just to fit them into the hole. In fact, it is better to clip a lengthy root off than to curl it in the hole. University of Minnesota research has shown that curled roots can come back and wrap themselves around the trunk, choking the tree. Roots that are not spread at planting never do straighten out.

It is important to remove all pots, all wire contraptions, and all burlap from around the root of a tree at planting time. Even biodegradable pots can restrict the root, and may even steal nitrogen from the tree as they decompose. In addition, removing the pot allows one to spread the roots out into the hole.

Exception: Spruce and pine should be planted with their biodegradable pots left intact to keep the root ball from disintegrating at planting.

Don't purchase trees until you are ready to plant

Whether planting bare root or potted trees, wait until you are ready to plant before picking up the trees at the nursery. Trees deteriorate quickly if left to languish between purchase and planting, no matter how well-intentioned the purchaser. People tend to forget that a fully-leafed tree in a pot needs to be soaked every day just to maintain its health. Bare root trees should be put in the ground within a day or two of purchase.

Do not fill the hole with water before planting the tree

Some planting instructions advocate filling the hole with water and letting the water soak in before planting the tree. This practice may serve some purpose in other parts of the country (we remain puzzled as to what that purpose might be), but in our area, filling the hole with water before the tree is planted does no good.

Take care to plant the tree at the proper depth

Trees planted too deeply can suffer damage to their trunks, and trees which are planted too shallowly can tip. *Potted trees* are rarely planted at the proper depth in the pot, and usually must be planted more deeply. The lump at the base of most trees, which is the graft, should be right at ground level after one accounts for the three-inch-deep depression left to hold water. The lump at the base of the tree should be three inches below the original soil level, but even with the new soil level.

Bare root trees may bear an obvious mark where the soil once was, or where the coloring of the bark changes into the coloring of the root. It is wise to plant the tree so the soil level reaches exactly that point, or at the level of the graft.

Keep in mind that the eventual soil level around the trunk should be two to three inches below the general level of the lawn to allow for a depression to hold water.

Dig the hole. Set the tree in the hole. Make sure it is deep enough. Pull the tree out of the hole and make adjustments to the bottom of the hole with the spade until the tree is at the proper depth and the roots spread.

Keep roots damp and shaded until the hole is dug.

Use the initial watering to pack the soil around the roots

After the tree is at the proper depth, fill in enough soil for the tree to stand on its own. Tamping down the soil by hand may be necessary to get the tree to stand up while you run and get the water hose. Water the tree thoroughly, filling the depression. Allow the water to soak in.

The most effective packing of the soil is accomplished by the first watering. Keep manual tamping of the soil to a minimum and allow the water to pack the soil to the greatest extent possible. Fill in more soil and water again. Holes will form as the soil packs. Fill in the remaining soil to the proper level on the tree, making sure the tree is straight.

Some settling may occur, and the tree may list to one side the first few days after planting. *Do not stake the tree.* Simply pull the tree back and step down on the soil with your foot to make the tree stay in place.

Exception: Princeton Elm have poor root systems and sometimes require staking for two years to keep them upright until they anchor themselves.

Make sure no tags or strings or wires are left around the trunk

It is common for trees to arrive with tags, twine, or even wire around the base of the trunk or stem. Although the tag may seem loose at planting, as the tree grows, it can choke the trunk. Get rid of all such things at planting to make sure the tree doesn't choke later on.

Some people keep the tags in a safe place in a baggie as a way of remembering what they purchased. Others keep a map they make at planting time. Keeping track of what you planted is essential to solving any problems which may arise in the future.

Protect the trunk with ugly plastic tubing

Plastic tree guard protects the tender bark of young trees from weed trimmers in the summer and from rodents and rabbits in the winter. It should stay on the tree until the bark turns rough. Do not used corrugated paper wrap as it traps moisture against the bark of the tree and can do more harm than good.

When the tree trunk grows large enough to press against the plastic tubing, it is best to take the tubing off during the growing season to avoid the risk of injuring the trunk.

CARE OF TREES

Improper care after planting results in the decline and death of many young trees. Sometimes the damage done by improper care is not evident for many years. Moderation is the key: aggressive but misguided care kills as many trees as does neglect.

Watering young trees

Bare root trees do not need much, if any, water after the initial soaking they receive at planting. Potted trees, in contrast, need careful watering for at least two years after planting. See Chapter 5 on watering.

Fertilizing

Most young trees can benefit from a handful of 10-10-10 fertilizer once per year, spread around the base of the tree. Gimmicks such as fertilizer spikes aren't necessary or worth the extra money. Fertilizer is treated in greater detail in Chapter 4 on fertilizing.

Keep the grass away

Grass takes more nutrients out of the soil than any tree or shrub. *Allowing grass to grow right up against a young tree or shrub will slow the plant's growth to a crawl.* Keeping the grass and sod away from plants is particularly important with young spruce trees, but grass will stunt any young tree.

Glyphosate herbicide can be applied at ground level before the leaves come on the tree without risk of killing the tree.

Young trees which have cultivated soil right to their base can grow at *triple* the rate of young trees that are choked out by weeds and grass. *Mowing the grass near trees does no good.* Sod up to the base of a young tree does almost as much damage as tall weeds and grass.

Should newly planted trees be mulched?

Mulch is merely a covering of ground-up bark or peat or straw, or even a layer of plastic or porous landscape fabric—any covering which serves to keep moisture in and weeds down around the base of the tree.

While mulching can keep weeds down and moisture in, mulch can do more harm than good if applied improperly.

Do not mound up bark, wood chips, or rock directly around the trunk of any tree. Such mounding has the same effect as if the tree were planted too deeply.

The most useful mulches are the more finely textured natural substances such as cedar bark, or cocoa bean hulls. A four-inch deep layer of cedar mulch spread to a width of about two feet from the tree's trunk will keep weeds down and moisture in, but take care not to place the mulch against the tree's trunk.

As an alternative to fabric or plastic, spread about 30 pages of newspaper down before putting the mulch on top. Newspaper will do the job and disappear when it is not needed, unlike plastic, which comes to the surface years later to taunt you with its ugliness.

Avoid using rock around young trees. Rock gets into the lawn. It seldom maintains its appearance. Rock also makes it difficult to cut away suckers which may come up from the root.

Circles of plastic lawn edging placed around a tree do not do the job of keeping grass and weeds out. As the years (months?) go by, the edging works its way out of the ground and looks uglier and uglier. Instead, spray glyphosate to keep the creeping grass at bay.

Weed trimmer blight

Too many gardeners are saddled with a spouse (who also can qualify as a furry pest) who lacks restraint with the weed trimmer and, in the interest of getting that last blade of grass, tears the bark off young trees. Weed trimmers kill trees as certainly as would a mouse or rabbit. There is no spray to cure weed trimmer blight, unless you spray your spouse with pepper spray so he or she can't find the tree.

PRUNING TREES

General pruning tips

Always use sharp clippers. Dull clippers are frustrating, and leave sloppy cuts which heal more slowly. Long-handled lopping shears have a lot of power and work great for branches thicker than one's thumb. A hand clipper works for branches smaller than one's thumb. Pruning shears, which cut many branches at once, and are meant to shape a hedge, and don't work for trees.

When is the best time to prune trees?

The best time to prune most deciduous trees is in spring, before the leaves have started to emerge. The exception is oak, which, for disease purposes, should never be pruned during the months of May, June and July.

Some experts consider February the best time to prune apple trees. Pruning of water sprouts and suckers around the base of the tree should be done when they appear, or at the moment they are discovered.

To the home gardener, there is no substantial penalty for pruning at other times of the year. In fact, Grandpa used to say, "Prune when the knife is sharp." That was his way of saying that, although there are times which are better than others to prune, it is better to do it at the wrong time than not do it at all.

Should I paint the wound after I prune?

No. Painting a wound can do more harm than good. So does tar. Allow the wound to heal naturally. Cut the branch off as close as you can to the trunk of the tree *without damaging the collar around the base of the branch.* That collar is what will heal over the wound.

Trimming vs. Pruning

Although the two terms are used interchangeably, there is a difference. *Trimming* is shaping of a tree or shrub by making it round, or square, or formal in any way. *Pruning*, for our purposes, is the selective removal of branches without attempting to make the perimeter of the tree or shrub confined or uniform.

Many people *trim* their evergreen shrubs to keep them looking uniform and round. Orchardists *prune* their apple trees to keep the branching from getting too thick, and to allow for maximum yield.

Don't trim shade and ornamental trees, prune them

It is almost always a mistake to *trim* a shade or ornamental tree so the perimeter of its crown is uniform. Once you trim a flowering crab, or a maple, or an ash to make it look like a perfect round ball, the line where the branches were cut will show for years. The shape of a tree can be permanently made unnatural. In addition, the branches that are sent out from near the wound are tender and weak, and grow much too quickly.

Pruning of trees, however, by the thoughtful and selective removal of entire branches, can improve a tree's appearance and can prevent eventual problems. What follows are the various reasons for pruning.

Prune to eliminate weak joints

When a tree develops twin, competing leaders of equal vigor, one of them should be completely removed. The sooner this is done the better. The joint where twin leaders join is very weak, and will easily split in windstorms down the road.

Any joint with a very narrow angle will split easily. Wherever they are found on a tree, it is best to remove one of the branches so that the weak joint does not eventually break. Generally speaking, joints which are narrower than a "Y" are weak. Those which are closer to an "L" are strong. This distinction is particularly important in fruit bearing trees, which need their joints to be as strong as possible.

Exception: upright-growing shade or ornamental trees such as Tower Poplar, Norlin Linden, Pyramidal Arborvitae, are bred to have narrow crotches. It is part of their charm, and they should be left, however weak those crotches make the tree.

97

Prune out water sprouts

Water sprouts are fast-growing vertical shoots which are most prevalent on flowering crab and apple trees. They emerge from large lower limbs. Because these shoots are tender and fast growing, they are susceptible to fire blight and other pests and diseases. Those diseases can spread to the rest of the tree.

Water sprouts should be eliminated quickly. Trim them off as closely as possible to the limb from which they grew without injuring that limb. If you get to them before they harden, it is sometimes possible to strip them off the limb with your bare hand.

Prune away suckers around the base

Suckers are shoots which come up from the base of any tree or shrub. They are a nuisance, and should be removed as soon as they appear. The larger suckers are left to grow, the tougher they are to remove.

On any grafted tree, the sucker is likely to be *wild* rather than *tame*. It is particularly important to remove all suckers which grow up from the base of any grafted tree to insure that the *rootstock* does not overcome the desired tree.

Avoid trimming suckers near the trunk of a tree with a weed trimmer. If the weed trimmer so much as touches the bark of the main tree, it can do tremendous damage.

There is no good way to prevent suckering. Do not spray suckers with a systemic herbicide, as the herbicide will get into the entire tree. It is fine, of course, to simply mow over the suckers, although the remaining sharp stubs can impale the feet of children.

Chokecherry, particularly the ornamental red-leafed variety, are the most determined suckerers of all.

Prune out redundant branches

Branches which come out from the side of the main trunk should be spaced evenly. When two of them are too close, one should be removed. Remember, *the space between branches does not increase as the tree grows.* Get rid of branches that are too close to each other early in the tree's life to lessen the trauma to the tree.

Prune to gently improve the shape of the tree

Although it is not a good idea to trim trees harshly into a particular shape, it is fine to lop off a single branch that appears odd, or that is growing out of proportion to the rest of the tree. If you are cursing a branch as you mow beneath the tree, get rid of it to improve your language.

Prune out dead or damaged branches

The sooner you get rid of dead branches, the less likely they are to fall and cause damage to buildings or people. Cut them clean at the base.

Do my trees need "topping?"

Topping trees is the violent heading back of large trees, supposedly so their branches don't fall off in winds.

It is a criminal practice.

No trees need topping, unless they are about to grow into power lines. If you have a fast-growing shade tree, such as a soft maple, or a seedless green ash, and it is looking tall and lanky, it is best simply to let the tree fill out on its own, which it always will.

If you "top" the tree, which means to cut off the lead branches and any others which seem to be stretched out too far, you encourage the development of a bunch of new shoots which are even less sturdy and more likely to break off in a wind than the original shoot. Topping of trees simply ruins the shape of the tree—forever.

Forming a trunk

Small shade trees planted in the open will naturally grow as a shrub, with branches almost to the ground. To form a trunk, remove a few of the lower branches each year. Always keep the tree looking in good proportion, however. The trunk should be firm to the point of unbendable at the point where lower branches are removed.

It is a myth that pruning out lower branches increases the growth of the top branches. A tree needs adequate leaf surface to form a strong trunk, and pruning off too many of the well-leafed lower branches can weaken the remaining trunk.

Windstorms

Our frequent violent summer storms do tremendous damage to trees. Often it is difficult to decide whether to attempt to save a tree or whether to just have it taken out.

Large trees which have been tipped slightly in a storm can recover. If the sod has risen just a little, the tree may well survive. However, if the surface of the ground was broken by the rising roots on the opposite side from where the tree has leaned, it is likely that it is best to get rid of the tree. Pulling a tree thus uprooted upright with the John Deere does nothing to repair the damage to the root.

Younger trees can be pulled back into place and staked after a storm. The sooner the better. Straightening the tree while the soil is still wet will be easier on the tree. Water the tree after the straightening to readjust the soil around the root. Stake the tree if needed to prevent it from leaning back to where the wind blew it.

If a larger tree develops a small split between two major limbs, it is possible to pull the split together by drilling a hole and inserting a threaded rod through the tree. Use large washers on either end of the rod.

If the tree is split to the core wood of the trunk, cut it down.

MOVING TREES WITH A TREE SPADE

There is nothing wrong with moving trees with a spade, as long as the tree is of the proper size to be moved. Spruce should not be moved if *over eight feet in height*. Deciduous trees *over two inches in caliper* suffer mightily at the hand of the spade.

Impatient developers and new homeowners often hire a tree spade to bring in very large trees. These large trees make an instant impression on the landscape, but they are expensive, and they start off at a disadvantage.

The roots of large trees have often been violently cut by the spade when they are moved. Often between one-half to two-thirds of a tree's root system is left in the ground when the tree is dug. It takes the tree years to recover from the loss. During those years, the transplanted large tree will leaf out, but will not add much growth. In addition, because roots function as an anchor, the tree may require staking to keep it from tipping in high winds.

By the time a large tree establishes itself, a smaller, bare-root tree planted at the same time will have passed the tree-spaded tree by, and will have a more vigorous appearance to boot. In addition, it is likely that the tree-spaded tree will have cost at least five times a smaller tree, perhaps ten.

CHAPTER 10

Useful Trees for the Northern Prairie

Trees should last a long time, and are a valuable feature on the northern prairie. It is important to not only select hardy varieties, but to plant the tree in a location where it will prosper for decades. For those reasons, the descriptions of the trees below will be more lengthy and involved than the descriptions of other plants in this book. *With trees, you want to do it right the first time.*

The first set of trees listed below are the staples on the northern prairie. Their success is to be expected, and their impact on the prairie landscape has been, over the short time since white settlement, substantial.

The following list is in alphabetical order by the name most often used.

FIRST TIER TREES FOR THE NORTHERN PRAIRIE

Ash, Mountain   *Sorbus*

The Mountain Ash is known for its clusters of orange-red berries. They appear in late summer, and can hang onto the tree well into the winter. The white blooms in spring are an added feature.

The Mountain Ash is a dignified ornamental tree. They rarely grow large enough to provide shade, usually living only thirty years or so.

However, an established Mountain Ash is a prize tree, and in parts of the northern prairie, the Mountain Ash foliage can turn an orange-red fall color, even planted in alkaline soil.

Mountain Ash can be stubborn to get started, particularly in heavy, akaline soils. Avoid planting Mountain Ash where the soil pH approaches 8 or above.

Mountain Ash attract sapsuckers, that little woodpecker which pecks rows of holes in the bark. When the sapsuckers appear, hang an old Michael Jackson CD or two in the tree with fish line, making sure the CD is able to twist freely in the wind.

Mountain Ash are susceptible to fire blight, particularly young trees. Watch the new growth of the tree carefully in June and July. If the tips of the new growth wilt and turn black or deep brown, immediately take the steps prescribed in the disease chapter of this book. *Fire blight seems to move faster on Mountain Ash than on apples, and it can be fatal.*

Basswood (Linden)   *Tilia*

The American Basswood is a hardy native tree with enormous leaves which provide a deep shade. Its sweet smelling blooms attract bees, and the resulting basswood honey is some of the clearest available. The soft but strong wood from basswood is a favorite of carvers. A mature basswood can rival a cottonwood in size in our area.

The two names, *Basswood* and *Linden* are inter-changeable. There is no such tree as a *Lindenwood*, although there is a park by that name in Fargo, which leads many local people to use the term as a name for basswood.

There are two types of basswood which work in our area. The American Linden is the native type, and it is most prevalent. It is what most people think of when they refer to basswood. It is the most frequently planted.

The imported European Linden, however, is a striking tree with a perfectly triangular crown. A most spectacular display of European linden runs along 8th Street South in Moorhead, on the campus of Concordia College.

The hardiest variety of European linden on the market is the "Norlin," which was developed in Manitoba.

Basswood have no serious insect or disease threats. As with Mountain Ash, sapsuckers can peck holes along the trunk of basswood to get at the tree's sweet sap, but the basswood is usually vigorous enough to shrug off the damage. However, if one sees fresh holes in the bark, it is wise to hang an old Barry Manilow CD from a branch with fish line, making sure it is able to twist in the wind.

Care of Basswood

When planting basswood, it is especially important not to plant the tree too deeply. Basswood balk if the soil level is even one inch too high on the trunk. Do not mound mulch around the trunk of basswood, as you will likely harm the tree. When you plant a basswood, pay attention to the line which separates the grayish bark from the yellowish root. Do not allow the soil to rise above the gray bark.

Take particular care to straighten basswood roots out in the hole at planting time. Do not curl the roots just to get them in the hole. Dig a plenty deep hole, and if there are roots which are ridiculously long—and basswood do have long roots—cut them off rather than curling them. Curled basswood roots can grow back towards the trunk and choke the tree.

Young basswood often send up a lead branch which curls off to one side. To keep the tree's leader on a vertical trajectory, use a bamboo stake as a splint and loosely attach the branch to the stake with twine.

Young basswood will send out shoots (suckers) from the base of the trunk. The only way to control suckers is to pinch them off as soon as they appear. Avoid letting these shoots get too large. Avoid cutting the shoots off with the weed trimmer. The smooth basswood bark is easily damaged.

Birch, White Paper   *Betula papyrifera*

White birch, also known as paper birch, are native in parts of our region and are famous for the papery white bark, as well as the beautiful bronze tint displayed by the bare branches during winter.

Although birch are native to our area, they do not thrive as easily in most yards as they do in their natural habitat, where they are able to select their own growing site. The birch seed spreads everywhere, but only those distributed to ideal spots grow into adult trees.

Where birch grow naturally

Birch prefer cool, moist soil, the conditions found on a typical north slope. If its root becomes hot, the birch tree weakens and becomes vulnerable to its main nemesis, the *bronze birch borer*, a worm which crawls under the bark, eats a trail through the vital cambium layer, and eventually causes the tree to die out at the top and sometimes die completely.

Birch trees whose roots remain cool usually remain strong enough to fend off the birch borer worm.

It is worthwhile to notice where birch grow in the wild. They love north slopes, especially those found on the south shore of a body of water. Out on the prairie, the few birch that volunteer do so on the shady slope of a ditch bank. Birch thrive in woodlands where their roots are covered with layers of dead leaves.

Creating conditions for a long-lived birch tree

Observation of long-lived birch on the northern prairie yields the following conclusions: Yards with irrigation systems tend to grow healthy birch.

Long-lived birch are often found on the northeast corner of a house, where their roots are shaded during the afternoon. Something as simple as a cluster of low growing junipers around the southwest side of the tree can save the tree.

Neglected birch which have very low branching have survived well, likely due to the shade the lower branches provide the root. Finally, people who build decks around their birch have sometimes unwittingly saved their tree by shading the root.

Other options are to plant a flower bed around the base of the birch, or to simply place a layer of mulch, either redwood shavings, or peat, or even leaves, around the birch tree out to the at least the tips of its branches. One can leave the lower branches on birch as a way of shading the root, but those branches take away from the view of the white trunk, and interfere with mowing.

Birch are sensitive to root damage. Do not till where there are roots. Do not cut off the occasional knob of root which breaches the surface, even if it gets in the way of mowing.

Purchasing and planting birch

Birch trees are easy to grow as young trees. They grow quickly in their first years. The most efficient way to purchase white birch is to purchase young bare root plants. A three-foot high seedling looks small, but will probably double its size and triple its trunk's caliper the first year.

If one purchases birch in pots, choose small trees which aren't overly root bound in the pot. The root is of greater importance than the top, especially with birch. If the tree is root-bound in the pot, make sure to forcefully spread the root out and water well after planting. The more root-bound the tree is, the more water it will require early on. Birch do not like to dry out.

Conversely, they cannot sit in water for any amount of time. When a lake rises above its usual shoreline, birch suffer and die more quickly than other trees.

The answer? More than ever, *moist but well-drained soil.*

Clump birch are not a separate genetic variety, but are merely a collection of several stems of white birch. Birch often form clumps in the wild, and clumping them in the yard mimics that successful arrangement.

106

To create a birch clump, simply plant four or five stems in the same hole. Planting more than three is a good idea because if one stem fails, you will still have a decent clump.

In recent decades, several new cultivars of white birch have been introduced. The most useful and spectacular improvement has been the *Dakota Pinnacle,* introduced by NDSU, a tightly-formed birch which one horticulturist has described as "rocket-shaped." More compact than the generic white birch, Dakota Pinnacle makes a formal centerpiece for a flower bed. It should not be planted in clumps, as it has its own shape.

Maroon-leafed birch such as "Crimson Frost" are hardy only to Zone 4, and should only be attempted in protected areas near rivers or lakes.

Birch, Cutleaf Weeping   *Betula pendula*

The Cutleaf weeping birch features branches which weep elegantly to the ground.

The weeping habit is not passed on by seed, therefore weeping birch must be grafted and are more expensive to purchase as a result.

Instructions for care, maintenance and birch borer prevention are the same for the weeping birch as they are for paper birch, discussed above.

Crabapple, flowering   *Malus*

The spectacular May bloom of the flowering crabs is a highlight in our northern seasonal cycle. Flowering crabs are of the apple family, but are bred for their ornamental features, which include the color of the bloom, the color of the leaf in summer, the color and size of their mostly inedible berries.

Our northern latitude and cold climate eliminate all but a few of the many dozen flowering crab options, making the job of choosing a good flowering crab pretty simple.

First, make sure that the flowering crab tree you purchase is rated hardy for Zone 3.

Second, decide what color of bloom you prefer, realizing that most of the better brands bloom pink. The search for a dark, dark pink bloom on a flowering crab tree hardy for the prairie is ongoing.

Third, decide whether you can tolerate fruit which falls on the ground, or whether you prefer a tree which hangs onto its fruit until the birds eat it, or whether you want no fruit at all.

My grandfather, Melvin Bergeson, introduced the "Red Splendor" flowering crab to the nursery trade in 1948. The "Red Splendor" blooms pink in the spring. The name "Red Splendor," however, came from the fruit which hangs well into the winter, until it is eaten by the birds. In November, the show of bright orange-red berries is so spectacular that Grandpa named the tree in its honor.

Although the "Red Splendor" needs frequent and aggressive pruning due to its somewhat chaotic branching habit, it remains one of the better flowering crabs for the Upper Midwest. Adhere to apple tree pruning instructions for keeping the tree open in the middle, realizing that the flowering crab branches *do not* need to hold up hundreds of pounds of fruit and therefore needn't be structurally perfect.

The best of the non-fruiting varieties is the "Spring Snow," a cute, neatly-oval flowering crab which blooms white.

Flowering crab issues

All of the pest-protection measures one performs for young apple trees must be provided the flowering crab as well, as rodents, deer and rabbits find the two equally delicious.

Fire blight can strike flowering crab, but with slightly less frequency than it strikes apples.

Apple scab, which causes flowering crab leaves to drop prematurely and can make the entire tree look November-gray in July, appears during damp years. It is less a problem on the prairie than in the more humid woodlands to the south and east. There is nothing to be done but hope for a drier season next year.

Elm, American   *Ulmus*

For the past fifty years, the American elm, which once lined the streets of prairie towns with soaring arched branches reminiscent of a gothic cathedral, was not sold or planted due to the pernicious Dutch elm disease which killed nearly all of them.

Then, after the carnage, it became apparent that some American elm survived and were indeed resistant to the Dutch elm virus. At least two such trees have been introduced. The "Princeton" and the "St. Croix" are of worth, and others are in the pipeline.

And so, after fifty years, American elm are back on the market—and just in time, too, for the elm's designated replacement, the green ash, is now on the chopping block due to the emerald ash borer.

After watching these new elm take off from small saplings, a privilege denied me in my first 40 years in the business, it is easy to see what made them so popular back in the day. American elm grow fast, with great shapeliness, and they seem to tolerate any sort of soil short of cement.

That said, American elm roots at planting are often quite poor, and the elm are the only shade tree on this list which may require routine staking to prevent the tree from tipping in winds until its root finally grabs hold.

In addition, the American elm share an odd trait with basswood: Their lead branch sometimes curves off to the side, only to be replaced by a second lead branch which eventually does the same. As the tree ages, this is not a problem, but in the early years, as one seeks to establish a single, straight trunk, it may pay to tie the errant lead branch to a long, smooth steel rod in order to foster straight growth. (The raised bumps of rebar will hurt the trunk. Smooth rod is best.)

The return of the American elm is to be celebrated on the northern prairie. We must hope that the Dutch elm virus does not mutate to the point where it kills the now-resistant trees. In the meantime, we can enjoy the revival of an American tradition.

MAPLE   *Acer*

There are dozens of types of maple available on the national market, but two basic types of maple trees are most useful in the northern prairie region. They are the *Sugar (hard) Maple* and the *Silver (soft) Maple*.

Sugar maple *(Acer saccharum)* are popular for the brilliant orange fall foliage.

Silver maple *(Acer saccharinum)*, although messy, are our fastest way to get a very large shade tree with arching branches.

Occasionally, some variant of Norway maple *(Acer platanoides)* will survive on the northern prairie, usually in town and on high ground. However, success is rare enough to eliminate Norway maple, which includes varieties with deep-maroon or variegated foliage, from the menu of dependable northern-prairie options. The "Crimson King," a popular deep maroon-leafed variety in Zone 4, tends to freeze back to the ground in Zone 3 and form a rank-growing shrub.

New varieties such as the "Autumn Blaze" maple mix the genetics of the Red Maple *(Acer rubrum)* with the hardier silver maple in order to create a tree which has cherry-red fall color and is also fast-growing. The results on the northern prairie have been mixed, with the best success happening on higher ground and in locations protected from the harshest winter winds.

Some perspective: The very large Norway maple and red maple families are highly popular in other parts of the country, and dominate national literature on maples—as well as the national tree market. Ignore the hype and stick to what works on the northern prairie.

Maple grow best where the soil is acid, and most soils on the northern prairie are alkaline. So, we have a problem, but one which is not without remedies.

The problem of alkaline soils manifests when a maple tree shows symptoms of *iron chlorosis*, a severe yellowing of the leaves. Although applications of iron fertilizer can help a young tree for a time, as the tree matures, the surrounding alkalinity will prevail and the tree will become stunted, or perish.

Sugar Maple (Hard)   *Acer saccharum*

There is no prettier landscape tree for the northern prairie than the sugar maple. Although slow-growing, the sugar maple crown forms a compact oval of impressive dignity at a relatively young age.

To have success, however, one must have (or provide) better conditions than exist generally on the northern prairie.

If you are lucky enough to have lighter, sandy soil, such as is found on ridges, you can grow sugar maple. It seems that good drainage can offset the alkalinity of the soil enough to allow a sugar maple to establish.

If you have heavy soils, the task is more difficult. A solution: haul in a few yards of better soil and make a mound of at least one foot in height and eight feet in width and plant the sugar maple tree on the mound.

Without acid soil, even if the soil is well-drained, sugar maple leaves do not turn brilliant orange in the fall. Sometimes they will be merely yellow. The absence of brilliant orange fall color from any tree is one price we pay for locating on the alkaline soils of the prairie.

Adding iron, or using an acidifying fertilizer such as ammonium sulfate can improve fall color on young trees.

So, there you have it. Sugar maple are rightfully coveted, but are difficult. The lesson for the home gardener: Plant one sugar maple as an experiment in a place where it will show off if it grows, but won't be seriously missed if it doesn't.

Silver Maple (Soft)   *Acer saccharinum*

So-named for the silvery underside of its deeply-cut leaves, the soft maple grows about three times as fast as the sugar maple, and with a rangy habit. Old silver maple in town inevitably lift the sidewalk, but can provide deep, pleasant shade for the entire yard.

Silver maple can tolerate some alkaline soils, and will power through slight bouts with iron chlorosis. However, during a wet year, the silver maple can start turning their bright-yellow fall color as early as July.

Silver maple make a mess. Not only are their branches weak and brittle, but the tree produces seeds which germinate in profusion on any cultivated patch of ground within a few rods. In addition, the vigorous root of a mature silver maple can steal the nutrients from a swath of ground as wide as fifty feet from the trunk.

Are silver maple worth it? If you have a large yard and want a real big shade tree with grand, arching branches in a relative hurry, yes. Like cottonwood, silver maple have nostalgia value.

Maple issues

The most frequent gripe of maple owners are the warts which can form on the leaves. Some warts are green, others red, some large, others small. These growths, called *galls,* are caused by the venom of mites, who bite the nascent leaves in May when they are still in the buds. The resulting galls are harmless, and the damage they do is mainly to the mental well-being of people who are repulsed by wart-like growths.

Sometimes, the smooth bark of maple attracts sapsuckers which drill rows of unsightly holes. As with basswood and mountain ash, the solution is to hang an old Andy Gibb CD on the tree.

During a cold winter, the smooth bark of young maples, particularly of the Autumn Blaze type, can crack. To prevent cracking, paint the southwest side of the trunk with white latex paint in late fall, as one would with Honeycrisp apples.

Once the cracking has occurred, there is nothing to do but hope it heals. Paint is a preventative, not a cure, and should *not* be applied *after* a tree's bark has cracked open. Wrapping the trunk after cracking does more harm than good by trapping moisture on the wound.

With all of these problems, why bother? Because an established maple tree is a treasure in the northern yard, and once a maple gets established, it will be a valued friend for the rest of your life.   ...

Poplar, hybrid   *Populus*

People wrinkle up their nose when they hear the term *poplar*, but hybrid versions of the poplar and cottonwood families are the fastest-growing dependable tree available for the northern prairie.

The tall, narrow columnar "Lombardy" poplar is *not* hardy here and should be avoided like the plague. But the sturdy varieties of hybrid poplar, the most prominent of which is the "Norway," are fast-growing, dignified, and an important staple of prairie plantings.

The developer of a new sub-division of homes on the prairie could do no bigger favor for himself and the development's future residents than to plant hundreds of hybrid poplar along the perimeters, at a cost of a few dollars per tree. In only a few years, the new development would be well-protected, well-shaded, and would have an established appearance.

The hybrid poplar have the benefits of the old-time cottonwood without the liabilities. They have large, rubbery, rustling leaves. They grow fast and live long and produce no cotton.

About one-in-a-hundred hybrid poplar will develop a big gall on the trunk and fall over in a storm. The problem is structural, and will not spread to the other trees.

Willow   *Salix*

Most forms of willow, including the weeping, drop branches all over the yard in windstorms, and they might not live forever, but they still are a much-loved tree. Willow work in moist areas, and can have spectacular bark coloring in the wintertime.

Willow can stand heavy moisture, even standing water, but they do not require it. The ideal location for a willow is right on the shore of a lake or pond, where the roots will have easy access to water, but will not be submerged. However, willow are tough enough to survive most soil conditions on the northern prairie.

Scrubby native species of willow grow prominently in and around area swamps. Do not be put off by the scruffiness of wild willow: domesticated varieties are better-looking by far.

The elegant Weeping willow are the sloppiest of all willow, but incurable romantics love them nonetheless. Motorists who enjoy the elegant tree will thank you for your willow-work as they speed past.

The "Flame" willow, a compact variety introduced by Melvin Bergeson, loses no branches and displays the most spectacular deep orange branch color of any willow available in our area. It grows in a perfect oval. It is best grown as a large shrub, with branches to the ground; however, because it gets twenty feet tall, Flame willow is still considered a tree rather than a shrub.

New varieties of willow, particularly the "Prairie Reflections" introduced by NDSU, are truly promising. They are dignified enough to qualify as a front-yard shade tree, yet they grow fast.

Pussy willow are desired by many, but the tree simply does not do well outside of its natural habitat in ditches and swamps, and it will not make an attractive specimen in the yard. No one will mind you taking stems from the ditch in early spring.

All willow reproduce easily by cuttings and are therefore quite affordable. Small, inexpensive willow trees take off more quickly than trees purchased with trunks more than an inch in caliper at the base.

With all these caveats, willow remain underrated on the northern prairie. One or two in the yard, whether weeping or not, will bring the home gardener a great deal of happiness and satisfaction (in addition to the exercise picking up the branches).

More new introductions are sure to come, as the value of the entire willow family, which is complex and diverse, becomes better appreciated.

SECOND TIER TREES FOR THE NORTHERN PRAIRIE

The following trees are hardy, attractive and useful in the northern landscape, but for various reasons they are not planted as frequently as the trees listed above. Some of the trees are not yet familiar to the public, others are difficult for nurseries to raise, transport and sell. Some are difficult to get going the first year, and others simply do not respond well to being in a pot, or to being moved. There are ways to overcome most difficulties presented by the following trees, and in many cases they are well worth the effort. This section offers the gardener cautions, as well as opportunities.

Unfortunately, due to alphabetization, we must start with the unfortunate ash family.

Ash, Black   *Fraxinus nigra*

Black ash are native in the wetlands of the forests to the east. Sporting a crown more dense than the green ash, as well as a more pronounced oval shape, the black ash is an ideal boulevard tree.

Black ash are well suited to the heavy soils of the prairie, and can tolerate more standing moisture than most trees.

However, the black ash is also as susceptible to the emerald ash borer as the green ash (see following entry). For that reason, they are rightfully disappearing from the market.

It is theorized, but not yet proven, that some hybrid varieties of black ash are somewhat resistant to the ash borer—but until resistance can be established without question, planting black ash is not recommended.

Ash, Green   *Fraxinus pennsylvanica*

Due to the apparently inevitable arrival of the emerald ash borer, green ash are no longer recommended.

If you have green ash, don't cut them down merely because they are doomed. Indeed, it may be decades before the borer, which is presently in the Twin Cities, gets out to the prairie. Meanwhile, enjoy your tree like you would any living thing with a limited life-span.

When the ash borer arrives at our respective locales, it will likely be trumpeted in the local press as the new Pearl Harbor. Do not panic, or get out the chainsaw. When that day arrives, do not purchase expensive treatments for your green ash tree without consulting impartial experts from the extension service.

Highly-publicized tree-disease panics create openings for con artists.

Meanwhile, the green ash have other problems. The most irritating to the home gardener is anthracnose, a fungal spotting on the tender, newly emerged leaf which can cause as much as one-third of the new leaves to drop to the ground in late May or early June.

There is nothing to be done about the anthracnose, and the tree will likely be fully recovered by mid-summer.

Green ash in established prairie windbreaks have been dying off, but not due to the borer. The culprit is likely spray. The problem is given the catch-all name "ash decline," which is a way of making our ignorance sound like knowledge. Again, as consolation: there is no better firewood than green ash. *Do not bring in ash firewood from other regions, as firewood is the primary way emerald ash borer advances great distances.*

Aspen, Quaking   *Populus tremuloides*

The world's most ubiquitous tree, the quaking aspen, are often thought of as a weed. They spread by the root and take over entire areas. They form groves which, depending upon your perspective, can be beautiful, or an invasive curse.

Despite their dominance in the wild, aspen are difficult to start. Single transplants lack the support that young aspen get from the massive, interconnected root systems of an aspen grove (entire aspen groves are actually a single, massive organism, with some in the mountain west estimated at 13,000 years old).

Yet, there is nothing wrong with emulating the wise landscapers in the Denver area who use quaking aspen in groups in the urban landscape.

Aspen bark is an attractive white, just as birch bark is attractive. However, aspen grow where birch won't. They do not mind sun on their roots.

Birch and aspen can be distinguished in the wild by their habits: Birch tend to grow in a series of V-shaped clumps. Aspen trunks, in contrast, run militantly parallel to each other. In accordance with that fact of nature, aspen planted in a group should be spaced a few feet apart.

Aspen are not a long-lived tree, and cutting one down is not, as it is with oak, an act of moral significance. All the more reason to try a few near a window of the house where their bark can be appreciated during the winter.

Buckeye, Ohio *Aesculus glabra*

The character-laden Ohio Buckeye is an extremely useful tree for the northern prairie. It can have a fall color which varies from bright yellow to a deep maroon, with many shades in between. The attractive mahogany-colored nut ripens in September, and although it is slightly toxic to humans, it is a favorite of the squirrels. The unique five-pronged leaves droop like miniature umbrellas in the spring, and later fan out to provide a deep shade. The bark becomes ruddy and rustic early in the life of the tree, and the stout trunk makes the tree look old and gnarled well before it is over head height.

Unfortunately, the Ohio Buckeye is seldom planted, for many unfair reasons:

The Ohio Buckeye is a difficult tree for nurseries to transplant and sell. The deep tap root doesn't lend itself to growing in a pot, and cutting the tap root off during moving can kill the tree. Ideally, the tree will be root-pruned in the nursery—that is, the nursery will cut the roots with a big U-blade which goes under the tree in the field, requiring the buckeye to send out more side roots.

Because the root of the young Buckeye tree can be much larger than the top, it is not an easy tree to convince customers to purchase: "I have to dig a massive hole for that little thing?" is the common objection. (An alternative is to plant a buckeye nut in the ground where you would like a tree.)

Finally, the Ohio buckeye is a rare tree that works *better* on the northern prairie than it does just to the east and south. For example, Ohio Buckeye seem more subject to a late-season problem called leaf scorch even as close as southeastern Minnesota. Therefore, writers and publications further south tend to ignore a tree which works well for the relatively few of us who live on the prairie.

Prairie dwellers who see an established Ohio buckeye in the landscape often fall in love with the tree, and are willing to go through the slight hassle of finding one on the market.

Chokecherry, Amur   *Prunus maackii*

Used frequently in city plantings on the northern prairie, the Amur chokecherry bears no fruit and is distinguished by its striking, shiny bronze bark. On the prairie, the largest trees reach about fifteen feet tall.

The Amur chokecherry requires well-drained soil, and in the absence of ideal conditions can rot at the base of the trunk. Take care not to plant the tree too deeply, as soil and mulch that creep up onto the bark can hasten the development of rot.

Amur chokecherry are another favorite of the pecking sapsucker. Hang an old Bette Midler CD in the tree to ward them off.

Chokecherry, Red Leaf   *Prunus virginiana*

The red leaf chokecherry, which is variously called the Schubert chokecherry, the Canada Red cherry, and other names, is the hardiest tree in our area to have maroon leaves during the bulk of the growing season.

The red leaf chokecherry's leaves come out green—at the same time that the tree blooms—and quickly turn to a deep maroon. It is a fast growing tree early in life, but will only reach 20 feet at maximum in its lifetime.

The red leaf chokecherry is ideally suited for our climate and our soils. Unfortunately, the tree is susceptible to *black knot*, a fungal disease which causes tar like lumps on the branches of the tree, and which can kill the branches it infects. There is no spray worth using.

Due to the black knot problem, it is advisable to plant only one red leaf chokecherry per yard. A large quantity of trees in close proximity increases the severity of the black knot disease.

In addition, the red leaf chokecherry, like all members of the chokecherry family, are prone to send out dozens of shoots from the base of the tree, as well as suckers from the roots well away from the tree. The suckers in the lawn can merely be mowed off, and the suckers near the trunk can be pinched or clipped off with a pruner.

Red Leaf chokecherry should be used only singly as an accent, and with full awareness that the tree has substantial liabilities which might make it more trouble than it is worth.

Dogwood, Pagoda   *Cornus alternifolia*

Native in the forests just to the east, the Pagoda dogwood is a delightful small tree. In its natural habitat, it grows beneath the canopy provided by larger trees. Not surprisingly, it doesn't do as well out in the open, unprotected, and in full sun.

However, in the deep shade of a yard with old, established trees, the Pagoda will add a touch of oriental elegance.

Elder, Box   *Acer negundo*

In Winnipeg, box elder are sold as "Manitoba Maple." In fact, the sap of box elder, a member of the maple family, makes good syrup.

Box elder grow well in the heavy soils of the northern prairie. In fact, they are the most common weed tree to take over neglected hedges and corners of back yards.

They have become despised due to their weak and chaotic branching.

Although it is probably unwise to plant box elder, it is not necessary to cut down existing ones. Like it or not, box elder are a part of our prairie heritage.

Ironwood   *Ostrya virginiana*

Ironwood are a striking native tree which grow very, very slowly and hang on to their leaves until spring. Ironwood are a rarity in our area as they prefer to grow under a canopy of larger, established trees.

The wood of the ironwood is much harder than oak, thus its name. It is unlikely that you will find ironwood on the market, but if you do, they make a fine ornamental tree in a shady back yard.

Hackberry   *Celtis occidentalis*

Hackberry are a solid, hardy and attractive tree for our area. As the hackberry matures, the tree develops an elegant shape. The svelte trunk quickly forms an attractive, corky bark which becomes deeply grooved when the tree is young.

On the prairie, hackberry are not troubled by any major insect or disease problems, and do perfectly well in alkaline soils. Hackberry should be planted more often.

Why aren't they?

Perhaps the main reason is the difficulty hackberry sometimes have leafing out the first season after planting. The leaf buds of the hackberry are so deeply embedded in the bark that a newly planted tree sometimes is unable to "break bud." That is, the buds are unable to force their way open.

If hackberry is completely unable to break bud that first year, it dies. If it is only partially able to break bud, the tree will have leaves here and there and will not look attractive.

Once the tree is established, breaking bud does not seem to be a problem. The harsh winter temperatures seem to soften the bark enough so the tree has no trouble leafing out.

To avoid this problem, purchase a hackberry tree in full leaf in a pot, or make sure that the bare root tree you purchase has been "sweated." Sweating is a process whereby the branches of the tree are wrapped with wet fabric and kept damp and warm, ideally in a greenhouse, long enough for the buds to emerge.

Mature hackberry sometimes form wart-like galls on the leaves, a problem which is nothing more than cosmetic. (See the maple section above for an explanation of galls.)

Lilac, Japanese Tree   *Syringa reticulata*

Better in protected areas in town rather than out on the open prairie, the Japanese tree lilac blooms with cream-colored plumes in mid-June. It grows to a maximum of 15 feet, so can work under power lines.

Oak, Bur   *Quercus macrocarpa*

The native bur oak makes a wonderful yard tree. Although they grow slowly as *older* trees, many people are surprised to find that their *young* bur oak can add up to two, even three feet of growth in a single season. The young trees develop a deeply grooved bark very early on, making the bur oak attractive early in its life.

The native bur oak is seldom planted, for two reasons: first, people don't want to wait a lifetime to see the oak mature, and second, the deep tap root of the bur oak makes it difficult to transplant as a larger tree.

The prairie homeowner shouldn't exclude a young bur oak from their yard for those flimsy reasons.

Where to plant oak?

Bur oak will not survive where water remains standing late into the spring. In fact, settlers often placed their homes in groves of bur oak because they knew those areas had not flooded since the oak established.

Plant the small bur oak just where you want it to be for the rest of its life, for moving an oak is not an easy task. The tap root can go deeper than the tree is tall, and if it is severed, the oak can pout, or just die.

Olive, Russian   *Elaeagnus angustifolia*

For silver foliage in the yard, the Russian olive can't be beat. The foliage hangs on well into the winter and makes a striking contrast to the deep black bark. A single specimen Russian olive in a yard, well-trimmed, can be very striking.

Brought over from Asia due to its tolerance of salty, alkaline soils and dry conditions, the Russian olive was a staple windbreak tree sixty years ago. It has declined in popularity, as it tends to die out when things get too wet. However, as a specimen tree in the yard it still has value.

Plum, Flowering   *Prunus nigra "Princess Kay"*

Discovered near Grand Rapids, MN only a few years back, and introduced by the University of Minnesota, the Princess Kay flowering plum is still a rare tree in the northern landscape. But what a splash it makes on the early spring landscape when it covers itself with rose-like double blooms in the first week of May. Those blooms come out white and fade to pink.

The tree will grow in an upright oval shape, and will reach a maximum of 12-14 feet. The bark on the flowering plum tree is a glossy black with white stripes, attractive enough to add some winter interest.

Princess Kay flowering plum bears no fruit to speak of, but it can develop a fall color ranging from a deep maroon to a bright orange red, making it a tree which carries its weight all four seasons of the year.

The problem on the prairie: Princess Kay flowering plum have a very week root system in heavy soil. Sometimes they rot at the base of the trunk, particularly if planted too deeply. The problem becomes evident when a mature Princess Kay simply tips over in the wind. Tying them back upright can prolong the tree's life for a time.

Poplar, Tower and Swedish Columnar Aspen

populus x canescens
populus tremuloides 'erecta'

Both are adequate and hardier replacements for the old columnar "Lombardy poplar."

If you really want a pillar shape out back, and you have decided against establishing the Pyramidal Arborvitae, plant one of these two poplar.

Warning! These two poplars send out roots far distant from the tree. Shoots come up everywhere, particularly where and when the ground is damp. The shoots can be simply mowed down.

Walnut, Black

Juglans nigra

Black walnut were once native along the Red River of the North, according to an analysis of the charcoal which remains from the fires of Native Americans hundreds, even thousands of years ago. However, the climate has gotten a bit colder over the past two-thousand years, and the black walnut are not quite as hardy here as they once were.

In well-protected locations, usually right along a river, Black Walnut can live to a ripe old age.

Black walnut roots emit a toxin called *juglone*. Grass will not be hurt, but other plants can be hindered by the toxin, which stays in the soil for at least one year after a black walnut tree is removed. Fortunately, on the northern prairie we have large enough yards, and small enough black walnut trees, that the juglone from the roots doesn't cause the problems it does in cities to the immediate south, where a black walnut's root can poison an entire back yard.

EXPERIMENTAL TREES ON THE NORTHERN PRAIRIE

Several trees which are hardy in the Twin Cities sometimes creep into the northern prairie despite their lack of hardiness. They are not recommended unless you live right down by the river, or are solidly in Zone 4a. Others, such as the Alder listed, are still so new to the market that they haven't been broadly tested.

Alder *(Ainus hirsute)* is gaining attention after a new variety with the ability to withstand the dry conditions on the prairie, "Prairie Horizon," was introduced by NDSU. It will be a big addition to have an alder appropriate for the landscape.

Honeylocust *(Gleditsia)* will grow elegantly until the first tough winter, at which time the branches will often freeze back to the trunk. New branches will come which are even more tender and liable to freezing back. This cycle will continue until the tree dies. Zone 4 only.

Kentucky Coffeetree *(Gymnocladus dioica)* can survive in sheltered locations, or right along a river or lake. It prefers higher ground. Its bark looks like it is peeling off in enormous strips, but if you grab a strip and try to pull it off, you find it is as sturdy as an old-time buggy spring.

Hawthorne *(Crataegus)* don't seem to be worth the trouble. Varieties promoted as hardy for Zone 3 just haven't made it to maturity.

Catalpa *(Catalpa)* tempt gardeners with their orchid-like blooms and enormous leaves. They die out or die back in most locations on the northern prairie. There seems to be one which survives to maturity in every small town in the area, but the winter of 1996 battered even those.

Northern Pin Oak *(Quercus ellipsoidalis),* as well as **Red Oak** *(Quercus rubra)* are striking due to their extremely red fall color, and their tendency to hold on to their sharply pointed leaves deep into winter. They just aren't as hardy as the bur oak, however, and should be treated as a novelty item. They most certainly don't work well in heavy, alkaline soils.

CHAPTER 11

Planting Shrubs Around the House

Types of shrubs

There are *evergreen* shrubs, such as junipers and arborvitae, and there are *deciduous* shrubs, such as spirea and potentilla, which drop their leaves in the fall.

There are low shrubs, like the creeping junipers, and there are tall and narrow shrubs, like the pyramidal arborvitae.

Some shrubs bloom, others are meant only for their foliage. Shrubs can be trimmed and formal, or, if they are naturally dwarf or in a large enough space, they can be left to grow naturally and informally.

Choosing shrub varieties for your location

A good way to choose shrubs for your yard is to see what has worked for others in your neighborhood. Walk around. If you see a shrub you like, snatch a leaf off of it and keep it for future reference—or take a close-up picture with your phone.

Walk around an older neighborhood in your area and see what you enjoy of the plantings that have lasted through the years.

Next, take your ideas, along with a half-dozen pictures of your house and its basic measurements to your nursery person. He or she can identify the pictures or leaf samples you have taken from shrubs that have caught your eye, and help you fit those shrubs in the right spot around your house.

How much do you like to work in the yard?

Generally speaking, *evergreen* shrubs such as arborvitae and junipers are more expensive and require more care. *Deciduous* shrubs, as long as they are carefully chosen, require less maintenance. If they are neglected for a long time, deciduous shrubs are much easier to rein in and refurbish than evergreens. Once evergreens get out of hand, you pretty much have to pull them out and start over.

What look do you want to accomplish?

Are you formal or informal? Evergreens form the bulk of *formal* yard plantings, although tightly trimmed deciduous shrubs can accomplish the same look.

When allowed to grow naturally, low-maintenance deciduous shrubs will accomplish an old-fashioned, *informal* look. It is more difficult to visualize an informal planting in advance, but once it is planted, an informal yard is much easier to maintain.

This writer is inclined towards informal deciduous plantings. Deciduous shrubs provide more for your money, last longer, and are forgiving of occasional or constant neglect.

Does it help to have a big, complete plan?

It may. However, following the steps below will allow you to progress on your yard gradually, starting with the most important shrubs and working your way down to plantings which are optional, but fun.

The ease-of-mind which comes from a full, professional plan is illusory, but sometimes necessary. *No formal, complete landscape plan ever works out completely in reality* as the years go by. Some plants die. Others might not look like one hoped. The best form of planning allows you to plant in stages. Always be willing to adjust the plan to your tastes as you learn more of what you like.

The joy of yard work, as well as the curse, is that it is never finished. However, if done in the proper order, plantings can look relatively complete at nearly every stage, and the work can be a pleasure, not an obligation.

Planning an old-fashioned, informal yard

In informal plantings, you must match the shrub with the location so the shrub doesn't get too large for the spot. Pay attention to the maximum heights of the shrubs listed on the signs where you purchase the shrubs, or in the descriptions later in this book. Often these maximum heights are understated, but they can give you a good idea. Then, fit the shrubs to the openings they will *eventually* fill.

THE PLAN

A basic, fool-proof plan for every home's foundation

What follows are simple options for foundation plantings which will work for most houses on the northern prairie. The plants mentioned are hardy and proven. The concepts are simple and easy to understand. Once the basic plantings of the yard are established, using the principles outlined here, there is no end to how one can improve matters further if one gets hooked on gardening. Establishing sturdy, simple, basic plantings around the foundation of the house will be rewarding for people of every level of gardening interest or experience.

Plan and plant the corners first

Instead of filling the entire front of the house with shrubs, plant the corners first. Corners are no place to experiment. Plant only hardy, tough shrubs on the corners, ones which will survive the whipping of the winds, as well as the short-cut routes of children and chickens.

For a formal look on the corner, *Techny arborvitae* can't be beat. If you prefer an informal look, *Red Twig Dogwood* is ideal. A grouping of three *Savin juniper* around the corner of a low-eaved ranch-style house can be satisfying.

Avoid using the tall columnar *Pyramidal arborvitae* near the house. They will shoot past the eaves of most homes and become a curse. Pyramidal arborvitae only work in proximity to large houses with eaves over 18 foot up. Even then, plant them 6 to 8 feet from the house to avoid trouble.

If possible, plant corner shrubs *diagonally* out from the corner of the house *at least four feet*. Such a distance might look strange at first, but will allow the shrub adequate space to fill in without looking cramped.

The corner planting is meant to soften the harshness of the corner. Planting directly in front of the corner does not accomplish this softening as surely as does planting *diagonally* off the corner.

Next, plan and plant on either side of the entrance

Shrubs planted by the front entrance should be slightly smaller than the shrubs used on the corners of the house. *Tor spirea* is the best deciduous shrub. *Techny arborvitae* work well for a more formal look. For a smaller scale house, or where there is only three feet or less of space, the *Globe caragana* is ideal. *Bridalwreath spirea* are delightfully old-fashioned, tough and dependable. If you are willing to do some trimming, *Dwarf Korean lilac* or *alpine currant* work well by the steps.

Although either side of the steps is a more protected location than the corner of the house, one should not use novelty shrubs, or marginally dependable shrubs, by the steps, no matter how intriguing. You want these basic shrubs to make a firm structural statement.

Embellish the open spaces with odd numbers of small shrubs

Do not seek to fill the entire front of the house with a mass of shrubs. The shrubs between the steps and the corner, if you choose to put some there, should be markedly shorter than the shrubs on the corners or by the front step. They should be planted in odd numbers, which will give the entire foundation planting a more natural look.

Little Princess spirea is a fool proof solution to fill middle spaces. They can be both formal and informal, depending upon how often you trim. In the hottest sun, potentilla or hardy roses work well. Hardy roses are truly old-fashioned, as are the old time Bridalwreath Spirea, sold nowadays as the Van Houtte Spirea. If the planting is more formal, Mugo pine will provide round shapes, and the Savin juniper will add a dignified fountain shape which is perfect under low windows.

The low creeping junipers aren't tall enough to make an impact from the street. You simply can't see them unless you are right on top of them. The most prostrate creeping junipers are best for rock gardens, or for locations where they are allowed to cascade.

Complete the landscape by accenting with odd, interesting and colorful shrubs

Having covered the crucial parts of the house with completely dependable shrubs, it is now time to add interest by putting in shrubs with more novelty value.

Red- or maroon-leafed shrubs such as barberry or ninebark work well planted singly as an accent against a light-colored house. More than one looks overbearing.

Yellow-leafed shrubs, such as the Goldmound Dwarf Spirea, contrast with the reds, or can be used for color in front of the darker green shrubs behind.

Wiegela, the non-yellow Potentilla, Mockorange, Burning Bush, and other marginally hardy but useful shrubs are best used sparingly, and not on corners.

Add a few of your favorite perennials

It is not wise to plant too many perennials around the foundation of your house just to fill the space. Very few perennial plants look solid all season. Stick with shrubs, particularly if you aren't a gardener.

Silver mound, day lilies, asters, bleeding heart, hosta and other staples are the best bets to embellish foundation plantings. Consider rhubarb as an ornamental perennial near the house.

Accent your permanent plantings with colorful annuals

It is not necessary to plant large masses of annuals to make a splash. Just a few brightly-colored annuals can add considerable pizzaz to a formal planting of evergreens, or trimmed deciduous shrubs. Plant $50 worth of geraniums in three or four clay pots, place them across the front of your house, and could add as much as $10,000 to the market value of your home. It is worth a try anyway, and you won't regret it.

Don't hesitate to plant veggies or fruits near the front step

A cherry tomato planted way out in the garden is seldom used to its potential. Hundreds of the fruit go to waste. But a cherry tomato planted in full sun by the step, or in any high traffic area, will provide nibbling for much of the summer. Parsley is ornamental, yet provides a good breath freshener for visiting salespeople. A single raspberry plant, or a grouping of three little strawberry plants will add flavor to the morning walk to the car.

PLANTING AND CARE

Purchasing shrubs

The ideal way to purchase deciduous shrubs is bare root. However, bare root shrubs are not broadly available, and most people are accustomed to purchasing shrubs in pots.

If you do purchase shrubs bare root, look at the plant's root and choose one that looks vigorous. The root is more important than the top. Branches should be pliable and look as if they are ready to sprout. Roots should be plentiful and hairy.

Bare root shrubs might seem insubstantial. The first-time buyer often feels sheepish paying $200 for a bundle of sticks that he or she can carry to the car in one arm. However, the results usually *exceed* the results of potted shrubs, even as early as the middle of the first summer, at much less cost, and with much less hassle.

Planting bare root deciduous shrubs

To save a lot of hassle, don't purchase bare root plants until you are ready to plant them within a day or two.

Wait to open the package of bare root shrubs until you are ready to plant. Once you have opened the package, keep the roots moist and shaded from the sun *at all times* until the plant is in the ground.

Do not soak the roots of the plant in a pail of water unless they came in the mail all dried out and need to be reconstituted. In any case, do not soak roots for longer than six hours.

To plant bare root shrubs: Dig a 2' x 2' hole and spread the roots out wide making sure that the shrub is deep enough so a 2-3 inch depression can be left around the base of the shrub. That means that the crown of the shrub (where the branches begin) is going to be 4-5 inches beneath the *original* soil level, and two inches beneath the *final* soil level.

Bury the roots without filling in the hole entirely yet. Leave a large depression at least 5 or 6 inches deep for water. Fill the depression once or twice and allow the water to soak down, then fill in the rest of the soil, leaving a depression of at least two inches around the base of the shrub.

The bottom inch or two of the branches of the shrub should be covered with soil. (Hydrangea are an exception to this rule.)

Potted shrubs

Potted shrubs require more care than bare root shrubs, but most people are forced to plant potted shrubs due to the unavailability of bare root shrubs.

Before purchasing potted shrubs, *it is best to choose plants which have a pot in generous proportion to the top of the plant.* The smaller the pot is in relation to the top of the plant, the more root-bound the shrub is, and the more watering will be required for the first year after planting.

For the important first plantings, choose only shrubs rated for Zone 3. It is not safe to assume that because a shrub is for sale on the northern prairie that it is hardy for the northern prairie. Although yews, weigela, boxwood and azaleas sometimes find their way onto discount store garden displays on the northern prairie, none of the four are completely hardy for our area.

Planting potted shrubs

Dig the hole about 1 1/2 times the depth of the pot, and about twice as wide as the pot's width. If the shrub is root-bound, as it likely will be, take care to pull apart the roots in the root ball before planting.

Plant the shrub deeper than it is in the pot. In most cases, the crown, that point at the base of the shrub where the first branches start, should be covered by about two inches of soil.

Make sure that the shrub is deep enough so a 2-3 inch depression can be left around the base of the shrub. That means that the crown of the shrub is going to be 4-5 inches beneath the *original* soil level, and two inches beneath the *final* soil level.

Make sure no labels, tags, wire or twine encircles the base of the shrub, or any of the main branches. Anything which circles the shrub's stems can choke the shrub later in its life.

Carefully remove all pots, even those which are supposed to be biodegradable. It is necessary to help the roots of a potted plant get out into the soil by digging the hole plenty big, and by pulling the root ball apart quite violently.

Watering your shrubs

Unless they are planted under an eave, bare root shrubs should not need watering after the initial watering at planting time until a prolonged dry spell. Potted shrubs, because they are full of foliage at planting and usually root-bound, need more frequent watering. Stick your finger down *near the base of the plant, into the original dirt ball.* If it is dry, water. If the soil is still damp, do not water.

Trimming shrubs

Trim blooming shrubs just after the bloom has faded. Trimming at that time not only gets rid of the unsightly spent blooms, but it shapes the shrub—and allows the shrub the rest of the season to prepare for blooming the next season. Trimming blooming shrubs at any other time than just after they have bloomed will reduce upcoming bloom.

Trim foliar shrubs, those which are just there to look leafy, when you think they look scruffy. When alpine currant and cotoneaster look like they need a haircut, get out the clippers. Dogwood are prettiest if they are left to grow naturally, but can be shaped if need be.

Trim evergreen shrubs when they are showing new growth, usually in June. Always leave some of the new growth or the evergreen shrub become stunted, woody and unhealthy.

An alternative to trimming: harshly cut back deciduous shrubs

Shrubs such as potentilla and dogwood, especially *variegated* dogwood, respond well to being cut back to the ground every two or three years. People hesitate to cut shrubs back to the ground for fear they will kill them. However, cutting a deciduous shrub to the ground can reinvigorate old, woody shrubs. If one cuts back the shrub during dormancy, it can return to presentability as early as mid-June. Cutting back a potentilla to the ground merely delays the bloom for a couple of weeks the next summer, and often completely reinvigorates the plant.

Evergreen shrubs *cannot* be cut back to the ground. Once they grow too large, they have grown too large. A tow rope and a four-wheel drive pickup are the only remedy.

An old-fashioned way to use large shrubs

Large shrubs can be used around the perimeter of the yard to enhance the natural landscape. Nannyberry, Amur maple, lilac, and other large shrubs can be planted in such a way as to blend into the landscape. Plant large shrubs singly, or in odd-numbered groups at the edges or in the corners of the yard, or to fill in large blank spaces along the house or along the big, blank side of a farm building. When they mature, these large shrubs will form an old-fashioned mass. The lilac will bloom in May, the Nannyberry and Amur Maple will turn bright colors in the fall.

Large shrubs strategically placed are the best way to make a big, open yard more cozy.

Consider hardy roses

The breeding of hardy roses brings forth new options each year. If you have a hot spot of ground against a white house, hardy roses are the best option. Because most people do not use hardy roses in the landscape, you will be the star of the neighborhood when they come into bloom.

Hardy roses come in nearly every shape or size. Some grow to six feet, others stay at two. Some grow wide, others grow narrow.

Dark pink roses are the hardiest and most showy. Most yellow hardy roses only bloom in June, but are spectacular then. Red roses are shorter, bloom less, and are best if viewed up close.

Figure out the measurements of your spot and choose a rose to fit the spot based upon shape and size first, color second. See Chapter 19 on roses for more information.

Color coordination

The yard is not the living room. Although a little color coordination might improve matters in the yard, blooming plants tend not to clash with each other. In fact, the various plants reach their peak bloom at different times, making perfect coordination unnecessary.

The primary color concern is to make sure plants along the foundation stand out against the color of the house, particularly houses painted in darker tones.

Darn near everything looks good against brick or rock facing, no matter the color.

CHAPTER 12

Useful Shrubs for the Northern Prairie

Below are the most commonly successful shrubs used on the northern plains. Most are common on the market, a few require some digging. And a couple, such as the first on the list, the barberry, are still on the market despite evident weaknesses.

Barberry   *Berberis*

Barberry are known for their colorful foliage, ranging from the most common deep maroon to bright chartreuse. Barberry stay small, both by force of their growth habit and by their propensity to die back in winters.

Because barberry can be so beautiful their first season, they retain their popularity despite their dismal performance in our winters. For years, barberry were the only small shrub with purple foliage. The breeding of dwarfed ninebark with maroon leaves, however, means the barberry is no longer alone in this niche.

If you love barberry, plant them where there is ample sunshine in summer and deep snow in the winter for best results. Use a single plant as an accent. If used in plural numbers, or in a row, it is likely that each plant will grow to a different height depending upon winter cover.

Rather than cut out the dead branches of the barberry in spring, a painful exercise give the shrub's wicked thorns, simply cut the bush back to one-half of its original height, more if necessary to remove all the dead branches.

Enjoy barberry plants one shrub at a time, one year at a time.

Note: Several barberry varieties have been identified as noxious weeds in Minnesota and will be phased out by 2018.

Caragana, Globe   *Caragana frutex "Globosa"*

The globe caragana, or dwarf peashrub, is a little gem particularly well-suited for the northern prairie. Globe caragana are rarely used outside our area, and sometimes they are difficult to find even here.

Globe caragana limit their own height to three feet, and usually grow narrower than they do tall, often with a definite little trunk at the base.

Globe caragana do not need trimming, except for the removal of an occasional errant shoot. They survive without much water. They thrive in junky soil. They never get overgrown. They leaf out with beautiful lime green leaves early in the spring.

Globe caragana are ideal for cemetery plantings because they never will get overgrown, they tolerate neglect, and they are at their most beautiful lime-green color at Memorial Day.

Globe caragana can work in shade, but they will not tolerate saturated moist conditions. They work in heavy soil as long as it is not constantly wet.

Globe caragana send out shoots from the base. These shoots can be allowed to grow, giving the planting a natural look, or they can be chopped out with a spade and, if dormant, planted elsewhere.

Globe caragana makes an idea small hedge alongside a house, especially in the limited space available in cases where the sidewalk has been placed too close to the house.

Globe caragana can survive in an area as narrow as 18 inches wide, and won't mind the heat of the south side of a building.

Globe caragana can fill the role of *boxwood*, a common small hedge plant used in much of the rest of the country which is not hardy here. However, unlike boxwood, the globe caragana is best if allowed to grow without trimming or shaping.

Chokeberry   *Aronia*

This relative of the chokecherry features glossy dark green leaves which turn fiery red in the fall. The berries are dark, and although not poisonous, they aren't particularly good to eat. They are popular in Europe for syrups, and for medicinal purposes.

Cotoneaster   *Cotoneaster acutifolia*

Cotoneaster can be one of the most satisfying hedge plants for the northern prairie. In some locales, cotoneaster can turn a spectacular orange color in the fall, a coloration rare on high-alkaline soils.

Planting cotoneaster in shade will produce a thin, open plant, and is probably not worth the trouble.

Cotoneaster respond well to trimming, whether planted singly or in a hedge. They should be trimmed in an A shape, not a V shape. Trimming them in an A shape will allow them to stay fully branched all the way to the ground.

Cotoneaster have always been susceptible to a host of insects and disease, including fire blight, spider mites and oyster shell scale. These diseases cycle through, depending upon conditions.

If your cotoneaster hedge starts to decline, cut it back severely to about one-foot in height. It will come back with fresh new growth which may not be as afflicted with disease. Hope for better times next season.

The deep purple berries of the cotoneaster hang on into the winter. They aren't edible, but neither are they poisonous.

Cranberry, Compact American   *Viburnum*

The Compact Cranberry grows naturally in a compact oval shape, seldom needing trimming to maintain a formal look. The foliage is a dignified orange-green all summer, turning to brilliant fall colors ranging from deep red to bright orange, depending upon soil and moisture conditions.

Compact Cranberry are somewhat difficult to establish. They pout when planted in pots, and they don't like cold storage, either. They want to be planted in the ground by your house, *now*.

Compact Cranberry foliage can be attacked by aphids in late spring. Aphids will not kill the plant, but will cause the leaves to curl. If you have the problem one year, spray with a systemic insecticide (rose spray in a can will work) early the next spring, as soon as the leaves emerge, and before the problem appears.

Cranberry, American   *Viburnum trilobum*

The non-compact American cranberry is usually planted for its fruit. Due to its vigorous growth, plain old native American cranberry makes a better hedge plant than the Compact Cranberry. And the waxwings and grosbeaks love the berries!

American cranberry is included here as an ornamental shrub, (in addition to its status as a small fruit) because dozens of new ornamental varieties of American cranberry are coming onto the market, many of them worth having both for their bloom and fruit. The newer varieties are being sold under the Latin name *Viburnum*. They feature an intriguing variety of bloom sizes, shapes and textures—however, they are not intriguing enough to justify planting one of every type.

It is worthwhile to try one or two viburnum out by the woods somewhere, as, unlike the Compact American cranberry, the newer viburnums are rangy and a bit irregular in habit—and should be left that way if they are to bear fruit.

Currant, Alpine   *Ribes alpinum*

Alpine currant is an ideal foliage shrub for the shade, but can be used in almost any situation that requires tight, dense foliage. It grows thickly, responds well to formal trimming, and can be cut back to the ground if it ever gets too large.

Alpine currant is the most useful plant for a small hedge available on the northern prairie. Its quarter-sized, glossy, maple-like leaves provide a dignified, semi-formal look whether the plant is trimmed or not.

Alpine currant foliage is susceptible to mildew in cool, moist summers. Mildew can cause the leaves of the alpine current to turn a crispy brown long before fall. If mildew becomes a perennial problem, spray with fungicide in June *before* symptoms of mildew occur.

Dogwood, Red Twig   *Cornus*

A hardy native plant, the dogwood should be a staple in the northern yard. If properly maintained, dogwood shrubs can last for decades.

Although they are merely green and leafy in the summer, the red-twigged dogwoods make a show in the winter, especially towards spring when their branches seem to become brighter red, and can positively glow when made glossy by an early spring rain.

In addition, some dogwoods can display good fall leaf color, ranging from deep burgundy, to red, to even some oranges.

Do not confuse our dogwood with dogwood further south which bloom with large blooms. The two are from different families. Our dogwood do not have the spectacular bloom. The dogwood tree from the south does not survive our winters, and they do not have the red branching of our northern varieties.

Dogwood are perfect for the corners of houses. They make excellent informal hedges. They can screen out a propane tank like no other shrub. If one ever moves the tank, you can cut the dogwood to the ground to allow the machinery in, and they will grow back as if nothing happened.

We are partial to a cultivar of red-twig dogwood discovered by Melvin Bergeson, my grandfather. Grandpa originally named it the "Gary" dogwood because it was found in a swamp near Gary, MN. Another nursery named it "Bergeson Compact Dogwood," which we thought quite nice—although it later was decided the shrub wasn't quite compact enough to have the word "compact" in its name. So, today it is the Bergeson Dogwood, and it is a dandy.

Bergeson Dogwood grow with a tighter habit and have a deeper red branch color than the generic dogwood grown from seedlings. The best feature of the Bergeson Dogwood, however, is its fall leaf color, which starts purple and turns to a brilliant maraschino-cherry red.

Red-twig dogwood render a valuable service in the large yards containing large houses on the northern prairie. Dogwood provide what I call "architectural green." That is, if you have a big blank spot which you want to fill with green, as an architect might pencil in a green blob on a rendering, the dogwood will do the trick and do it quick.

Never hesitate to cut the dogwood back to six inches height in order to reinvigorate the plant. Some dogwood owners do this each year, with good effect.

Dogwood, Variegated   *Cornus alba*

The white and green foliage of the variegated dogwood made it a popular choice for foundation plantings over the years. However, the old-time variegated dogwood were notorious for their lankiness. They needed to be cut back to a few inches height each year in order to stay attractive. And then they would shoot straight up to eight feet! They were neither as tough nor as thick as the plain old green-leaved red-twig dogwood. Their leaves, which were their only reason to exist, got spotty with disease as the season progressed. In addition, the winter bark color of the variegated dogwood was nothing to write home about.

Just when we were about to give up on the idea of variegated dogwood, along comes the "Ivory Halo" variegated dogwood, a compact version of the shrub which grows only to about four feet tall and four feet wide.

The leaves on the Ivory Halo feature a deeper contrast between the white and green. They last throughout the season. The shrub stays dense without trimming.

In short, the Ivory Halo rescued variegated dogwood from the brush pile and gave it a renewed place in the northern prairie yard.

Euonymus, "Burning Bush" *Euonymus alata*

Burning Bush should be planted more frequently on the northern prairie. Compact *Euonymus alata*, the official name for the species of Burning Bush which works best here, produces a delightful cherry red fall leaf color.

The summer appearance of Burning Bush is that of a neat, dark green globe. Euonymus tend to form a single trunk at the base. They do not form uniform hedges due to the openness at the bottom, but they work well as a single plant.

Euonymous aren't quite tough enough to be relied upon on the corner of a house in our area. Better to use them along long, blank walls, or out at the edge of the yard where they will be seen when they are doing their thing in the fall. In a flower bed, they can also form a centerpiece that will never get out of control.

Be patient with Burning Bush in the spring as they can be very slow to leaf out. The dwarf version features corky fins on the bark.

Forsythia *Forsythia*

Until the introduction of the *Meadowlark Forsythia* by North Dakota State University, forsythia were not regarded as hardy for the northern prairie. Now, however, gardeners on the plains are free to enjoy this most useful shrub.

Forsythia are famous for bright yellow blooms which emerge first thing in the spring, even before the plum blossoms.

142

A tough winter can reduce the forsythia's bloom. In fact, one can sometimes see the snow line on a hedge of forsythia—below the snow line the branches are rich with bloom, above the line blooms are sparse.

Apart from the bloom, the forsythia makes a thick and vigorous hedge plant. To keep forsythia smaller than six feet requires frequent trimming, as they send out lush shoots with abandon.

The attractive, thick foliage of the forsythia makes it useful as either a trimmed, formal hedge or an untrimmed, informal, eight-foot hedge.

Meadowlark is the variety of forsythia recommended for the northern prairie. Insist upon it, absolutely.

Hydrangea *Hydrangea*

The old-time hydrangea *(Hydrangea arborescens)* have long been a popular shrub for deep shade on the northern prairie. The hydrangea's huge white globular blooms and lush, soft green leaves brighten the darkest corner of the yard.

Two varieties of the old-time hydrangea remain on the market: "Snowhill" and "Annabelle." It takes an expert to tell the difference between the two, so don't fret whether you get one or the other, or a few of each.

If your old-time hydrangea simply won't bloom, it isn't your fault. Sometimes non-hybrid batches of hydrangea sneak their way onto the market. Blame your nursery and have them give you a new one.

Old-time hydrangea can be cut back to 6-8 inches each spring. They will bloom on new wood. The blooms dry well, so leave them stand throughout the winter for winter interest.

For a long stretch of house in the shade, particularly at a lake cabin, a row of old-time hydrangea will fill the bill.

Hydrangea love peat. Dig out the heavy soil and fill an area two feet wide and a foot deep with pure, local peat for great results.

Old-fashioned hydrangea are one shrub which will not do well if planted too deeply. Barely cover the fresh little shoots on a bare root plant, and do not plant a potted hydrangea any deeper than it is in the pot.

May we have the blues?

Oh, the temptation to plant blue hydrangeas on the northern prairie after seeing them on your vacation to the Pacific Northwest, where they are numerous and spectacular. Forget it! Blue hydrangea can't take the cold, and they can't take our soil. Even the famous "Endless Summer" hydrangea, which was sort of a pinkish-blue, needs cover and a lot of fertilizer to survive here.

No blues, but we now may have the pinks!

Luckily, breeding of hardy hydrangeas for the northern prairie has taken off. Although we cannot yet grow blue (acid soil is required to get blue blooms), we can get pinks, some of them deep.

The new hydrangea are of a different breed than the old-fashioned— they are classified as *Hydrangea paniculata,* or, as we call them "Pee-Gee-type," because the first of the type was called Pee Gee.

Pee Gee-type hydrangea (*paniculata*) differ from the old-fashioned in three crucial ways. First, *Hydrangea paniculata* require more sun than *Hydrangea arborecens*, more than a half-a-day. Second, *Hydrangea paniculata* cannot be cut to the ground each season as they only bloom on old wood. Third, their leaves are darker and more firm than the old-fashioned *Hydrangea arborescens*.

The most rewarding all-around shrub of the new type is the Limelight, which can grow to seven feet and features conical blooms one-foot wide at the base and one-foot tall. The shrub has no problem holding the massive blooms erect above the dignified dark-green foliage.

Breeders have now attempted to add pink to the blooms, with pretty good results. Although the blooms emerge white, they quickly turn to pink. The pink-blooming *Hydrangea paniculata* have a little trouble holding their massive blooms upright, but can be helped with a little staking, or perhaps a peony cage.

144

Other types of *Hydrangea paniculata* feature looser, airy blooms instead of the traditional full globe. "Quick Fire" is the best example, a shrub which may soon qualify as a staple on the northern prairie due to its apparent tolerance of alkaline soils and cold winds.

The development of new hydrangeas has been the most exciting change in the shrub department on the northern prairie in decades. Check out the new ones each spring at your local garden center!

Lilac, Common   *Syringa vulgaris*

The smell of lilac blooms heralds the last days of school and the beginning of summer vacation. What can fill a room with a scent more rich and glorious than a bouquet of lilacs?

The common lilac is the most important lilac for the northern prairie, and includes a number of French hybrids with blooms which can range from single to double, dark purple to pink to lavender to white, each with a slightly different twist to the intoxicating lilac scent.

The seedling common lilac, sold in bundles by the hundreds by the soil conservation service, is best for long rows. Common lilac send out suckers from the base, so the eventual hedge is very thick at the bottom, sometimes wider than the hedge is tall, which can be 12 feet.

The French hybrids do not sucker as vigorously, and neither do they grow as quickly, or to be as full. Because they are reproduced *vegetatively,* they are more expensive.

The common lilac, French or not, are best if planted out in the open, as a screen between your yard and a neighbor's, or in a place which could use some architectural green. They are too big and rangy to put next to the house.

Lilacs will grow in shade, but weakly, and their bloom will not be as prolific as in full sun.

The very best of the hybrid common lilac is the "Pocahontas." It grows quickly, blooms on young plants, and blooms from the tips of the branches down to the ground. The color is the typical lavender and the scent is spicy. One "Pocahontas" lilac will make a dramatic specimen out in the wide open space.

Where do common lilac grow best?

Lilac do not like low areas on the northern prairie. They particularly don't like salty soil, which can be identified by a white crust which forms on the soil surface as the soil dries after a rain.

Lilac, Canadian   *Prestonian hybrid lilac*

Canadian lilacs, otherwise known as *Prestonian hybrids,* have been developed to be more tolerant of heavy, wet soils. They bloom two weeks later than the common lilac, and tend towards pink. The bloom clusters are prolific, but not as tightly-formed as the common lilac's. The leaf of the Prestonian hybrids is rougher and more elongated. They do not sucker.

The "Miss Canada," a true pink, has been the most vigorous of the Canadian varieties.

Lilac, Villosa   *Syringa villosa*

For those who want a lilac hedge, but who don't like the suckering habit of common lilac, the "Villosa" lilac from China provides a seedling (and therefore cheap) alternative.

From a distance, this late-bloomer makes quite a show. Up close, the blooms simply lack the elegance of the common lilac. Their bloom clusters are true pink, but quite loose. Villosa are more appropriate for hedges or windbreak than they are as a specimen shrub.

Lilac, Dwarf   *Syringa meyeri*

Unlike the common lilac, dwarf lilac can be used as a landscape plant against the foundation of the house.

The most popular, the "Dwarf Korean," grows to six or seven feet, but in a very dense fashion. Their blooms are small, but very numerous. The scent is overpowering. They bloom slightly later than the common lilac. Their leaves are the size of a quarter.

Dwarf Korean lilac look best if trimmed formally right after the bloom fades. As the years pass, they tend to look like tight round balls. If you like formality, they are the shrub for you.

A second dwarf lilac, the "Miss Kim," *(Syringa pubescens)* should be used more often. With a vigorous, vase-like shape and elegant, upward-pointing leaves, the Miss Kim has an oriental look to go with its Korean origins. Its late, very light lavender bloom clusters extend upward from the shrub. The scent is very pleasant and quite strong.

Miss Kim should be trimmed more lightly than the Dwarf Korean lilac, as they have a beautiful natural shape which should not be constrained.

Maple, Amur Compact   *Acer ginnala*

The compact form of Amur maple makes a spectacular globe specimen shrub in the middle of the yard. Compact Amur maple frequently display a fall color more brilliantly orange than the generic Amur maple (featured in the windbreak chapter).

Finding the compact Amur maple varieties on the market is getting more difficult as the seedling form loses popularity further to the east due to its alleged propensity to spread by seed. We can only wish they were that easy to reproduce out on the prairie!

If you see a compact Amur maple in a pot on a lot somewhere, pick it up. You may never see one again.

Bare root plants of Amur maple can be stubborn about leafing out in their first season. Be patient.

Mockorange   *Philadelphus*

A recent introduction, the "Blizzard" mockorange represents a big improvement in the mockorange family. With dark green, narrow leaves and a columnar shape filled out with foliage right to the ground, the Blizzard looks like an entirely different shrub than the traditional Minnesota Snowflake mockorange—until it blooms.

And boy does the Blizzard bloom! Coinciding with the first flush of bloom from the hardy roses, the Blizzard can take full sun well enough to be planted right alongside a larger rose such as the William Baffin. The visual effect of the two together is stunning, and the overpowering orange-blossom scent of the mockorange will drift throughout the yard.

In addition, unlike the traditional mockorange varieties listed below, the Blizzard is completely winter hardy and can grow in full sun.

The "Minnesota Snowflake" mockorange has historically been the most common for our region. They are prized for the vividly sweet scent of their mid-summer blooms. The Minnesota Snowflake seldom impresses one with its value in the landscape, but gardeners who enjoy the stimulation of all of the senses often find a place in the partial shade for a specimen.

Minnesota Snowflake mockorange tend to get lanky, and can be cut back to a few inches above the ground during dormancy to produce luxuriant, thick new growth. Because they can grow to be an eight-foot shrub, Minnesota Snowflake are best planted on a big back wall of a house where they can be enjoyed when they are blooming and ignored for the rest of the year.

The dwarfed "Golden" mockorange, a more tender plant, used primarily for its bright yellow foliage rather than its bloom, is no longer needed for that purpose on the northern prairie and should be avoided.

Nannyberry   *Viburnum lentago*

A native plant, and a close relative of the American cranberries, the nannyberry could be used more often, if only for its striking glossy-red fall foliage. The nannyberry is a large shrub, growing up to twelve feet, in an unorganized manner. Use the nannyberry to screen out your propane tank, or to make for a natural looking barrier between yourself and the neighbors. Or simply place a few in a grouping near the edge of the woods, where they will blend in throughout the season, but come into glory in autumn with a brilliant red splash.

Nannyberry produce small oval black fruits, which look like miniature black olives. They are not tasty, but they are not poisonous, either.

Ninebark $\hspace{10em}$ *Physocarpus*

The old golden ninebark are known for their bright golden foliage all season long. The yellow leaf color merely gets more intense in the fall.

However, the golden varieties were losing popularity due to their vigor and propensity to get very woody after only a few years.

Along came the plant breeders to rescue the scruffy old ninebark from oblivion! First in the parade of new varieties came the maroon-leafed "Diabolo" variety, which is quite large and should be allowed to grow to seven feet. Then came other maroon-leafed varieties, some dwarfed, and others with cascading white blooms in the fountaining habit of a bridal wreath spirea.

Finally, we have new varieties with orange-tinted leaves, and others which are multi-colored. Although the ninebark fad hasn't quite taken off like the hydrangea fad, given these exciting new introductions, it may be a matter of time.

The larger ninebark require trimming in most situations, but the new smaller varieties are quite nice if left to their own devices.

On some very alkaline soils, the golden-leafed ninebark's foliage can become whitish rather than yellow.

After a few years of growth, it pays to cut ninebark back severely, even down to one foot, in order to refresh the growth.

Plum, Flowering   *Prunus triloba*

Also known as Rose Tree of China, the flowering plum's pink, double, rose-like blooms open in early May. The blooms are quite impressive and can last for well over a week, enticing those who have never seen the plant before to run to the garden center for one of their own—only to find that they're already out. When it's a good year for flowering plum, everybody wants one!

And not every year is a good year. Sometimes the flower buds will freeze during the winter. In fact, a full, spectacular bloom happens about once every three years. Plant the flowering plum in a location where it will stand out when it blooms, but fade into the background for the remainder of the season.

Potentilla   *Potentilla fruticosa*

The dependable, hardy and native potentilla should remain a favorite for years to come. The strongest varieties bloom yellow. Some of the off-colors, like white, pink, and even orange, have been improved in recent years, but the yellow blooming potentilla remain head and shoulders above the rest for vigor and impact on the landscape.

Potentilla perform best in the hot sun. They are native to the dry prairies. Because of their dependence upon sun and heat, potentilla don't seem to bloom as much right up against the east side of the house, and should be avoided completely on the north.

Proper care of potentilla is easy, but very important. Potentilla should *not* be trimmed regularly or tightly. Shaping potentilla into little round balls by trimming the tips of the branches only cuts off the bloom and makes the branches underneath more woody.

When a potentilla becomes woody and ugly, *cut the plant back to four inches above ground level.* Then, let the potentilla grow and bloom naturally. If you cut the potentilla back every two or three years, a plant can last for fifteen to twenty years.

Do not to let the grass creep in to the base of the potentilla. No shrub can compete with sod or grass, but the potentilla are particularly vulnerable to such competition. Because potentilla grow up like a fountain from a definite base, it is easy to allow the grass to grow in. Keep the grass away for the best results.

Dozens of bright yellow potentilla varieties are on the market, all of about equal value and habit. The "Katherine Dykes" variety is more of a creeper and features pale yellow blooms atop bluish foliage. It is more appropriate in a hot rock garden beside some sedum.

Snowball   *Viburnum opulus*

A member of the American cranberry family, the snowball is a nostalgic favorite for the old-fashioned yard. Many people confuse the snowball with "Snowhill" hydrangea; in fact, they are very different.

The old-fashioned snowball is best planted in the middle of a large yard, where it can be allowed to grow to its natural height of 8 to 10 feet. Trimming the snowball is permissible, but it reduces the bloom.

The snowball will become covered with golf ball-sized and shaped white blooms in late spring. A specimen snowball plant can stop traffic during that time.

Snowball, like others in the American cranberry family, can be attacked by aphids early in the season. Aphids will cause the leaves to curl and sometimes turn brown. If you have had an aphid problem in the past, spray with a systemic insecticide early next spring, before the problem appears.

Snowball that get too large, or get old and woody, can be rejuvenated by cutting them back to the ground. They will not bloom for a couple of years following a severe hacking. For constant bloom, it is best to prune out old, unattractive and woody canes of the snowball one at a time.

SPIREA   *Spiraea*

The spirea family is huge. Too huge, in fact. For our purposes, we will narrow things down to two categories, the *old-fashioned white-blooming spirea*, the most prominent of which is called "Bridalwreath," and the newer *dwarf spirea*, such as the "Goldmound," "Little Princess" and the "Goldflame," which feature pink and red blooms, as well as different colors of foliage. The two types are very separate in appearance and use in the yard, and the fact that they share the name *spirea* is confusing, although botanically correct.

Old-time Spirea

The old-fashioned bridalwreath-type spirea was frequently planted around the big old Victorian mansions in the 1880s. The most popular of the type on the northern prairie was the venerable "Van Houtte." Today, the "Renaissance" is the most available on the market, as are some dwarf varieties which fountain out like the old Van Houtte, but take up less space.

The important thing is not the particular variety of old-time spirea you choose, but the eventual *height*. Because it is best to leave old-fashioned spirea to grow naturally, free flowing and informal, you want to put them in a place where they won't have to be cut back. Trimming an old-fashioned spirea into a round ball is an egregious affront to its natural shape. The spirea will send out a cluster of new branches right where the cuts are made, creating an obvious line for the next few years.

The old-time spirea grow virtually anywhere, against the house or in the yard, in sun or shade, even on a corner. They are perfectly hardy, showing winter damage only once in the past forty years.

Spirea, Dwarf   *Spiraea*

Dwarf spirea, which to the casual observer bears little relation to the old-fashioned white spirea, have become a staple for landscapes in the urban areas of the Midwest. In fact, they are overused. Professional landscapers plant them by the thousands. Overly formal, they look like beach balls stranded on barren stretches of landscape rock around banks and fast food joints, where they collect candy wrappers and beverage cups in their branches for winter viewing once the leaves drop.

Inevitably, dwarf spirea are used around homes, with mixed long-term results.

The best of the dwarves

If they are going to be used in a home setting, it is important to select the strongest varieties of dwarf spirea. What follows is a list of top recommendations for this area.

Little Princess Dwarf Spirea

The best dwarf spirea is the "Little Princess." A sturdy, forgiving shrub, the Little Princess features delicate pink blooms in late June and throughout much of July. Trimming the Little Princess once after the bloom fades will keep it in a neat globe.

The delicate leaves are attractive from spring to fall, starting a soft-green and turning a deep maroon in autumn, even adding hints of orange. The Little Princess will grow to a maximum of 3 feet high and 5 feet wide. It can easily be kept slightly smaller. It is dependable and consistent enough to plant in groupings of three or five.

Anthony Waterer Dwarf Spirea

The "Anthony Waterer" is a dwarf spirea which has been on the market for decades, and is still difficult to beat. It blooms a purplish-red. Rather than forming a squatty globe, as does the Little Princess, the Anthony Waterer spread wide and send vigorous shoots straight up, topped by the bloom. They are more informal than the Little Princess, and fit well in a perennial garden.

Gold-leafed Dwarf Spirea

Although they are irresistibly cute in pots at the nursery, the gold-leafed varieties of dwarf spirea seldom look as good two years after planting as the day they were put in. However, there is no other shrub which stays quite as small (18 inches) without trimming.

Tor Spirea —*The best of both spirea worlds*

Straddling the divide between the old-fashioned, drooping white spirea, and the dwarf, mounding, multi-colored blooming types is the "Tor" ("Tor" being the Gaelic word for "mound") spirea, which blooms white in late spring, but on a neat, contained mound. The Tor is irresistibly cute, and its round, lobe-like leaves can turn blaze orange, or sometimes purple, in the fall. The Tor limits itself to three feet in height, and three feet in width.

Sumac   *Rhus*

The very first plant to turn red in the fall, sumac (staghorn) tends to grow along ditch banks. *Sumac spreads.* Yet, there is no reason sumac can't be planted as a filler around the edges of a yard, or along a bank. Get permission to dig up the dormant shoots from a ditch bank.

The relatively new "Tiger Eyes" sumac is of an entirely different character than the staghorn sumac. It stays contained in a single clump, and features golden foliage which comes back from the bottom of the shrub most years, or from the branches after milder winters.

Weigela   *Weigela*

The weigela (a word nobody knows how to pronounce) is of borderline hardiness, but produces the only bright red bloom of any shrub on the northern prairie. It is best planted near lakes, rivers, and in towns and cities where the bottom few degrees are subtracted from the coldest nights of winter. It prefers the east side of the house.

"Red Prince" weigela is the crown prince of the weigela family. It is vigorous, and usually comes back from winter with minimal tip-dieback on the branches. It blooms in June, at a time when its red blooms truly stand out.

Other varieties are being introduced with purple and pink blooms which are very attractive, although the Red Prince remains the most tested.

Wiegela should not be expected to look all round and prim. They grow irregularly, and if you trim them early in spring, you cut off the bloom. Trim immediately after blooming to allow the new wood to develop which will bloom next spring.

A row of weigela will look silly due to their stubborn individuality, but a single plant in the middle of a flower garden will stand out due to its bloom in June and then be overshadowed by other plants the rest of the summer.

As an added bonus, weigela blooms attract butterflies!

CHAPTER 13

Evergreens

What is an evergreen?

To many people, the word evergreen means *spruce*. However, evergreen merely means a plant that stays green all year. Evergreens keep their foliage through the winter, and that same foliage maintains its vitality and begins growing again in the spring. Common evergreens in our area range from the creeping junipers to the grand Scotch pine.

In the upper midwest, one can safely say that all of our evergreens are *conifers*. Conifers are plants which produce seeds in cones. Cedar, pine, spruce, and junipers, our area's most prevalent evergreens, all produce cones ranging from very small to quite large.

Non-coniferous evergreens, which are common in warmer parts of the world, simply have leaves which do not drop, as opposed to *deciduous* trees, which drop their leaves in the winter. Holly would be an example of a non-coniferous evergreen, of which there are none native or common in our area.

Just to confuse matters, there are conifers that are *not* evergreen. One, the tamarack, a native to this area, is a needled tree which produces cones, but whose needles turn a bright yellow and drop each fall.

Why aren't there more evergreens on the northern prairie?

The alkaline nature of the soil on the northern prairie discourages evergreens from establishing themselves on their own. However, evergreens can grow well here once established, and the rows of pine and spruce that were planted by the early settlers did much to protect farmsteads from the northwest winter winds.

The dry winds of winter, as well as the broad temperature fluctuations as spring approaches, damage evergreens. Evergreens can *burn,* which means that their foliage loses its moisture without it being replenished by the root. Spruce turn brown. Pine turn red. Some come out of it in the spring. In severe cases, however, some trees die.

This can happen in the deep cold snaps—which are almost always accompanied by very low humidity—just as easily as it can happen in March when the days are warm and the sun is higher, yet the nights are still cold and the root is still dormant and inactive.

Think twice before pulling out your old evergreens

It takes a long time to grow an evergreen. Arbor vitae are cedar, and cedar have beautiful trunks once they get old. Cedar can live hundreds of years, even thousands in some climates. Junipers, too, have gnarled trunks which, if shown off properly, can have an interesting effect. Old neglected Mugo pine, if they aren't so close to the house that they are crimped, can develop into an interesting small tree with multiple trunks.

Why not take the chain saw and prune out most of the branches in these old shrubs, exposing the trunk? Prune all dead foliage and branches out. You might end up pruning out over half the branches on the tree. Step back and see what is left. You might have created a thing of almost oriental beauty. And if you don't like what is left, you still have the luxury of pulling the tree out with the pickup.

SPRUCE

Spruce are the most common evergreen planted on the northern prairie. The pinnacles of old spruce tower above the deciduous trees in many remaining farmsteads, a living tribute to traveling tree peddlers who sold tiny seedlings from farm to farm in the very early years of the last century. Some of the grandest windbreaks on the northern prairie are those planted in spruce.

Black Hills and Colorado Spruce   *Picea*

Two varieties of spruce work best in our area, the "Black Hills" spruce, which is a variety of white spruce, and the "Colorado" spruce. Of the Colorado spruce, about one in seven have a lovely light blue tint, and thus earn the title "Colorado Blue spruce."

Homeowners who wish to establish spruce trees in their yard have the following options:

Seedling spruce

The most economical way to establish spruce is to plant small seedlings and take very good care of them. Such care includes keeping them completely free of weeds and watering frequently. Small seedlings will, if maintained, grow very vigorously.

Potted spruce

Medium-sized potted spruce (2-4 feet) are a good bet as well, but you must be careful. There are two types of potted spruce: 1) those which have just been dug in the field and plopped in a basket (see *Field dug spruce* below) and 2) those which have spent many of the last years in the pot. Ask the nursery which you are getting.

Medium-sized spruce which have spent the last few years in a pot are root bound. *This includes almost all spruce available at discount chains and box stores.* Such spruce actually *need* to have the roots disturbed at planting so they get out into the new soil.

If you do not disturb the root ball, the spruce can dry out even though the surrounding soil is damp. A healthy looking spruce in a small pot can decline quickly once it is in the ground when water cannot penetrate the root ball.

Field dug spruce

"Field-dug" spruce do the very best. The people who raise such spruce know what they are doing. Field-dug spruce usually have been root-pruned in the field over the years, a practice which keeps the root in a compact ball and minimizes trauma when the tree is eventually moved.

Most such spruce are potted in biodegradable baskets. It is absolutely necessary to leave the pot on field-dug spruce at planting, as disrupting the root ball will likely kill the tree.

Local nurseries are the best way to locate field-dug spruce. Plan ahead, as it is a major project to find, ship and plant field-dug spruce in any quantity.

Spruce moved in with a tree spade

The bigger the tree spade, the better the success of moving spruce.

In addition, the smaller the spruce, the better the success moving them with a tree spade. Moving spruce over eight feet tall, especially if they are from a windbreak and haven't been root pruned, is a waste of money even if the trees are free. You still have to pay the tree spade guy to move trees which have a low survival rate.

Tree-spaded spruce tend to grow quite slowly in the years following their move. As much as one-half of the root system is usually sliced by the spade, and it takes time for the tree to recover.

Indeed, some tree-spaded trees go into an irreversible decline. In the worst case we have seen, an institution moved over 100 spruce trees of 10-12' in height. Because a nearby farmer wanted to thin his spruce windbreak to avoid disease, the trees were free!

But moving them was not. Six years later, fewer than a dozen were left, and they were tied in place with cables to keep them from tipping. They looked pitiful.

To succeed with tree-spaded spruce, buy nursery-grown trees under eight feet, hire the biggest spade possible, and then water newly tree-spaded spruce with a garden hose run at a dribble into the crevasse left by the spade. For the first years, keep the area inside the circle made by the spade cultivated and clean rather than allowing it to revert to sod.

When is the best time to plant spruce?

Bare root seedling spruce are best planted early in the spring, soon after the ground becomes tillable. Planting after mid-May lowers the survival rate. Potted spruce can be planted any time they are available on the market.

When is it safe to move spruce?

Spruce should be moved either before their new shoots have emerged in the spring (usually before the first week in May) or after their new shoots have hardened and new growth has ceased (usually after August 15). Moving spruce during the heat of the summer is risky.

Digging spruce out of the ditch

People enjoy digging spruce out of the ditch to avoid paying high nursery prices. Bargain hunters who dig spruce trees two feet or smaller, who make sure to take all the root, even if one veers off six feet to the east, and who water regularly after transplanting, have the most success.

The keys to success in transplanting spruce from the wild: take your time and get all of the root possible. Water heavily at planting, and whenever the soil is dry. Keep all grass away at least out to the tips of the branches for several years after planting. Fertilize with ammonium sulfate.

A spruce grown in a nursery will have a compact root system, and will lose many fewer of its roots in moving. It is usually worth the extra money in the long run. You get what you pay for.

Trimming spruce

Young spruce can benefit from *light* annual trimming. Trimming should be done about July 4, just after the new shoots have firmed up enough not to droop, but before they have become tough and woody.

The purpose of trimming spruce is not to give a tight shape to the tree immediately. Rather, one should concentrate upon nipping the tips of as many of the new shoots on the perimeter of the spruce as possible.

In the absence of trimming of the new tips, spruce send out long single shoots which can become lanky.

Where the new growth is nipped, a cluster of new buds will form which will emerge next year and which will thicken the tree's appearance, but leave it appearing natural.

Moderation is the key. In late June, when the new growth on a small spruce is still soft, pinch the tips of a few dozen buds individually with your fingers to thicken the tree the next spring. Of course, you will then end up with hands tacky with pine tar!

In the process of trimming, it may be necessary to cut back the *leader,* the shoot which is aimed straight up. It is important for a spruce to have a single leader. If the leader is cut, a new leader must be developed.

To encourage a new leader after pruning a lanky one, allow the remainder of the former leader to send out a few horizontal shoots. Use twine to tie two or three of those shoots together in late June, when they are still soft. The shoots should aim straight up. In about a year, untie the shoots and completely cut off all but the best one, which will then form the new leader.

If a competing leader forms, cut it off at the base, the sooner the better. You do not want two competing trunks, which can split later in windstorms.

It is not suggested that spruce be trimmed tightly, unless you plan to continue to keep the spruce tightly trimmed for the remainder of the tree's life. Even then, tightly-trimmed spruce never look natural. The tight round shapes are more appropriate for a European royal palace.

Removing lower spruce branches

The debate over whether to leave spruce branches hanging down to the ground has led many couples to the brink of divorce. One spouse thinks spruce should have a bare trunk for a couple of feet, which also makes it easier to mow. Another thinks the apron of the spruce should extend to the ground, or it looks like its knobby knees are showing.

Here is a case where one spouse is right and the other should either submit, or move out.

If you are lucky enough to have a spruce with thick foliage right to the ground, by all means leave it!

However, if there is a need to compromise with the person who does the mowing, it is not harmful to prune out a few lower branches at the trunk so there is a six-inch gap between the lowest foliage and the ground.

If the lower branches of spruce die off to the point of showing no life at the tips, they will *not* come back. Cut all such branches off and see if the tree which remains is worth keeping.

Winter burn on evergreens

Drastic fluctuations in temperature, such as might happen on a sunny day in March, can do tremendous damage to the foliage of evergreens.

On a sunny day in March, an evergreen shrub, particularly those on the south side of a house, or near a large white building, might become warm enough during the day for sap to start to flow. Because the roots and trunk are still dormant and unable to replenish the moisture lost, the foliage will dry out and turn a burnt red color. The plant usually recovers, as long as the new buds remain alive, but it sometimes may be more than a year before the tree looks healthy again.

Scotch pine are the most resilient evergreen. They can emerge from winter a toasty brown and look completely green one year later. It pays to wait and see. Arbor vitae, on the other end of the evergreen spectrum, have a difficult time recovering from severe burn and are usually best replaced right away.

The drying out of plant tissue is called *desiccation*. Anti-desiccant sprays can prevent browning of evergreens, but are a pain. Such sprays consist of a wax-like substance which prevents moisture loss. Anti-desiccants are difficult to mix and spray, and are expensive.

A better solution is to cover or wrap small evergreens (the smaller the plant, the higher the risk of winter burn, but the easier the job of

162

covering) with burlap, or a similar fabric that breathes yet provides shade. Do not use any form or color of plastic, as plastic covering seems to make the winter burn problem worse.

Spruce diseases

Spruce have become subject to several fungal diseases, some of which can kill the tree. Colorado Spruce are more susceptible to disease than the Black Hills Spruce.

Diseases are worse when we have a wet June, and we have had more wet Junes than dry in the twenty years prior to 2017. Indeed, some of the old spruce windbreaks have nearly died out.

Notice that the problem of dead branches is worse on the north side of a grove, where the droplets of dew can linger on the needles until noon, causing diseases to produce spores by the billion.

At present, spraying spruce for disease is neither practical nor, in most cases, effective. If this changes, the university extension services are the place to go for information. *Using farm fungicides on spruce rows has not been shown to do any good.*

Prevention is the only cure

To prevent disease, plant your spruce at least twenty feet apart. Proper air circulation and sunshine can almost completely prevent spruce diseases. It is also vitally important to keep *all* weeds and grass away from spruce out to the tips of the branches.

Only spruce trees planted relatively far apart will continue to maintain low branches. Trees planted closely will lose their lower branches to disease and lack of sunshine just as surely as do the conifers in the large forests to the west. It is natural and unavoidable.

Due to decreased humidity, the prevalence of spruce diseases decreases as one moves westward across the northern prairie.

Keep young spruce free of weeds and grass

Young spruce forced to compete with sod or weeds will not do well. They often stop growing, turn yellow, and eventually decline and die.

Spruce grown in tilled ground will outgrow spruce grown in sod by *three times*, and will be far thicker and healthier. Take a look as you drive down the highway at the difference between spruce which are tilled and spruce which are trying to grow in sod. The difference is dramatic. Examples of both approaches abound in our area.

There is an easy way to keep weeds and grass away from spruce. Lift the branches and spray underneath with Roundup (glyphosate) once per season.

Grass allowed to grow underneath spruce is the most common reason spruce do not do well, and a probable reason they get disease.

ARBORVITAE

Arborvitae, from the cedar family, are probably the most common evergreen foundation planting in our area. Arborvitae have a flat, narrow foliage which is luxuriantly green. In our area, arborvitae seldom grow over twenty feet tall. In the Pacific Northwest, and in other parts of the world, members of the Arborvitae family can grow two-hundred feet tall.

Pyramidal Arborvitae

The Pyramidal Arborvitae is the most distinguished of the arborvitae which grow in our area. It grows in stately columns, many of which can be seen in almost any prairie cemetery. Indeed, the Pyramidal Arborvitae are the best way for prairie people to replicate the columnar cedar common in biblical pictures.

People who live in a house where a Pyramidal Arborvitae was placed on the corner often come to despise the tree, as it will grow into the eaves and simply overwhelm a ranch style house.

The most useful place for Pyramidal Arborvitae is in odd numbered groupings on the edge of the yard, or near buildings well over two stories high. The spires go well with old-time church steeples.

Pyramidal Arborvitae are prone to winter burn, especially when they are newly planted, and especially if they are planted on the south or west side of a building. The problem is made worse if the building is white.

To prevent burn, newly-planted Pyramidal Arborvitae should be covered with a burlap sack in mid-winter to prevent the sun from burning the foliage.

Pyramidal Arborvitae has tender foliage which deer seem to prefer over anything else in the winter. Arborvitae foliage is rich in vitamin C, and is the quickest way for deer to fill their daily minimum requirement without supplements.

If you have deer problems, wrap the tops of the Pyramidal Arborvitae with burlap all winter.

Trimming Pyramidal Arborvitae ruins their shape. It is best to plant the Pyramidal Arborvitae in a place where it can be allowed to grow naturally.

When forced to grow in shade, arborvitae can survive, but can become thin and airy in appearance, with virtually no foliage on the lower branches.

Techny Arborvitae

The very toughest arborvitae for the prairie is the "Techny." Techny arborvitae are almost completely hardy against winter burn. The Techny's foliage is a darker green than that of the Pyramidal, and much darker than some arborvitae used in warmer climes.

If left to grow naturally, the Techny becomes triangular in shape and quite loose in appearance. Most people trim their Techny arborvitae into globes or upright ovals.

One can purchase both "globe" and "upright" Techny arborvitae, but the difference between the two is merely a matter of trimming and training. They are genetically identical.

Techny arborvitae responds well to tight trimming, as long as it is done consistently. Do not allow arborvitae to grow too large, and then try to cut them back severely as they will look woody.

Techny, like all arborvitae, produce little cones. The production of inordinate amounts of cones can be a sign that the tree is under stress.

Water, fertilize—and hope.

Less common varieties of arborvitae

Holmstrup Arborvitae

The "Holmstrup" arborvitae is a dwarfed version of the noble Pyramidal Arborvitae. It will likely only get to seven or eight feet high in its lifetime, yet still retain an upright, columnar shape.

Unlike the more common Pyramidal Arborvitae, which features multiple spires, Holmstrup grows to a single point. It is not as hardy as its larger cousin against winter burn the first few winters, but once established, the Holmstrup has done well.

American Arborvitae

American arborvitae is a rounded form usually planted as small seedlings. It can be shaped to make a truly impressive formal hedge.

Dwarfed Globe Arborvitae

"Little Elfie," "Little Giant," and others are popular dwarfed globe arborvitae. Such dwarfed versions are of borderline hardiness in Zone 3, but can last many years in a protected area. They are undeniably *cute*.

There are several varieties of arborvitae with lighter, more vivid green, even golden foliage. You'll see them in yards on the West Coast in particular. None of them have proven hardy on the prairie over the long-term, although they sometimes appear on the market. Beware.

Purchasing and planting arborvitae

Arborvitae used for foundation plantings are generally sold in pots. Because they have grown most of their life in that pot, it is important to spread the roots at planting.

Dig a hole twice as large as you need. Pull the tree from the pot. If it is completely root bound, stomp on the root ball to loosen it up. Use a knife or screwdriver to break up the root a bit. Spread the roots with your hands.

Make sure there is nothing wrapped around the trunk of the tree which could eventually choke it. And finally, make sure that the arborvitae is not planted in pure clay, or in an area which is frequently saturated with water.

Small bare root arborvitae are available for larger plantings. It is important to keep young arborvitae plantings clean of weeds and grass. Follow the instructions above for young spruce. Plant deep.

Fertilizer

Arborvitae thrive in acid soils. An acidifying fertilizer such as ammonium sulfate will always help arborvitae, especially where the soil is very alkaline.

Possible problems with arborvitae

Arborvitae are low-maintenance. However, it is necessary to be aware of the few problems which can occur, as they are troubling, but usually can be addressed.

Tiny red dots

Arborvitae can rarely become infested with *red spider mites*. If the tree seems to be losing its vibrant green color, one should check for mites by shaking a handful of foliage over a white 3x5 card. Look closely at the debris on the card.

167

If you see tiny red dots moving around, the tree has red spider mites, and you should probably douse the tree with a miticide. Keep in mind that *most insecticides have no effect on mites.* You must purchase chemical labeled specifically for mites.

Male dogs

Dog urine on the foliage of arborvitae will cause the foliage to burn and die. It is important to keep male dogs away from arborvitae, especially when the trees are young, as constant dousing with urine can end the tree's life in a manner which lacks all dignity.

A truly weird (and luckily rare) disease

Arborvitae and junipers can be infected with *cedar-apple rust.* Cedar-apple rust is rare in our area, but not unknown. It shows up on the evergreens as an ugly, slimy, rust-colored mass. This bizarre disease must have both cedar and apple trees present in order for it become active. The fungus alternates between the two trees, using each tree for a particular part of its life cycle. Its spores are a bright red, thus the name "rust."

Although fungicides can be effective against cedar-apple rust, the best cure is prevention. Avoid planting arborvitae closer than a dozen yards from any tree in the apple family or rose family. If you have an apple orchard, avoid planting anything from the cedar family in your yard.

Burned by the cold

Winter burn is a problem in our area with any variety of arborvitae other than Techny, which is tough as nails. Winter burn affects younger trees more than it does established trees. Arborvitae can recover from moderate winter burn, but severe winter burn can kill the tree.

Once arborvitae foliage turns brown, there is no bringing it back. Come spring, strip the brown and crispy foliage off and see what is left before deciding to pull the tree. It is a common misperception that spraying the tree's foliage with a mix of acid fertilizer can bring it back. Yes, such treatment can green up the remaining living foliage of an arborvitae, but it cannot revive a tree, or parts of the tree, which have turned crisp and brown.

Siberian Arborvitae and Gettysburg

If you run across a Siberian arborvitae on the market, buy it without question and plant it. Siberian is an ideal form of arborvitae, very hardy and slow growing. They never burn, yet remain a beautiful green.

Why are they rare? Siberian arborvitae are so slow growing that nurseries find them hopelessly expensive to raise.

An historical footnote: The original architect of the Gettysburg cemetery included a long hedge of Siberian arborvitae. However, when the bureaucrats in Washington saw the price, they blanched and decided to use a less expensive variety and save the taxpayers a lot of money.

Bad move. The trees died. The original architect knew the climate at Gettysburg, Pennsylvania, and knew that only Siberian arborvitae would do the job.

Whoever has a Siberian arborvitae in their yard (we have one that is nearly 90 years old) has an obscure piece of Civil War history.

JUNIPER

Arborvitae vs. juniper

Arborvitae and juniper are both in the cedar family. Arborvitae have flat, soft foliage, while juniper have a rounded foliage which sometimes can be prickly. Some juniper foliage has a bluish tint similar to the Colorado Blue spruce. Arbor vitae require more water, while juniper are able to withstand a bit of drought.

Spreading junipers

There are dozens of varieties of creeping juniper, ranging in colors from green to blue to lime, and in shape from completely flat to those with a branching habit similar in shape to a low fountain.

Spreading junipers are a staple in the commercial landscape, and are a popular way to fill large spaces, slopes, and other challenging situations found around the very large concrete buildings in industrial parks.

The use of spreading juniper in the home landscape should be limited. Spreading junipers become woody if not allowed to expand. Their centers can become exposed as they age. They encroach on sidewalks.

Savin Juniper   *Juniperus sabina*

For prairie dwellers, one form of spreading juniper is both hardy and noble in appearance, the Savin. The fronds of Savin juniper grow like arms stretched out, palms up. Planted under a bank of windows three feet off the ground, the Savin will appear as if they are supporting the windows. Savin provide a shape otherwise unavailable to the prairie gardener. The look at home here.

Savin are hardy. They rarely winter burn. They can survive in the open in a grouping, say around a lamp-post in the middle of the yard. The Savin has a dignity and a usefulness more prostrate junipers lack.

Pruning vs. Trimming spreading juniper

Spreading junipers should be allowed to retain their natural, informal shape. They do not respond well to being trimmed tightly, or simply chopped off at the edge of the sidewalk.

The tips of the new growth may be clipped lightly to stifle the growth in a non-confining manner.

If you wish to keep spreading junipers a certain size, or reduce their size after they have become overgrown, do so by taking the longest fronds by the tip, shaking them out from the rest of the plant, and cutting the branch off at the very base.

Upright Juniper   *Juniperus scopulorum*

In areas of the northern prairie leaning towards the warmer Zone 4, upright junipers such as the "Medora" can work. They provide a blueish color with a dignified, upright, nearly columnar shape redolent of the mountain west. However, in Zone 3, upright juniper become impractical due to their propensity to burn. They are less workable as one moves from southwest to northeast in our region.

Red Cedar

Red cedar are so-called because of the reddish-brown tint of their foliage in the fall and winter. Although they are common in older windbreak plantings, red cedar are rarely used in the yard.

Red cedar make an ideal mid-sized evergreen windbreak. Their informal fountain shape is a pleasant variation from the other evergreens. As one moves south in our region, the red cedar have seeded themselves and become weeds in pastures and ditches. But what a nice weed!

Red cedar are hardy to Zone 2, and tolerate alkaline soils.

Red cedar are easiest planted as small, cheap seedlings bought bare root from the soil conservation people. They grow fast. To get them going, plant them deeply, with the soil a couple of inches above the crown, and yet in a depression. Planting more deeply than one might think appropriate will preserve the moisture in the plant while the roots establish.

Do not plant red cedar *anywhere* near apple trees due to cedar-apple rust. Better to have healthy applesand no cedar.

PINE

Spruce vs. pine

Pine are distinguished from spruce by the length of the needle. Spruce needles are generally one-inch long or less, while pine needles are generally from two inches up to six inches in length.

The best pine trees for the prairie

Pine are very popular as Christmas trees, as they are faster-growing and more easily shaped than spruce. For the prairie gardener, however, shaping of pine should be left to the Christmas tree farms further south and east. Pine on the prairie should be allowed to grow naturally, even irregularly.

Every yard should have one pine tree, if only for the sound in winter when the wind rustles the needles.

Two varieties of pine trees are useful in the prairie yard, in addition to the dwarf Mugo pine, which is a staple shrub used nearer to the house.

Scotch Pine   *Pinus sylvestris*

Without a doubt, the most useful and successful pine on the northern prairie is the *Scotch*, also known as *Scots*. An established row of Scotch pine, left to grow in its gnarled, windswept manner, is a poetic sight. As the tree matures, its trunk develops an attractive, papery, orange bark.

A severe drought, or winter burn, will turn even mature Scotch pine a reddish-brown. The entire tree can look dead, only to recover within a few months.

Scotch pine should be planted as seedlings. They grow fast the first few years, before slowing down to a crawl later on. Cover the lowest needles of the small tree with about an inch of soil to prevent loss of moisture as the tree develops root. Keep a three foot circle around the tree utterly clean of weeds and grass for the first several years. Although they survive drought, boy do Scotch pine respond to good watering during dry spells. Add a little acidifying fertilizer to the water, and the results will astound.

Ponderosa Pine   *Pinus ponderosa*

Faster growing than the Scotch, the Ponderosa feature a longer needle. The Ponderosa's bark is rough, gray, and not attractive in any way. However, the speed of growth and larger eventual size make the Ponderosa worth considering.

Mugo Pine   *Pinus mugo*

The dwarf Mugo pine is popular for its round, compact, thick appearance. It is more a shrub than a tree. Mugo pine grow very slowly, and if trimmed once per year, can be made to stay compact for many, many years. The ideal eventual size is two feet tall by three feet wide.

Proper trimming is essential. The Mugo pine will send up *candles*, new shoots which eventually open up into needles, in late May and early June. When these candles reach their maximum growth, but before they open, their tips should be cut off.

To allow the Mugo to get a little larger, only trim off the very tip of the candle. If one wants to keep the Mugo at its present size, one can trim back virtually the entire candle, although it is important not to cut off all of the new growth. Trimming of Mugo pine is best done in June.

Without trimming, the Mugo lose their density, and you begin to see branches and eventually a trunk. If left untrimmed, Mugo can grow to eight feet tall and perhaps ten feet wide.

Mugo pine can burn in the winter, but because they are so compact, they are often protected by snow cover. Mugo recover well from winter burn once their new growth emerges.

Other Pine Trees

Although a few have survived to maturity on the prairie, the *Norway Pine*, so predominant in the forests to the east, are not a good bet for us.

Jack pine are too slovenly, and so inferior to the Ponderosa and Scotch that there is no reason to consider them.

OTHER EVERGREENS

Fir Trees

Douglas and Rocky Mountain fir trees so rarely succeed on the northern prairies that their use should be confined to experiments.

Tamarack   *Larix laricina*

Tamarack, and its close relative the *Siberian larch,* are classified as *deciduous conifers.* They have needles and cones, but the needles turn brilliant yellow and drop each fall. They are common in the bogs to the east, but rare out on the prairie due to their fussiness. In my lifetime, I have seen three mature tamarack on the prairie, one on the Sandhill River near my home, one in Fargo, and one in Crookston.

So, should you try one? Why not! Small seedling tamaracks cost very little, and they grow fast. You'll know soon if the tamarack, against all odds, likes your yard. If one of them matures, you will have a true rarity.

Yew   *Taxus*

The flat-needled yew is popular as a foundation planting in the Twin Cities. Unfortunately, they rarely last on the prairie due to winter burn. In short, yews might work in Sioux Falls, while in Fargo one bad winter will kill them off. If you love yews, plant one of them on the north side of the house (in order to shield from the sunshine in March) and do not become attached to them.

Do fallen pine and spruce needles acidify the soil?

Not enough to help or hurt. Many people think plants struggle under their pine or spruce trees because the needles make the soil acid. Baloney. The real reason things won't grow under big evergreens is that the shallow root system of a large evergreen takes most of the moisture and nutrients out of the soil. In addition, the shade of an old tree limits what could be planted there in the first place.

The myth that needles acidify the soil continues, but it is a myth, and one with only the slightest foundation in fact.

CHAPTER 14

Hedges

In the yard, the equivalent of windbreaks are hedge. A *hedge* is little more than a bunch of shrubs or bushes planted in a row which functions to block a view, or keep the neighbor kids from coming into your yard.

Formal vs. informal

When people think of a hedge, they usually think of a formal, tightly trimmed hedge. Although the popularity of formal hedges goes back centuries and won't disappear soon, informal, untrimmed hedges are every bit as attractive, and on the whole are a lot less work.

FORMAL HEDGES

The best shrubs for a formal hedge

A formal, trimmed hedge requires plants which respond well to tight trimming. It is best to use shrubs which are vigorous enough to become full, yet not so vigorous that they send fresh shoots out within a few days after trimming. What follows are a list of shrubs that will work when used as more formal hedging:

Alpine Currant—For a small formal hedge, nothing beats the Alpine Currant. It responds well to trimming, and becomes impenetrably thick. One should expect an Alpine Currant hedge to be a maximum of four feet tall.

Cotoneaster—No shrub makes a better medium-sized hedge in the valley than the cotoneaster. Beware of the disease and insect problems on this plant, but don't let that scare you away from considering cotoneaster. In parts of the prairie, where it is difficult to find fall color, cotoneaster hedges become a spectacular orange color in the fall, depending upon the soil.

Dogwood—Although dogwood grow more naturally as an informal, untrimmed hedge, people who have sought to turn a row of dogwood into a formal hedge have had good luck. Dogwood respond well to trimming. A more natural look arises when the whole plant is cut down to the ground every few years to encourage fresh growth. The new growth will have better red winter color than the old. Dogwood can be trimmed to five or six feet.

Caragana—Although it is known as a windbreak plant and will grow to twelve feet, if caragana are consistently trimmed, they can be kept as low as four to five feet tall. It is hardy and fast-growing, although nondescript. The common caragana provides a fuller trimmed hedge than do the dwarfed, or "Globe" varieties.

"Miss Kim" Dwarf Lilac—This odd inclusion on the list is due to the spectacular performance of the Miss Kim in the University of Minnesota Arboretum hedge garden. It was the opinion of the author that the Miss Kim was the finest hedge on display there. Lilacs are usually used for informal rather than formal hedges because trimming the tips for a formal look usually prevents all bloom. With the Miss Kim, this problem is less pronounced. The Miss Kim's foliage is an attractive purplish-green, turning to deep maroon and purple in the fall. The leaves are cupped and pointed, with a very definite oriental look. They can be kept trimmed to six or seven feet.

Forsythia—The Meadowlark forsythia, the first forsythia bred to be hardy in our area, can make a very dense, wonderfully green hedge, with the added benefits of its early spring yellow bloom. Most people who have planted a forsythia hedge have been pleasantly surprised by the results. Forsythia can be reasonably kept in formal shape from six to eight feet.

Arborvitea—A Techny arborvitae hedge can be very attractive and hardy. It will take a few years for the plants to fill in, but once you have an established arborvitae hedge, you will have year-round protection from the wind, as well as year-round beauty. An arborvitae hedge can be kept trimmed to anywhere from six to ten feet in height.

Bridalwreath Spirea—It is a cardinal sin to shape the old-time white spirea—unless you don't care if you ever see the white bloom, and just want a petite formal hedge. Like the Miss Kim lilac, the unlikely inclusion of the Bridalwreath Spirea on the list of good plants for a formal hedge comes from observation of trimmed spirea at the hedge garden of the U of M arboretum. The Bridalwreath are best if kept at two to three feet in height when used for hedge purposes. Do not expect significant bloom, just thick growth.

Avoid these shrubs for formal hedges

Compact cranberry and *globe caragana* do not make for good formal hedges because of their refusal to fill around the base. *Ninebark* do not make good formal hedges because they grow so blame fast that you will do nothing but trim all summer.

How to trim a formal hedge

The cardinal rule: Trim a formal hedge in an "A" shape rather than a "V" shape. This goes against every human impulse. Most people trim in "V" shapes. However, a "V" shape results in the bottom leaves of the plants thinning out because they are shaded by the upper leaves. Those leaves will eventually disappear. As my father has said repeatedly, trim in a V shape and pretty soon the chickens will be able to run in and out underneath your hedge.

Trimming in an A shape allows the sunshine to reach the bottom leaves, thus promoting thick, healthy growth right to ground level. It is okay to flatten the top of the A, but round looks more natural.

INFORMAL HEDGES

An informal hedge allows one to let the shrubs bloom to their heart's content, and have their natural shape. An informal hedge can be allowed to grow to any size.

Because informal hedges are little more than shrubs lined up in rows, you can pretty much make a hedge out of any of the selection of shrubs hardy for our area. However, there are some informal hedges which are particularly spectacular, and others which are traditional, even nostalgic.

Lilacs—The most old-fashioned hedge of them all is the common lilac. Common lilac are easy to grow and hardy as nails. We should keep planting them so future generations can fill their homes with lilac bouquets about the time school gets out at the end of May.

Common lilac send suckers out from the bottom of the plant, which causes the lilac hedge to grow in width as well as height. In the end, the width of the hedge usually exceeds the height, which can be 10 feet. Lilac are meant for full sun, and can get thin in their old age if they have become shaded.

You must have an area at least 10 feet wide if you are planning to have common lilac hedge there for long time. There is no way of preventing a common lilac from sending out suckers.

The Canadian types of lilac, most notably the Villosa, do not sucker. They work in heavy, high alkaline soils where the common lilac sometimes suffer, or are inconsistent. However, the Villosa-type lilacs do not fill in at the base like the common lilac, and for many years it is likely that you will be able to see the individual plants.

Some people plant French Lilac hybrids in a row as a hedge, but hybrid lilacs are costly and not as vigorous as the common. A suggested alternative would be to intersperse a few French hybrids, with their wide range of bloom size, shape and color, with the common lilac. Years down the road, the French hybrids will provide a nice surprise to anybody seeking a bouquet in the old lilac hedge.

179

Old-Fashioned Spirea—Although the Bridalwreath-type spirea is common in foundation plantings around our area, very few people have thought to plant them as a hedge. The Bridalwreath Spireas can work as a small, trimmed hedge, but they really can be spectacular if left to grow in their natural shape. Perhaps people don't think of using the Bridalwreath Spireas as a hedge plant because of their fountain shape, but a hedge of them along a driveway would stop traffic in the spring.

Hardy Roses—Any of the hardy roses can be made into a spectacular hedge for a sunny, hot location. The William Baffin rose is the tallest, reaching 8 feet tall. Sometimes unnamed rugosa (shrub) roses are available on the market for a fraction of the cost of named varieties. However, the Morden roses and any of the named varieties of the old-fashioned shrub roses will make a fantastic, showy hedge which will be well worth the cost.

Red Twig Dogwood—Red Twig dogwood, if cared for properly, make an ideal informal hedge. What a colorful display their branches make in the winter! To keep the branches from getting old and woody, mow the dogwood to the ground every three or four years and let it come fresh. That is, if you have one of those brush mowers. Otherwise, you can use the chain saw.

Expect an untrimmed dogwood hedge to be at least 8 feet tall, and just as wide. Dogwood are native, hardy, and will grow in moist places. According to research conducted in North Dakota, the Bergeson Dogwood withstands moisture even better than the common Red Twig dogwood.

Amur Maple—Straddling the divide between hedge and windbreak, the Amur Maple is a striking informal hedge. With its smooth bark, irregular habit, and spectacular fall color, it will add an element of oriental artistry to any yard. Consider planting Amur Maple in a grouping in the corner of the yard rather than in a row. Amur Maple are far from uniform, and will look more appropriate if planted randomly.

Potentilla—Yellow-flowering potentilla make a showy informal hedge for along a sidewalk or driveway. They need the hot sun, and the same sun exposure from one end of the row to another if they are to be uniform. Cut them back to the ground every third year.

An informal hedge for tiny spaces

Globe Caragana — Building contractors often leave very small spaces between sidewalks and houses. What can you do in an eighteen-inch space? Plant Globe caragana. They will fill in beautifully, and they work in sun or shade *as long as they do not get too much moisture.* A sprinkler system which comes on every night is very hard on Globe caragana, as is wet clay soil.

PURCHASING, PLANTING AND CARE OF HEDGE PLANTS

The most economical way to purchase hedge plants is to buy small, bare root plants. A bundle of bare root plants can go a long way, and will cost as little as one tenth the money of larger shrubs in pots. Bare root hedge plants do not need to be watered after the initial watering at planting time unless there is a prolonged dry spell.

In the nursery trade, a *hedge-grade* plant is simply a shrub which is smaller than those used as a *specimen plant*, a shrub which must stand on its own. Hedge-grade plants are genetically identical to their larger brethren.

Planting a hedge

It is a good idea to prepare the ground for a hedge well in advance. If the hedge is going to be planted where there is now lawn, spray with glyphosate (Roundup) in a strip about three feet wide the length of the hedge before doing any tilling. After the grass has died, which should take about a week, till the ground several times. It is best if the ground is prepared the fall before the hedge is planted, or even kept fallow a full year in advance, if you think of it.

Some have had good luck planting hedges in a mulch of landscape fabric. The fabric keeps the weeds down and the moisture in. Since it is essential that the soil around a young hedge be weed-free, those without time to cultivate or hoe should consider mulch.

If the ground is properly tilled, planting the bare root plants is a breeze, especially with two people. Lift the soil with a spade, have a second person slide the root of the hedge plant behind the spade, let the soil fall back where it was, and pack the plant in with a single step of your heel. Water the newly planted hedge plant, using the heel imprint as the depression to hold the water. Planting in landscape fabric should be only slightly more difficult. Simply cut two incisions in the fabric in a cross shape, fold back the fabric, and plant the small tree as described above.

Long, single-stem hedge plants should be cut back about half-way at planting. A second harsh trimming the second season can insure that the hedge will branch out fully to the base.

Spacing between plants

Generally speaking, hedge plants should be planted at least half as far apart as they are expected to grow tall. For example, hedge plants you wish to grow six feet tall can be planted three feet apart. If you want a solid mass very quickly, plant close, but never closer than eighteen inches. If you aren't so fussy when the hedge gets solid, you can plant farther apart and save a little money.

Establishing a hedge

A hedge will do nothing if it is competing with grass or weeds. Keep a three-foot-wide strip of ground weed free for at least the first three to four years. Weeding can make the difference between success and failure. *Do not allow the sod to creep in to the base of the hedge plants.*

The first year or two, it is okay to let the shrub grow longer between trimmings, but once the hedge is at the height you wish to keep it, it is wise to trim again as soon as the hedge becomes visibly scruffy.

Watering is important if you purchase potted plants, not so important if you purchase bare root. Fertilizing once per year with an all-purpose fertilizer will speed the growth of the hedge.

CHAPTER 15

Windbreaks and Shelterbelts

No human effort has had a greater impact upon the northern prairie's flat, open spaces than windbreaks planted by our forebears. Without them, our landscape would at times be truly barren.

With windbreaks, the open spaces become bearable during winter, and more beautiful in all seasons. There is no way to measure the impact of a solid windbreak on the fuel consumption of the homes it protects, but it is likely to be substantial.

A *windbreak,* or *shelter belt,* is usually a row of larger trees planted around a farmstead, or on the perimeter of small prairie towns, or in rows in the field, with the idea that the trees will slow the wind, reduce soil erosion, lower heating bills, and ease the drifting of snow during blizzards.

Windbreaks and *shelter belts* have been planted for over a century on the northern plains.

In the 1880s, it was thought that planting of trees would bring more rain, so the federal government sponsored "tree claims," an arrangement by which settlers would agree to plant a certain number of acres into trees in exchange for the right to homestead the land.

During the Great Depression, it was evident that established windbreaks helped keep the soil in place during dry years. The federal government formed Soil and Water Conservation Districts, which have assisted farmers in establishing trees ever since.

Anybody who has driven in a winter storm in the open spaces of the northern prairie knows that a *windbreak*, even one as distant as a mile away from the highway, can slow the snow enough to increase visibility dramatically.

Shelter belts perform the function of protecting farmsteads and entire towns from the harsh northwest winds of winter. A good shelter belt can take the bite out of an Alberta clipper, and can make a house feel more cozy.

Ideas change. At one time, it was a trend to plant ten to fifteen rows of trees close together around each farmstead. Then it became a trend to plant a single row of brushy plants like Siberian elm every few dozen rods or so in the open fields. Now it seems that the trend is to plant fewer trees, in rows further apart, and to keep the branches of each tree trimmed up higher, as one might trim a shade tree in the yard, so as to spread the blowing snow out over a greater area across the field.

Whatever the present doctrine, there is no doubt as to the value of an established row of trees on the prairie.

Qualities of a good windbreak tree

A windbreak tree has to be hardy and proven, for it will undergo some of the toughest conditions of any tree. It will face the brunt of winter's harsh winds. It will need to cope with the stresses of cultivators clawing at its roots, as well as farm sprays injuring its foliage. The tree must be vigorous and rangy in habit, rather than compact and round.

As a practical matter, windbreak trees must be easy to reproduce, raise, transport, and plant. They are planted by the thousand.

Grafted trees are impractical. Semi-hardy trees are a bad bet. Trees which aren't tough enough to get established on their own in harsh circumstances must be avoided. We are left with a small selection of tough, proven, and easily-reproduced trees.

QUALITY WINDBREAK TREES

Hybrid Poplar—*the best all-round windbreak tree*

For a prairie windbreak in our area, there is no more attractive and fast-growing tree than the hybrid poplar. A farmstead surrounded by a row of hybrid poplar will very soon be enclosed by a shelter belt of grand heights, rustling leaves, and graceful appearance. Hybrid poplar live to an old age in our area. They are free of any serious diseases. They are inexpensive, easy to reproduce, and easy to grow.

Cottonwood were the first tree planted on the prairie. Cottonwood have always been known for their survival in both cold weather and in alkaline soils. They survive floods and drought.

However, cottonwood are messy, as anybody who has ever cleaned the cotton out of their window screens knows.

Since the 1940s, various hybrids of cottonwood and poplar have been introduced. The poplar half of the hybrid provides a fast growth, up to six feet per year in some cases. The cottonwood half of the hybrid provides the tree with its relative strength and longevity. The varieties of hybrid poplar on the market have the added benefit that they are sterile and do not produce the messy cotton.

The term "poplar" causes many people to turn up their noses. They immediately think of the, tall, narrow, short-lived Lombardy Poplar, a truly undesirable tree.

The hybrid poplars and cottonwoods recommended here, however, are tough and hardy. There is simply no faster, more dependable windbreak tree for our area.

Green Ash—*no longer of use*

The dowdy green ash once made for a sturdy windbreak tree. However, due to the inevitable arrival of the pernicious emerald ash borer, green ash should no longer be planted.

Remaining green ash windbreak are struggling from other diseases, and from sprays.

Spruce—*best wind-stopper, an all season barrier*

A mature spruce shelter belt is a priceless possession. There is no better protection from the winter winds than that provided by a row of spruce. The rich green color makes a yard cozy in the winter, and the roar of the wind through the needles reminds one of the mountains.

Establishing a shelter belt of spruce takes years of time and effort. It is best to plant small, bare root plants, and *keep them cultivated.* Growing spruce in tilled soil is what makes the difference between success and failure.

Planting the spruce close together—at a distance of less than fifteen feet—will create a wind barrier more quickly. However, the closer together spruce are planted, the sooner they will lose their lower branches.

When spruce begin to crowd each other, diseases move in, and the first casualties of disease are usually the lower branches of the spruce trees. This problem is worse on the north side of a shelter belt, where the sun only hits the needles very early and very late in June's long days.

To keep the soil around the spruce perfectly clean, it is safe to spray glyphosate herbicide (Roundup) near the base of the spruce, especially early in spring before the spruce buds emerge.

Cultivation is also important. Space the spruce at planting so you can cultivate both directions with a small cultivator. You won't regret it.

Planting seedling spruce purchased from the Soil Conservation Service is the cheapest way to go. It is not important that the little trees look the greatest at planting. The poorest quality seedling will flourish if given proper care, just as the most beautiful seedling will struggle if it has to compete with sod.

Plant young bare-root spruce transplants deeply, covering up a couple of inches of the lower branches with soil. Planting that deeply *looks* wrong, but it can raise the survival rate of young spruce from 2/3 to nearly 100% by preserving the moisture in the unestablished young tree when we are hit with hot and dry winds early in the season.

Of course, make sure that each tree has a depression around its base to allow water to collect.

In sandy soils, watering young spruce can truly benefit them. It is not possible to overwater in sandy soils. However, in heavy soils, it is probably best to treat small spruce just as you would small deciduous bare root plantings: Water at planting, and then water only if the soil dries out.

Small spruce planted from pots require frequent watering for the first couple of seasons.

Pine—*listen to the whisper*

A row of old Scotch pine is a precious thing. Their striking orange bark peels away like birch bark. The wind through the needles sometimes rises to a low roar. In comparison to the more formal spruce, a row of Scotch pine looks and sounds romantic and windswept.

A legacy left in pine is more lasting and appreciated than that of any other tree, it seems. Spruce lose their shape and some of their dignity as they get very old. Cottonwood start to drop branches and may fall over in windstorms. Old pine just become more grand, gnarled and dignified with age.

Scotch pine are the most dependable for the northern prairie. They tolerate alkaline soils and drying winter winds better than other pine.

Red Cedar—*not used enough*

On some parts of the prairie, red cedar have spread via birds to the point where they are a weed. However, a drive across the pasture-lands of the prairie west is made more beautiful by the scruffy, reddish-green bushes.

188

Tolerant of all the prairie deals out, from alkaline soils to dry winter winds, the red cedar grows faster than other evergreens available for windbreak plantings.

Flowering Crab Seedlings—*great for wildlife*

The seedlings of flowering crabs make an ideal source of food for wildlife. They are inexpensive, and they bloom spectacularly in May.

Seedlings grown from the seed of a deep pink flowering crab will range in bloom color from deep pink to white, perhaps even a maroon one here and there. The fruit will range in size from no fruit at all, to pinhead size, on up to two-inch wide crabapples, and everywhere in between. Some will be edible, most not.

Leaf color, branching habit, speed of growth, every one of the characteristics of the flowering crab can change from one seedling to another. No two are alike. Who knows, the next great patented flowering crab tree could be in your windbreak.

It is not recommended to plant a flowering crab windbreak if you want a neat, trimmed row of trees. They are best if left to grow as brush.

Amur Maple—*best fall color*

Although the Amur Maple, otherwise known as *ginela maple,* is coming under pressure from naturalists, who claim its seeds are spreading the species into natural woodlands to the east of the prairie, there is no easier way to achieve spectacular color on the prairie. The Amur is more tolerant of heavy soils than other maple.

Nurseryman Alf Benson of Valley City planted Amur Maple around the rest areas along I-29 in North and South Dakota. Their fall color is spectacular, a memorial to a grand old nurseryman.

Dogwood—*functional and handsome filler*

Those who prefer to plant native species might consider the red twig dogwood for a shorter snow-catch. Red twig dogwood grow thick to the ground. During the winter, their red bark glows in the late evening sun.

When the red twig dogwood get older and woody, it works to mow them off with a bushwhacker. The new growth will be fresh, vigorous and a brighter shade of red in winter.

Plant seedlings three feet apart for best results.

Willow—*add a touch of gold to the winter*

In combination with the red twigs of the dogwood, a row of Flame Willow, with its bright orange twigs, will be striking. Flame willow are not sloppy like other species of willow. Their branches are upswept, not weeping. Their winter branch color is deeper.

A dense row of Flame Willow can be seen from miles across the prairie in March, when it seems the branches almost glow.

TREES TO AVOID IN WINDBREAKS

The above trees are highly recommended. The trees listed below, although historically used in windbreaks on the plains, are not.

Russian Olive—*a Bolshevik plot*

Actually, the Russian Olive was brought across long before the 1917 revolution in Russia, but those who dislike the tree might be forgiven for thinking the tree was a plot hatched in Moscow during the Cold War.

A specimen tree of Russian Olive can be attractive if trimmed so the striking black bark of the trunk is visible in contrast to the gray leaves.

However, an entire row of Russian Olive is a headache. Their thorns can puncture mower tires. They drop branches, and some branches die out. The trees can become misshapen.

Siberian Elm—*dying, dying, dead*

My grandfather Melvin Bergeson once confessed to me that he was probably responsible for introducing Siberian elm to the Red River Valley, and that if the word got out, his life might be in danger.

Yes, the Siberian (or Manchurian and other Asiatic varieties) elm grew fast, provided brushy wind protection, and actually could be attractive as an older tree; but it also dropped seeds by the million which sprouted everywhere, creating seedlings with a root so tenacious that they were almost impossible to pull out by hand.

If trimmed into a specimen tree, an older Siberian elm can look like a gnarled bonsai tree, so it might pay to rescue a few of them.

Caragana—*tough as nails*

The most miserable prairie soils will still support the caragana. If trimmed, the caragana can make a passable formal hedge. If left untrimmed, the barrier they create will slow winds and stop animals.

Caragana produce miniature pea-like pods of seeds which, when ripe, actually pop open in a way which throws the seeds quite a distance.

So, you end up with caragana everywhere.

Plant caragana only if your soil is so salty or alkaline that nothing else grows.

Honeysuckle—*besieged by pests, no longer recommended*

At one time, the pink- or red-blooming honeysuckle made for a good windbreak. No more! An aphid has attacked them which stunts the growth and creates a phenomena known as "witch's broom," a fist-sized cluster of tiny, ugly, usually dead branches at the end of each stem.

Lombardy Poplar—*should be banned this far north*

The pillar-shaped Lombardy poplar last only 10 years on the northern prairie, if that. At that point, they die and must be removed.

WINDBREAK LAYOUTS

The problem with rows

It drives some people nuts to have a row of trees which isn't uniform. However, no amount of fertilizer, spray or other forms of love and care can make a stunted tree catch up with another if it just doesn't like the spot it is planted in.

If the land in a row of windbreak trees dips, or varies in a way which creates a stretch of stunted trees, it is better to rip the trees in the bad soil out and have a gap in the row than to leave the weak trees to struggle.

The aesthetics of rows

If you do chose to plant in rows, make them straight. Curved rows will cause northern prairie natives to question your character for the next several decades.

Above all, *do not alternate varieties of trees within the same row.* Attempts to create variety in this fashion look haphazard.

Do not attempt to soften the lines by curving the row around your farmstead. This just looks wrong.

Do not run rows at odd angles to the roads or property lines unless you have a compelling reason.

An exception: If a shallow ditch sweeps through an area in an S-curve or some other dignified pattern, lining the ditch with a similarly curved row of dogwood can look elegant.

The easiest, best, and cheapest shelter belt

You have a big lot on the open prairie. What should you plant on the north side to protect your eventual house from the wind?

Starting from the outside of the lot, here is an ideal sample solution:

Row 1: Norway Poplar, planted 15 feet apart.

Row 2: Flame Willow, planted at least fifteen feet from the poplar and at a rate of two for every poplar (7.5 feet apart).

Row 3: Red Twig dogwood, planted fifteen feet from the willow, and at twice the density (one every three feet or so).

If one still has room, spruce planted 30 feet apart and treated as specimen trees will add even more winter color inside the corral created by the rows of deciduous trees.

CHAPTER 16

Vines

The number of vines available to the northern prairie gardener is limited by our cold climate, which freezes the long stems of vine varieties used further the south. We can be thankful, for vines such as kudzu are taking over entire counties in Dixie!

The vines we *can* grow will do the job, and they will never get out of our control.

Engelmann Ivy   *Parthenocissus quinquefolia var. engelmannii*

Also known as woodbine, this native vine climbs trees in the woods. The leaves turn bright red first thing in the fall. The true Engelmann Ivy will cling to masonry (and most anything else) in a very tight, dignified fashion. It can grow to 50 feet in height!

There is confusion on the market about Engelmann Ivy and Virginia Creeper, listed below. Many nurseries treat them as the same plant. On the northern prairie, they are not.

If you want a vine which clings tightly to masonry, make sure you get the true Engelmann Ivy. Your nursery-person should know the difference.

The Engelmann features smaller leaves and finer branching than the Virginia Creeper, and also features "holdfasts," the little squiggly growths which do the clinging.

194

Virginia Creeper   *Parthenocissus inserta*

Closely related to the Engelmann Ivy, the Virginia Creeper *lacks* the "holdfasts" which grab walls. However, it will climb trees. It is even more vigorous than the Engelmann Ivy, and makes a good ground cover as well.

With both Engelmann Ivy and Virginia Creeper, *one plant is enough to give you a thousand.* They set root and spread. However, their perimeter is easy to control with a mower.

Both vines grow best in full sun, where they will display superior fall color, but can withstand shade as well.

Together, the Engelmann Ivy and Virginia creeper are the toughest, fastest, and most useful vines available on the northern prairie.

Honeysuckle Vine   *Lonicera x brownii*

A vigorous vine which can tolerate some shade, the honeysuckle vine, sometimes known as "Trumpeter," or "Trumpet Vine," features orange blooms in a trumpet shape. The trumpet blooms are very popular with the hummingbirds!

Honeysuckle vines will climb, but unlike the Engelmann Ivy, they do not cling tightly and will require training and pruning to look neat. They sort of grow in a pile unless given direction.

However, the honeysuckle vine are a nostalgic favorite, and old-time gardeners relish their exuberance.

American Bittersweet   *Celastrus scandens*

Bittersweet are native, and are famous for their brilliant orange berries, which dry well and can be used in dried winter arrangements.

American Bittersweet have an odd characteristic: Seedlings of the plant are roughly 40% male, 40% female, and 20% a little of both! In the old days, it was difficult to know which you had, so you had to plant several bittersweet plants to make sure pollination took place.

Very recently, however, a breeding breakthrough has enabled the nursery trade to know that they are selling bittersweet plants with both female and male characteristics. In addition to assured fruit-bearing, the plants are much stronger than plants with only male or female characteristics. *Make sure the bittersweet plant you purchase is one of the new varieties.*

Grapes   *Vitis*

We do have native wild grapes on the northern prairie, but if you want a vine which will thrill you with edible fruit, plant the "Beta," "Valiant," or "King of the North." One plant will cover an entire arbor!

Prune out vast amounts of the grape vine in early spring to keep things fresh. Unpruned grape vines gradually become so thick and brushy that they stop bearing.

Grapes will not climb brick very well, but they love lattice work. Plant them in full sun to get the best fruiting.

Climbing Roses

There is no true climbing rose hardy on the northern prairie. The sometimes-gangly "William Baffin" rose can be trained to a trellis and will reach as high as the eaves if encouraged.

Perennial Vines (Non-woody)

The clematis, which dies to the ground almost every year on the northern prairie, is considered a perennial and is featured in Chapter 21 on Perennials.

Annual Vines

Sweet pea and morning glory are the best annual vines.

CHAPTER 17

Growing Fruit Trees in the North

Because apples are the most dependable fruit tree on the northern prairie, most of this chapter will concern them. Plum trees are the second most dependable fruit tree, but tend to be short-lived. Apricots can survive, but large crops are rare. Pears provide the occasional novelty of a few delicious fruits, but little by way of annual sustenance. However, our success with apples and plums more than makes up for the lack of other fruit trees.

The rewards of growing fruit trees on the northern prairie

The flavor of northern homegrown apples can't be beat. From the larger Haralson to the smaller Chestnut, apples grown in the back yard in the north country exceed in flavor and character anything you can buy in a store.

Northern plums taste so sweet and vivid that you wonder if somebody added sugar, or artificial flavoring.

Hardiness, hardiness, hardiness

Hardiness in fruit trees is measured by the minimum temperature they can survive without damage. Believe it or not, a single -40°F night can severely damage an apple tree that is hardy only to -36°F.

In our area, cold hardiness in fruit trees has less to do with *average* low temperatures, length of winters, or depth of snow than it does with the lowest temperature reached at some point during winter.

Any fruit tree variety on the market is rated for hardiness by USDA Zone. Most of the northern prairie region can be considered Zone 3. Varieties which are rated for Zone 4 should be purchased and planted with an experimental mindset. If you are close to a river or other body of water, or well within the city limits, a Zone 4 fruit tree is more likely to survive than if you plant it out on the barren prairie.

APPLES   *Malus*

Where should you plant an apple tree?

Apple trees can be beautiful, especially when covered with blooms in the spring. However, apple trees planted for their fruit should not occupy a spot in the yard which is important for the landscape. Apples are not as hardy as shade trees, and they can become broken down, or oddly shaped—but still be well worth keeping for their fruit.

An ideal spot for an apple tree would be on the south side of a grove, just to the east of a big farm building. The grove protects the tree from the cold drying winds of the winter, and the building would block the rays of the southwest sun in March, which can cause sun scald on the southwest side of the tree.

In town, apple trees are better off in the back yard rather than the front. Apple trees can do a bit better in town because they are protected from extremes in wind and temperature by the many buildings.

Crabapples can be the sweetest of them all

A member of the apple family is designated a *crabapple* if its fruit is less than two inches across. There is no other criteria. Actual sweetness or sourness of the fruit is not considered. And yet, people wrinkle their nose at the term *crabapple* and refuse to plant the hardiest apple trees available because the word *crab* implies sourness.

Crabapples range from sweeter than big apples to completely sour. To get the name *crabapple* out of people's heads, perhaps we should label the smaller fruit of some apple trees *lunchbox apples.* The two best of the lot, the "Centennial" and the "Chestnut," are on the list of desirable apple varieties below.

What is most worth remembering is that crabapples thrive in the north. Our most recent difficult test was the winter of 1996-1997, which featured record-setting low temperatures for several days. So-called crabapples came through with flying colors.

Avoid dwarf apple trees

Dwarf apple trees are more popular than *standard* apple trees in urban areas. Because they are stunted by their root stock, dwarfed trees do not take up as much space in the yard, and they may bear fruit earlier in their lives.

Apple trees are made dwarf by grafting them onto what is called a dwarfing *root stock. Dwarfing* root stock is not as hardy as *standard* rootstock. During a cold winter with little snow cover, the root of a dwarf apple may freeze out, killing the entire tree. In our area, where space is plentiful and the winters are cold, dwarf apple trees are not the best idea. Ask for *standard* trees, which have a hardier root.

Out on the prairie, apples trees endure enough stress to slow down their growth to allow for bearing in 3-5 years. The argument that non-dwarfed trees will be slower to bear (because they grow too fast) doesn't apply as it might further south and east.

Hold back on fertilizer

Apple trees don't generally require a lot of fertilizer. In fact, over-fertilizing apple trees stimulates fresh, green growth which will cause the trees to delay bearing. Such fast *vegetative* growth is more susceptible to *fire blight* (see Chapter 6 Insects and Disease).

They only time one truly needs to fertilize an apple tree is if it is obviously suffering from iron deficiency—that is, if the leaves are turning yellow, or if it has completely stopped growing, in which case a good dose of an all-purpose water soluble fertilizer can jolt it awake.

When will my newly-planted apple tree bear?

Apple trees generally begin to bear fruit three-to-five years after planting. The later the apple tree bears in the season, the longer it will take for the tree to begin bearing fruit in its lifetime. The faster the tree grows as a young tree, the longer it will take to bear fruit. So, apples which are planted on rich ground tend to take longer to bear. Again, on rich ground the apple tree produces growth which is more vegetative than reproductive.

If your apple tree doesn't bloom

Blooms are necessary to produce fruit. Trees which do not produce bloom will not bear. If an apple tree has grown well for several years without producing bloom, the tree may be growing too fast.

To speed up bearing, it is possible to injure the tree in such a way as to slow the sap flow. Calculated damage discourages vigorous green growth and encourages the development of fruit spurs, the little spikes on the branches which eventually produce blooms, and therefore fruit.

To inflict calculated damage, some people beat the trunk of their trees with a log chain. Less violent types can simply make a cut with a knife on several branches of about thumb thickness, cuts deep enough to go below the *cambium layer,* the green part just under the bark, but running only half-way around the branch. Two inches away from the first cut, make a second cut around the opposite side of the branch. The cuts force the sap to weave its way out to the tips of the branches, which slows the growth of that branch. Perform this procedure in June for probable increase in bloom the next year.

To encourage earlier bearing, do not plant apple trees on rich soil. Fertilize them only if they look deprived of nutrition. Eventually allow the sod to creep in to the trunk of the tree. Such deprivations can cause the tree to grow slowly enough to encourage bloom.

What about pollination?

It is true that apple blossoms must be pollinated by pollen from another tree in the apple family in order to bear fruit. However, so many members of the apple family grow in our area that pollination is seldom a problem. Keep in mind, ornamental flowering crabs will pollinate apple trees. Whatever bee comes to your apple tree likely found a flowering crab tree first.

If you plant two apple trees in hopes of improving pollination, make sure the trees are not of the same variety. Two trees of one particular variety are no better than one.

When apple trees do not bear, it is usually because they do not set bloom in the first place. When pollination is an issue, it is usually because cold, wet weather in May prevents the bees from working while the blooms are out. A hard frost while the bloom is out will also prevent fruiting. Such problems are out of our control, and thus not worth fretting about.

Why does my apple tree bear every other year?

Some apple trees are prone to cycles of bearing heavily one year and very little or not at all the next. Alternate year cycles are natural and common. To coax the apple tree out of the alternate year cycle, pull off half of the young apples soon after they have grown large enough for you to find them. This is easier said than done, but it is the only way to flatten out the cycle of a tree bearing in alternate years.

Better to find a friend or neighbor with a tree which bears in the year yours doesn't. Split the crop with them each year. In the case of Haralson apples, both parties will likely have enough to get you through the winter.

Can apples take frost on the tree?

The Haralson and other late bearing apples actually benefit from one or more light frosts before they are picked and put away in storage. Light frosts improve the flavor by raising sugar content. The frost should just touch the apple. If the fruit freezes into the flesh, it will turn to mush.

As a rule, if the temperatures threaten to sink into the lower twenties for several hours during the night, it is time to get out the ladder and pick every last apple.

How do I get larger apples?

Sometimes, the apples on a tree don't become as large as advertised. Drought can reduce the size of apples, in which case watering can help.

However, when some trees start to bear, they overdo it and set too much fruit. The tree can only support a certain number of full-sized apples. If it sets too many fruits to support, the apples will be small. In that case, removing half the apples in June can nearly double the size of those which remain.

As trees mature, the job of removing apples becomes too much. To save time, chose one limb and remove half the apples from that limb only. The remaining apples on that limb should be larger than those on the rest of the tree.

Protecting apple trees from deer and rodents

It is absolutely necessary to protect young apple trees from rodents during the winter, and from deer both in winter and summer. See Chapter 7 on Furry Pests for more details. The cost of proper protection will likely equal the cost of the trees, but trees wrecked by deer are worth nothing.

Preventing wormy apples

The single most important action a gardener can take to prevent wormy apples is to clean up all fallen apples before they become rotten. Do not allow apples to rot on the ground, as worms crawl from the apple into the ground and lay thousands of eggs which will become the worms which ruin *next* summer's apples.

If worms have been a problem in the past, you might spray with a general fruit tree spray. We find that spraying every two weeks beginning when the small apples show the first tint of red, and ending two weeks before they are harvested, can prevent worms. This usually means only three or four sprays.

But with proper sanitation—disposal of fallen apples—worms can be prevented without chemicals.

Proper pruning of apple trees

Proper pruning is more important for apple trees than any other tree for the simple reason that branches of an apple tree will be asked to bear a tremendous burden when the tree produces a good crop.

The strongest apple tree has a strong, single, central stem. Emerging from that stem should be evenly-spaced side branches. Those branches should come out from the main trunk at a 90 degree angle, or as close to a 90 degree angle as possible. *The smaller the angle, the weaker the joint, and the more likely that the branch will break off when loaded down with fruit.*

In addition, branches which are closer to horizontal than vertical bear much more fruit, and more quickly. Commercial orchards actually weigh down branches to get them to bear more prolifically.

The goals of pruning a young apple tree are to preserve, encourage and strengthen a single, straight main trunk, and to eliminate weak joints years before they become a problem.

Priorities while pruning:

•*Remove all water sprouts.* Water sprouts are tender shoots which grow very fast, and tend to grow vertically out of much larger horizontal branches. Water sprouts are weak. Their tender growth is more easily attacked by fire blight. Remove them when they appear. If you get to them early enough, you can rub them off with your bare hand. Leave them for three years and you'll need a chain saw to get rid of them.

•*Remove all suckers around the base of the tree.* Suckers shooting up from the root serve no purpose. They are genetically different from the tree's top. They are unsightly. Get rid of them when they appear.

Do not use a weed trimmer to remove suckers right around the base of the tree. One touch of the trunk with the line can rip off a large chunk of bark, damaging the tree for years. Yes, the damage might result in more fruit if the tree lives through it, but a weed trimmer is not the way to go about it.

•*Remove branches at cross purposes.* Branches which rub against one another both become weak. Remove the one which looks least important. Also, remove branches which come from the outer branches of the tree and head back towards the tree's center.

•*Clean out the center of the tree.* Apple trees bear their fruit on the perimeter of the canopy. Getting rid of the brush deep within the canopy of the tree encourages air circulation and prevents disease. Children *should* be able to climb in the interior of an old apple tree without getting cut up by brush.

•*Make mowing fun and easy.* Don't fight with low hanging branches. Cut them off. Late in the season, if your tree is loaded with fruit, it may pay to support some of the branches with 2x4s. The branches should spring back into place when the fruit is removed. At that time, remember that apple trees are meant to produce apples, not look pretty all the time.

What varieties are best?

What follows is a suggested list of apple varieties which are best for the northern prairie. Some of us have favorites which are not on this list, but the bottom line is that you will not go wrong planting the apples listed here. The beginning gardener who chooses from this list will be well-rewarded.

The varieties below are listed roughly in the order that a new gardener should plant them.

Centennial

Introduced in honor of the Minnesota centennial in 1958, the Centennial apple is the earliest bearing and most prolific apple for our area. The tree is totally hardy. Trees under five feet tall have been known to produce many ice cream pails full of apples. Bearing inevitably begins the year after planting. The fruit is egg shaped and egg sized. It does not need to be peeled for use in pies. Great for sauce or pickling. For a young family eager for quick results, there is no better first apple tree to plant.

Chestnut

Introduced by the University of Minnesota in 1949, the Chestnut apple is the "best-kept secret in Minnesota," according to one old nurseryman. A small apple, it often falls unfairly into the *crabapple* category in catalogs and literature. However, the Chestnut makes up for lack of size with its wonderful taste, which, as the apples ripen, can include aromatic hints of pear. The texture is firm and crunchy.

The apples can hang on the tree for a month after ripening without going bad. A strong tree, the Chestnut survived the terrible winter of 1996 in fine shape. The large blooms in the spring contain a hint of pink.

The Chestnut fruit can be *russeted,* which means it may have patches of skin which are potato-skin-like. Those patches are harmless, and merely add character.

Haralson

The old favorite, the Haralson was introduced by the University of Minnesota in 1922. For steady performance, it can't be beat. The late-ripening apples will keep in the fridge or in a cool basement until April or later. Sour apple people like the fruit right off the tree in October. Others prefer the Haralson after it has sweetened in storage for a couple of months. All will agree that apple pie made from Haralson is tops, whether made in October or April. Secondary varieties such as Haralred and Red Haralson have been introduced, but the straight old Haralson is still the best.

Goodland

A hardy apple introduced by the Morden Research Station in Manitoba in 1922, the Goodland bears clear-skinned, blushed pink fruit late in summer. The squatty, but attractive fruit snuggles closely to the branches. The flesh of the Goodland apple is the purest white, and it stays white even if you take a bite and set the apple down for an hour.

The tree itself is fast growing and upright in habit. The fruit is good for all purposes. Goodland ripens in mid-August, and keeps in a cool place unusually long for an early apple. Goodland apples are mild in flavor. Some would consider them bland. But for hardiness, as well as ease of care and early bearing, the Goodland is ideal.

Honeycrisp

The University of Minnesota hit the jackpot with the 1991 introduction of the Honeycrisp, which has since developed world-wide popularity. One bite will tell you why.

Originally rated for hardiness Zone 3 due to a steady, sturdy multi-decade performance at the Grand Rapids experiment station, it became clear in the first few years that Honeycrisp *is not* completely hardy on the open northern prairie. Indeed, it was likely sheltered in Grand Rapids by a hill to the north and a rolling terrain. The hardiness rating was quietly changed.

So, what is a prairie dwelling apple lover to do? With minimal precautions, one can increase the likelihood of a Honeycrisp tree surviving on the northern prairie.

Here is the problem: as we get into late-February and March, the increased sunshine warms the bark on the southwest side of the Honeycrisp's trunk and branches. The thaw is followed that night by a return to freezing temperatures. The cell structure of the Honeycrisp is not equipped for the fluctuations. The bark turns to mush. The damage is called *sun scald*.

Most people do not notice the damage until spring turns to summer and the dead part of the bark is made black by soot mold. Shelf-like mushrooms may start to grow on the dead wood. Neither fungus is a problem in itself, but it shows that part of the tree has died. *Do not paint the wound, or wrap the tree after damage is done.*

To protect the Honeycrisp from sun scald, paint the southwest side of the trunk, and as many branches as you can reach, with white latex paint late in the fall. The white paint will reflect the sun, preventing it from warming the bark to the point of doing damage. Next season, the paint will wear off.

On younger trees, which are more susceptible to sun scald, the hard plastic wrap used to protect from rodents will do the job.

Once the tree develops rough bark, it no longer requires painting.

A bearing Honeycrisp apple is a true prize. Northern prairie gardeners might be able to establish a tree, and enjoy the demonstrably superior flavor of Honeycrisp apples grown at home and not shipped in. However, those of us in Zone 3 should maintain a realistic attitude about the famous tree's ability to withstand the prairie's winters.

Honeycrisp have one other weakness which has manifested on the prairie: They sometimes develop a calcium deficiency which can make the fruit's skin wrinkled and the flesh brown-streaked. If this happens, next year spray the foliage throughout the season with the same calcium spray used to prevent blossom-end-rot on tomatoes. The calcium will be absorbed by the foliage and the apples should revert to their normal perfection.

Zestar

A 1999 introduction from the University of Minnesota, the Zestar has produced the largest apples we have ever grown at Bergeson Nursery. Tender, juicy and sweet, the Zestar ripens in late August. In taste tests, many people prefer the complex flavor of Zestar to that of Honeycrisp. Additionally, Zestar, is a stronger tree of the two on the prairie. Unlike many mid-season apples, Zestar fruits keep quite well in refrigeration.

Red Duchess

An old-time favorite, the Red Duchess is a large, early apple with striped yellow and red fruit. The fruit can be very large. The Red Duchess bears on young trees. They are deliciously, even sloppily, juicy. The trees are hardy and durable.

Wodarz

A North Dakota introduction, the Wodarz apple languished in obscurity until the recent apple craze brought the tree to market. It is the hardiest yellow apple available. The flavor has a hint of banana. The flesh is firm, and if dehydrated, maintains a delightful chewiness.

Sweet Sixteen

Introduced by the University of Minnesota in 1977, the Sweet Sixteen has developed a devoted following of fans who love its exotic, cherry-like flavor. However, many people have been frustrated by the tree's reluctance to bear. Some have waited more than ten years!

The problem is likely that the Sweet Sixteen has an upright habit. Few of its branches come out from the trunk at a low angle, and it is the lower angle branches which set the most fruit.

In order to correct the problem, apple orchards have hung weights on the branches of the Sweet Sixteen, increasing their angle from the trunk to closer to 90 degrees. Care should be taken not to put on so much weight that the branch aims down.

PLUMS *Prunus domestica*

Plums are a short-lived (twenty years is a good run) fruit tree on the prairie, but the flavor of northern grown plums is unbeatable and unique.

The tame, *large-fruited plums* hardy here all produce yellow-fleshed and red-skinned fruit.

The *cherry-plum hybrids* produce smaller fruit, but bear like crazy.

Gardeners with a large yard should consider planting a cluster of *wild plum*, also known as American plum, out back. Wild plum are seedlings. Each is different. A patch will produce varied fruit which makes wonderful sauce and beautiful jellies. Many old wild plum plantings have died out on the farms, but planting a cluster of the inexpensive wild plum seedlings in your yard can bring back the nostalgic fall pleasures of picking wild plums, and finding the trees in the bunch which bear the sweetest fruit.

In addition, the wild plum blooms, which come out first thing in May, have a delightful scent and will effectively pollinate tame plum varieties.

Hazards for plum

Plums are subject to the same hazards as apple trees: Rodents can eat the bark of young trees and the bark of young trees is susceptible to sun scald. Deer can emasculate young plum trees. The same protection measures advocated for apple trees apply to plums.

Plum mummies

Sometimes plum fruit is afflicted with a rot which eventually leaves some of the plum fruit dead, empty and moldy, a mere mummy of what they once were.

The best cure is prevention: clean up all fallen fruit. Remove mummies from the tree when you see them. Prune out the interior brush, as one would with apple trees, to increase air circulation and prevent the mold from taking hold. Chemical spray regimens are too complex and risky for the home gardener to attempt.

Where should I plant a plum?

Plum tree roots do not like it wet. Plant plum on the highest spot possible in your yard. Realize that most plum trees are remarkably unattractive unless they are pruned into a presentable specimen.

Pollination of plums

Pollination is more often a problem with plums than with apples. *Plums bloom earlier than apples,* and are more at risk for frost. The smaller petals of plum blossoms are not as effective in attracting bees. There aren't so many plum trees planted, even in towns, and many of the wild plums seem to have died off in area windbreaks.

To pollinate your plum trees, plant two trees of different varieties close to each other. The "Toka" plum, with its long bloom-time, has earned a reputation as the best pollinator. It is a vigorous, sturdy tree and the flavor of its firm fruit, although spicy-sour, will grow on you.

To make darn sure plums pollinated, Grandpa used to clump two tame plum trees of different varieties in the same hole. Then, he would shake a bouquet of wild plum near the blooms of the tame plum to ensure pollination.

Protecting plum blossoms from frost

Plum blossoms can be caught by the last frost, particularly in seasons with an early warm spell, followed by the inevitable cold snap. To delay the blooming of plums, some people plant them in a slightly shaded area. Although the tree will appear more sparse in shade, you are free to interpret the sparseness as elegance, and the lovely, shiny black, white-striped bark of mature plums will help maintain the illusion.

Growing plums as shrubs

Plums vary in growth habit, from variety to variety and from location to location. Some plums, with pruning, turn into elegant small trees with an oriental twist, worthy of a position of honor in the front yard. Most grow into an unsightly pile of brush.

Oddly, plum trees which develop into an unsightly pile of brush tend to bear more fruit. When the lower branches of a plum are covered with snow in the winter, those snow-buried branches bear more the next summer than the higher unprotected branches.

The *Sapalta* cherry-plum tends to grow as a shrub, while the *Underwood* is the most upright and tree-shaped of the plums hardy in our area. In between are all of the other plum trees.

What follows are the first varieties of plum the beginning gardener should consider:

Sapalta Cherry Plum   *Hybrid*

The Sapalta is a cherry-plum hybrid. The fruit is roughly the size and shape of the circle made when you press the tip of your index finger against the tip of your thumb. It is purple-skinned, with a deep purple flesh. The pits are relatively large. The tree bears heavily, especially on branches which were covered by snow. For a sure bet on the prairie, start with a Sapalta. For pollination purposes, it will need to be joined by its fellow cherry plum hybrid, the Compass.

Compass Cherry Plum   *Hybrid*

The Compass, unlike the Sapalta, is more cherry than plum. Its berries are round rather than pointed. The fruit's flesh is yellow. If you lack space, plant a Compass in the same hole as a Sapalta. The two will then pollinate, and the resulting bush will provide a banquet in late summer.

Underwood

Underwood plum, like all the larger hardy plums, produce red fruit with a hint of purple, with yellow flesh. The Underwood is an old favorite, and is a vigorous tree.

Pipestone

The Pipestone, another old favorite, are likely to produce the largest fruit. They explode with flavorful juice upon the first bite! You will need to wipe your mouth—and much else—after the experience.

Toka

The best pollinator, the Toka plum features firm fruit which ripen later than the larger plums. If you let the fruit hang on the tree long enough, the flavor and juiciness improve, to the point where it can become one's favorite.

Waneta

A tad more crunchy than juicy, the Waneta plum is closest in texture to the store-bought plums.

Pembina

The Pembina plum, which produces fruit almost indistinguishable from the Underwood and Pipestone, has shown a superior ability to adapt to heavy soils.

The above plums are the hardiest for Zone 3. If you live closer to Zone 4, other plums such as the Superior, La Crescent, and Gracious are worth a try.

However, planting a random sampling of the hardiest plum trees listed is a sure way to enjoy one of the most vivid pleasures in the northern orchard: the first bite into a slightly over-ripe, juicy red plum.

APRICOTS   *Prunus armeniaca*

Apricots bloom so early that their blooms seldom pollinate. The trees aren't entirely hardy, either. They will work only with the natural protection provided by a hill, grove, or group of buildings. At best, one can expect a crop every four years.

Apricots can pollinate themselves, but it is best to have another apricot around for the purpose. A hardy seedling apricot will do the job. In fact, as an alternative to purchasing an expensive, grafted apricot, one might consider planting a little grove of cheap seedlings in hopes that one of them might produce good fruit in a good year.

213

"Wescot" and "Scout" come from Manitoba and are a better bet on the northern prairie.

The "Moongold" and "Sungold" were introduced by the University of Minnesota, and are well-known on the northern prairie market. However, they are rated for Zone 4, but are short-lived in Zone 3. They have been known to bear in protected areas along rivers.

Planting apricots is like buying a lottery ticket. If you get lucky, one year you will have enough apricots for yourself and everybody you know.

PEARS   *Pyrus*

Pear trees have been more successful than apricots over the decades. The author has, on one occasion in his life, bitten into a locally grown pear which was every bit as juicy and delicious as anything purchased in the store. Others are hard as rock, but good for canning.

Pears can bear without a pollinator, but are best in pairs. Seedling pear trees of soil conservation grade work as a pollinator as well.

The "Ure," "Early Gold," and "Golden Spice" are rated Zone 3 hardy.

Pear trees, more than plum or apricot, grow into attractive trees. Their glossy green leaves are a treat. Their branching habit is dense and well-shaped. Some develop a fiery red fall color. Their blooms are showy in early spring. Plant pear trees in hopes of getting fruit, but enjoy their beauty no matter what.

CHERRY   *Prunus cerasus*

Most of the better cherries for the northern prairie grow as shrubs, and are included in the "Small Fruits" chapter. However, the Bali cherry, (also known as "Evans") makes a cute ornamental tree. When the cherries ripen to a bright red, the contrast with the dark, glossy leaves makes for Christmas in July. You must put netting over the tree or the birds will get all the fruit, even before it ripens. The cherries are sour, but make great pies.

A sense of proportion

There you have it, a discussion of fruit trees for the northern prairie with an emphasis upon *that which produces results with the least effort.* The space given in this chapter to each type of fruit tree is in rough proportion to its importance on the northern prairie: Apples are first. Plums are a distant second. Apricots, pears and cherries are for novelty.

NUTS

Black walnut *(Juglans nigra)* are the hardiest nut tree for our area. The walnuts are good to eat, provided you can break them open. The tree is a wonderful addition to the yard, and eventually one of your great-grandchildren can turn it into exquisite furniture.

Butternut, hazelnut, hazelberts and other nuts can survive our climate, but their fruit is negligible in both quantity and quality.

Unfortunately, most of our nuts on the prairie will continue to be human.

CHAPTER 18

Small Fruits

Small fruit is a catch-all category for edibles which are neither annual vegetables, nor fruit trees.

Members of the small fruit family bring back memories of old times for many people. Gooseberries are sour, but those who ate them when they were young don't seem to mind. Juneberries have a more fruity flavor than blueberries, and, unlike blueberries, they are perfectly suited to our soil and climate.

Elderberries, long forgotten, are making a comeback. There are new red cherries from northern Alberta which promise to grow in our area. Hardy grapes should be a staple for northern gardeners, even though many new to gardening don't imagine them doing well this far north.

Plants in the category "small fruits" are distinguished from vegetables because of their woody, perennial stalks. *Small fruits* are distinguished from *fruit trees* by the small size of the bush, and the size of the fruit.

There is an overwhelming wealth of information available from university extension services and on the internet for raising small fruits commercially. Here, we assume you want to plant small fruits for your enjoyment. The information presented here should enable you to reap the enjoyment of small fruits without becoming overwhelmed by the work involved to raise them commercially.

Asparagus

Nothing tastes better than the first spears of asparagus taken in the spring. Although asparagus grow in the wild and are planted by birds, they can be difficult for the gardener to establish. However, with proper instructions, gardeners can maintain an asparagus patch that will produce for decades.

The asparagus spear one eats is merely an early sprout which will eventually, if left to grow, become a large, ferny frond of foliage. Tender while young, asparagus shoots become woody and tough with age. The ferny foliage can be ornamental late in the season, and turns a bright yellow fall color, with red berries.

Asparagus roots should be planted deeply for several reasons: Deeper plants produce thicker spears, while shallower plants produce spindly spears. Deeper plants are more likely to survive a harsh winter, and are less subject to heaving out of the ground from alternate freezes and thaws.

Asparagus roots can reach twenty feet in depth. Therefore, once an asparagus plant is established, it is not possible to move the plant.

Asparagus roots should be planted in a 10-inch deep trough. The roots, which radiate from the crown like the tentacles of an octopus, should be fanned out and covered, but the crown, with its sprouts, should be covered only with a dusting of light soil.

After the shoot grows, soil can be filled in so that the crown is eventually about 8 inches below the soil level.

Asparagus like higher ground, as they will send roots down to find water. The crown should not sit wet at any time during the annual cycle.

Many asparagus are planted by birds. Birds sit on wires. Wires tend to span the shoulders of a ditch bank, which, fortunately, is an ideal well-drained place for asparagus to grow.

Asparagus do not require fertilization. They are also one of the rare plants which thrives in salty soil.

217

Cranberries   *Viburnum*

The cranberry native to our area is the American Cranberry *(Viburnum trilobum)*. American Cranberry produce juicy, soft, bright orange-red fruit in clusters on the tips of the branches. The fruit is a little sour to eat, but makes a colorful jam. The berries are a favorite of grosbeaks and waxwings.

The bog-type cranberry *(Vaccinium)* which produces the firm cranberries used for Thanksgiving is not generally grown in our area due to lack of hardiness and the complexity of creating proper growing conditions.

The American Cranberry prefers moist, well-drained soil, unlike the bog-type cranberry. Like all fruit-bearing plants, the American Cranberry will bear more if planted in the sun.

CHERRY

Yes, we are able to grow cherries on the northern prairie. Thanks to advances in breeding in the prairie provinces of Canada, our choices are expanding with each passing year.

The cherries we can grow are categorized as sour cherries. They have soft, juicy flesh. They make delicious pies, and if left on the bush long enough are quite sweet to eat.

Cherries for the northern prairie can be divided into tree types and shrub types. The Bali is a cherry tree. The newer promising cherries from Saskatchewan grow as a shrub.

Cherries are a favorite of the birds as well, so covering the bush with netting may be necessary if you want any fruit left for yourself.

Cherry, Nanking   *Prunus tomentosa*

The Nanking Cherry bears small but eminently edible fruit of about 1/3 of an inch in diameter. Because Nanking cherry are grown from seed, only between one-half and two-thirds of the plants bear fruit. Nanking

Cherry are available on the market as small windbreak plants. Purchase a dozen or so and plant them thickly to ensure an eventual crop.

Despite its natural tendency to grow as a shrub, it is possible to prune a Nanking to have a distinct trunk. Such pruning will show off the deep bronze, shiny, white-striped bark of the Nanking Cherry.

Cherry, Bali   *Prunus cerasus*

The Bali Cherry originated as the Evans Cherry in Alberta, Canada. It is the first cherry *tree* proven hardy for Zone 3. It has grown and produced fruit in Alberta since the late 1960s.

The Bali produces bright red fruit a little larger than the width of a dime. It pollinates itself, so only one tree is needed. The fruit is sour at first ripeness, later turning mild if allowed to hang on the tree.

The Bali's bark turns a shiny bronze with pronounced white striping as it ages. The glossy, deep green foliage contrasts with the bright red fruit for a striking, Christmasy effect. There is no reason the Bali cannot be used as an ornamental tree in our area.

Although there have been isolated instances of cherry tree varieties such as the "North Star," "Mesabi," "Montmorency" and "Meteor" producing in our area, these varieties are far more suited for Zone 4.

Recent cherry introductions from Canada

Bush-type improvements on the Nanking cherry are yielding great results, namely varieties from Saskatchewan such as "Carmine Jewel" and "Romeo and Juliet." They do not need a pollinator.

Cherry trees will balk in wet soils. Try to find a spot which is slightly raised. Only fertilize if the tree shows signs of malnutrition, which is unlikely.

Elderberry   *Sambucus*

Elderberry are a native. They tend to die back to the snow line, but grow back to 5 or 6 feet tall and wide, and bear their BB-sized fruits in clusters at the tips of the branches even after a tough winter.

Ripe fruits can be used for a delicious pie, or for wine, or dried for tea.

The vigorous elderberry bush can double as a large screen to block out unsightly yard features such as propane tanks.

Grapes   *Vitis*

A highlight of early fall is tasting handfuls of northern-grown grapes. Their flavor is like nothing available in the store.

Two varieties of grape are proven over the long term to be hardy and productive on the northern prairie, the "Beta" and the "Valiant." The Beta are marble-sized and make great juice, jam and jelly. The Valiant are a bit smaller, and form tighter clusters of fruit, but they are a bit sweeter right off the vine.

Those two standards are joined by the "King of the North," which has shown no weaknesses during its fifteen years of production on the prairie.

None of the above three varieties require winter cover.

Viticulture, the art and science of raising grapes, is as old as civilization itself. There is enough information out there on growing grapes to scare one away for good!

The harshness of northern prairie winters makes grape-growing simple: Plant hardy varieties, give them a simple trellis, and wait for the pleasures of ripe grapes in August and September.

An acceptable trellis can be a fence, an arbor, or simply two or three wires strung between two posts. Raising the grapes off the ground keeps the berries clean, and increases the crop.

Prune grapes in the *early spring* before they leaf out. Simply thin out the plant by pulling out individual strands and removing them at the base until the plant is about one-third of what it was before you started the massacre. Grapes which aren't thinned in such a manner will slow their bearing after the third year.

Grapes not only need full sun, but they cannot compete with roots of trees. Keep the grass away as well.

Do not panic if new plants, or even established grape vines, are slow to leaf out in the spring. Grape vines can look dead until the end of May, and then, when you aren't looking, they explode with growth.

There is simply no reason why every northern prairie yard doesn't contain at least one hardy grape plant.

Gooseberries   *Ribes*

The sour gooseberries make a tasty pie which is enjoyed by a small circle of fanatics.

The University of Minnesota developed the "Pixwell" gooseberry during the Depression. It was touted as a source of vitamin C which could be grown in dry, weak soils.

The gooseberry's unique, clear-skinned fruit starts green, turns slightly pink, and finally ripens to an opaque purple.

The aggressive sourness of the berry makes it a hard sell to those who weren't forced to eat them as a child, only to later love them out of nostalgia.

Gooseberry plants are notoriously susceptible to leaf diseases and insects. Sometimes you come upon a bush in late summer which is full of purple fruit, but is without a single leaf left!

Plant gooseberries in an open area to minimize the effects of leaf disease.

Juneberries   *Amelanchier*

Once common in the wild, juneberries are now a rare treat. Known as *saskatoons* in Canada, and *serviceberry* in some locales, juneberries produce a super-nutritious fruit with a crunch created by small seeds.

Because blueberries do not work on the northern prairie, juneberries are seen as a substitute. In the prairie provinces of Canada, juneberry are grown commercially.

Commercial juneberry production has not taken off south of the border, in part due to several disease and insect problems which can inhibit bearing. It is the opinion of some experts in Canada that raising juneberries without chemicals is impossible.

For the home gardener, disease and insects are an explanation of why their juneberry plant doesn't always bear, but are nothing to worry about.

The most the home gardener should do is cover the juneberry bush with netting immediately after fruit sets to prevent the birds from eating the green berries before they ripen.

The juneberry is an attractive, airy plant with good fall leaf color. If kept free of weeds, it will become established and possibly bear in three years.

Raspberries, Red   *Rubus*

Fresh raspberries and cream are one of the great delicacies of a northern prairie summer.

Red raspberries are head and shoulders above the purple, black and yellow varieties in hardiness, vigor and production, and should be the first type of raspberry one plants.

Raspberries need full sun and good drainage. Any spot where water sits after a big rain, even for a few hours, can be fatal to raspberries.

Raspberries thrive in a bed of six inches of peat. The peat also makes the chore of weeding the raspberry patch a good deal easier.

The raspberry family can be divided in two, the traditional summer-bearing, or *floricane* varieties, and the fall-bearing (sometimes called ever-bearing) *primocane* varieties which have come into vogue more recently.

Summer-bearing raspberries produce a large crop in July. Fall-bearing varieties produce their largest yield between Labor Day and the first hard frost.

Summer-bearing raspberries bear on second year shoots, after which the stalks die and need to be pruned out of the patch to make way for next year's shoots. Fall-bearing raspberries bear on new shoots, which means the entire patch can be mowed to the ground annually.

Traditional summer-bearing varieties are the "Boyne," "Killarney," and "Latham," of which the Boyne has been the strongest for many decades.

The most prominent fall-bearing varieties on the northern prairie are the "Red Wing" and "Caroline."

It is unwise to plant summer-bearing raspberries in the same row as fall-bearing types, as one will overtake the other. However, a separate patch of each can mean fresh raspberries and cream for both summer and fall.

To start a raspberry patch, add peat or compost to an area four feet wide. Kill the grass and weeds with glyphosate first. Till the area well.

Ten starter plants planted 3 feet apart in a row 30 feet long will, by the second year, develop into a patch which will provide ample berries for a single family.

Raspberries send out suckers by the root which will turn the ten starter plants into hundreds of producing plants within a year. The suckers are so plentiful that it is recommended that you hoe out ones which emerge outside the confines of the patch.

Adding a thin layer of peat to the patch each year will make weeding easier, and will encourage the suckers to set root.

Adding 10-10-10 fertilizer each season is recommended. In addition, if there is hot and dry weather as the raspberries ripen, and assuming the patch is well-drained, watering will produce larger berries of superior flavor.

As a raspberry patch ages, it becomes more susceptible to insects, disease, and weeds. It is best to simply start another patch every five years or so. One can purchase new plants, or move a dozen fresh shoots from the old patch during dormancy.

Faithfully removing the dead canes will help prolong the life of the patch, as will thinning the new shoots to about one each square foot.

Raspberry roots are shallow. Care should be taken at planting not to plant the starter shoots too deeply. The root should be no more than one inch below the surface.

Raspberries, Black

Black raspberries are famously nutritious, and the fruit is usually quite expensive in the store. Often black raspberries are confused with blackberries, which simply aren't hardy on the northern plains.

Black raspberries *do not* sucker with any vigor. The plants must be forced to reproduce by manually layering branches under the soil. Therefore, single shoots of black raspberries are far more expensive to purchase, and are a bit more work to establish.

In addition, black raspberry plants are not as tough as the red. Plant in a protected location, yet in full sun. A south side of a building is ideal.

Raspberries, Purple

The best purple raspberry is the "Royalty," which produces huge berries that ripen on the stalk over a long time, becoming even better as they age. However, Royalty are only hardy to Zone 4, and are temperamental on the open prairie. They do not sucker as vigorously as the red, and bear best if frequently pruned.

Raspberries, Yellow

Perhaps one's eyes fool the taste buds, but it seems that fruit which is yellow always contains a hint of banana flavor. So too with the yellow raspberries. They are delicious. But the plants are somewhat weak, and they do not bear enough to get a dish full. Try as a novelty only.

Rhubarb   *Rheum*

Some textbooks consider rhubarb to be a "perennial vegetable." We'll call it a small fruit. The stalk is edible, but the leaves will make you quite sick.

An easy and rewarding plant to raise, rhubarb grows only in northern climates due to its need for a cold season.

A few people prefer green rhubarb stalks, but most prefer varieties which are red all the way through the stalk. The red varieties are what one finds on the market.

In fact, a single rhubarb plant can go from producing thick red stalks early in its life to producing small green stalks later on. In that case, if you prefer red stalks, it is best to purchase new starter plants and put them in a different location.

It is better to pull rhubarb stalks up from the base of the plant than to cut them off with a knife, leaving a stub which can rot.

It is best not to harvest rhubarb the first season, although no harm would be done by taking enough stalks to make a pan of muffins.

It is best to stop harvesting rhubarb about July 1 to allow enough leaves to develop for the plant to store up food for the winter. Removing any flower stalks which bolt up is also good for the long-term health of the rhubarb plant.

Rhubarb can be used in the perennial garden as an ornamental foliage plant while doubling as a source of food.

Simmering rhubarb when cooking it, taking care not to let the sauce get too hot, will keep the rhubarb intact and prevent it from getting stringy.

Plant rhubarb in full sun. Rhubarb likes a lot of organic matter, and a lot of compost. They will not survive in saturated ground, even for just a few days after a big rain.

Once established, rhubarb are difficult to kill. Slicing off a section with a sharp spade during dormancy is an easy way to share your plant with neighbors. As long as the division has both root and a shoot, it will take off. Plant with the shoot right at the surface of the ground, no deeper.

Strawberries   *Fragaria*

Strawberries are so-called due to the practice of spreading straw around the plants in order to keep the fruits clean and suppress weeds.

Strawberries love manure, heavy compost, a lot of peat, or a combination of the three. They do not do well in mucky heavy soils. A raised bed of peat is ideal. Old manure is wonderful for strawberries, but the weeding can be a chore.

A strawberry patch will do best if replaced with new plants every two to three years. Patches wear out quickly, and attempts to reinvigorate a patch by thinning the plants are seldom successful.

It is important to plant strawberries in early May. They must be planted at the proper depth, with the soil level exactly at the crown. Purchase bare root plants, and get them in the ground right away.

Strawberry starter plants send out runners. Allow those runners to set root, and you will have a productive patch for the next two years.

Commercial growers live by different strawberry rules than are necessary for the home gardener. They have to look at the big picture: maximum production over the years. They pinch the runners and blooms off new plants to that end.

For the home gardener, the rules are simple: get the plants in the ground, keep the weeds down, water the patch when dry, and pick the fruit when it happens, even on newly planted plants.

There are thousands of varieties of strawberries. They can be divided into three categories: June-bearing, ever-bearing and day-neutral.

June-bearing strawberries

June-bearing strawberries bear one large crop at the end of June into early July. The berries tend to be large and sweet.

June-bearing strawberry plants are photosensitive, meaning they are able to sense the length of the day. The plants produce bloom as long as the days are getting longer. Once past June 21, the plants stop putting on bloom and concentrate upon producing one big crop of fruit, which generally ripens in early July.

Ever-bearing strawberries

Ever-bearing strawberries keep blooming in cycles all season. They can produce up to four separate crops. In theory, the berries are supposed to be smaller than June-bearing varieties, but in practice, with water and good soil, the ever-bearing can produce fruit of an inch or more across.

However, the real joy of ever-bearing varieties such as the Ogallala is the superior flavor. Red through and through, firm but juicy, the Ogallala has enough wild strawberry left in its genetics to produce an intense flavor one will never experience from a store-bought strawberry.

Day-neutral strawberries

The more recently introduced day-neutral strawberry plants bloom and bear all season. They are ideal for snacking right off the vine. Day-neutral plants produce the first year and are not likely to make it through the winter. Plant them as annuals by the front step for season-long snacking.

CHAPTER 19

Roses

If you've ever run across a wild rose blooming pale pink at the base of an old cottonwood on the prairie in June, you know the beauty of roses native to our region.

However, the expectation most prairie people have of roses has been changed by the presence of long-stemmed tea roses in every cut flower dispensary for the past many decades. Today, when you say *rose*, the first thought is not of a prairie rose, but of a cut rose grown in Venezuela.

Yes, we can grow tea roses on the northern prairie. However, it is usually best to consider tea roses an annual in Zone 3. To get them through the winter, one must cover them to the extent of burying them in soil.

Tea rose people

Every town in our area has one or two gardeners devoted to tea roses. Value them. They invariably love to show off their roses, so they won't be offended by a visit. If you ask them their secrets, however, you will get tired just listening to what they do to maintain and protect their roses over the years. *Most tea rose people in the north develop back trouble!*

The good news for the more casual gardener? Tea roses are overrated! A garden of tea roses is beautiful if you examine each rose close up and inhale the delicious scents, but from a distance, a bed of tea roses makes no impact at all. Tea roses also have more disease problems than their hardier counterparts.

Hardy roses

Thankfully, new hardy roses are introduced each year as breeders compete with each other to develop or discover the next great hardy rose, an accomplishment which the market can reward with millions of dollars of patent royalties.

Many of those hardy roses can be covered with hundreds of blooms at their summer peak. The show they make from the street can slow traffic.

Roses have been bred for thousands of years. Rose breeding is a complex science. A rose breeder has several traits to consider, and he or she has to decide the order of priority:

•Color of bloom

•Size of bloom

•Density of petals (single or double, or somewhere in between)

•Quantity of blooms

•Attractiveness of hips (the fruit left behind after the petals fall)

•Attractiveness of the leaf

•Fall foliage color

•Drought tolerance

•Vigor of plant

•Scent

•Cold hardiness

•Disease resistance

•Shape of the plant

•Re-blooming ability

•Strength of stalks

The bloom color is likely the first quality a customer considers, but to those who breed hardy roses, cold hardiness comes first, disease resistance second, quality of bloom third, and with the remaining qualities, you hope for the best!

Disease resistance in roses is linked to hardiness, as roses which are perpetually fighting diseases are weaker going into the winter.

In the quest for a showy, hardy rose, scent often is overlooked—but that does not mean that hardy roses have no scent. Indeed, the "Hansa" rose, the hardiest of them all, has the strongest and most distinctive scent of any rose I have ever yet smelled.

To get the expectations created by tea roses out of our head, here are some over-riding facts about hardy roses which shape the choices we have on the market at present:

Pink and white roses are the toughest

There is just no denying that pink and white blooming roses are the strongest plants. There are, consequently, a great variety of shades, shapes and sizes of pink and white hardy roses on the market.

Red roses are second toughest

Next on the scale are the truly red hardy roses. Yes, there are varieties which put on deep red double blooms, such as the "Hope for Humanity". Overall, however, the reds do not yet rival the pinks.

Other colors trail behind

Any bloom color beyond red, pink and white, and various shades in between—say orange, or lavender—is simply going to be on a weaker, smaller plant with somewhat less spectacular results.

Hardy yellow roses bloom once

The yellow rose requires an entirely different set of genes, and is sort of the holy grail of breeders. They aren't doing very well in coming up with hardy varieties, particularly those which re-bloom.

At present, the best yellow roses bloom only in June, and very spectacularly at that time. They only bloom on last year's wood, so they will not bloom the first year after planting. Their branches have a pretzel-like coloring. Yellow hardy roses frequently die back in winter and need quite a bit of pruning to maintain an acceptable appearance.

In a protected spot, a "Harison's Yellow" rose (also known as the "Yellow Rose of Texas") can grow into an impressive six-foot shrub which will stop traffic at peak bloom. I admit that I have only seen three of them at full maturity in our area in my life. It says something that I remember all three.

The "Persian Yellow" is shorter, and a deeper yellow, but of the same general appearance as the Harison's. Both Harison's Yellow and Persian Yellow were introduced in the 1830s, and have not been improved upon since!

However, breeders are working on yellow hardy roses all the time, and some of their early results will be coming onto the market over the next years.

Rose breeder (and the author's brother) Joe Bergeson claims, "The reason there are not more hardy yellow re-blooming roses is that it has only been 117 years since the yellow pigment was first combined with modern characteristics. We just need more time!"

Take however much time you need, Joe!

Each hardy rose has a unique habit

Breeding a hardy rose is not a matter of plopping different colors of blooms on the same plant. That is, if you love the "Morden Centennial," a dark pink, that does not mean that the "Morden Blush," a sister rose, will have the same shape, vigor or leaf color. In fact, the Blush has a bluish foliage and grows about six inches shorter on average than the Centennial. Although they still work together in the garden, if you cut off all their blooms you could still tell them apart.

In short, a garden of assorted hardy roses is *not* as uniform as a garden of tea roses. Therefore, a person who loves hardy roses is faced with the task of fitting in the various sizes and shapes into a larger garden landscape.

Enjoy the non-bloom attributes

The increased breeding and introduction of hardy roses has brought forth roses with unusual characteristics—such as a variety with red leaves, and a single pink bloom (*Rosa glauca)*, and another with spectacular fall color to the leaves, "Therese Bugnet."

Nearly all of the hardy roses require less maintenance than tea roses, and qualify as shrubs in their own right. Hardy roses need not be confined to a single garden out back. They are more rewarding if sprinkled around the yard, each according to its unique size, shape and color.

Finding places for roses in the yard

On the northern plains, roses thrive best in the hottest, sunniest spots in the yard or against the house. Roses work where other plants whither.

Roses do poorly against the *east* side of the house, and should only be planted against the *west* side of the house if there is no additional shade from the west.

If a rose is planted fifteen feet or more from the house, the house has no effect and is not a consideration.

If you live in an old part of town with established shade trees, you may not have many places in your yard with enough sunshine for roses. Solution: Plant roses in a pot as an annual, and put it on the deck or the slab in front of the garage.

Purchasing roses

Roses are best purchased bare root. Catalogs specializing in bare root roses are generally reputable—if you make sure to purchase roses hardy for our area. If a rose is rated as hardy for our area, it does not matter if it spent its infancy in Oregon or California.

Most bare root roses on the market are tea roses, which are not hardy.

Grafted vs. Own Root roses

Most roses are grafted onto a genetically generic root. Some hardy roses, however, are grown from cuttings and therefore are considered to have their "own root." *Own root* roses are superior in that if the rose freezes to the ground, the shoots which may come from below the ground level are just as good as the original plant.

If a grafted rose freezes back to the graft, shoots which come from the base will be wild and will not be desirable.

Own root roses are more prevalent on the market with each year and can be easily found in local nurseries. When one can get an *own root* rose, do it.

However, planting grafted roses very deeply, with the graft at least 4 inches below the soil level, can both preserve them from the cold, and ensure that if they freeze to ground level in a harsh winter, the shoots which come from *below* the soil level will still be *above* the graft, and will be desirable.

Own root roses usually have the initials "OR" somewhere on the tag. Retailers who recognize the difference between *own root* and *grafted* roses know what they are doing and can be trusted.

Planting Zone 4 roses

If one plants roses very deeply, according to the instructions below, Zone 4 rated roses can do well in Zone 3.

Selecting healthy bare root plants

Never purchase bare root roses that aren't moist and healthy-looking. Late in the planting season, some bigger stores run sales on bare root roses which are essentially dead from being on display too long. A dead rose at half price is not a bargain.

The root is more important than the top. Most rose roots are relatively poor, but there still should be root in good proportion to the top. Pick the rose on display with the most root.

Hardy roses vary greatly by variety in heaviness at purchase. Simply make sure the plant you choose has the healthiest roots of the bunch.

Purchasing potted roses

Roses purchased in full leaf and full bloom in a pot should have no yellowed leaves whatsoever.

If the rose was recently potted, it is very tender and must be planted with the utmost care to not allow the root ball to fall apart between the time the pot is removed and planting. Those tense seconds are crucial to the rose's survival. If the dirt falls off a rose's roots while it is in full leaf, plant deeply, water well, and pray.

If a rose has lived in a pot for a long time and is root bound, the opposite is true: you *should* break apart the root a bit before planting. The risk with root bound roses is that the root ball will not get adequate moisture the first season after planting. Breaking apart the roots allows them to more easily tap into the existing soil.

Preparing the soil

Roses love soil which is about 50% good, local peat. If you are planning a rose bed, raise the entire bed up with six inches of peat first. If you are planting a rose singly, dig the hole bigger than necessary and plant the rose in a mix that is half peat, half the original soil. Mix a 10-10-10 general fertilizer into the soil at planting. Bone meal helps roses develop good bloom, but must be mixed in at planting to have real effect.

Plant deeply

Typically, directions for planting roses say to plant the rose so the soil level matches the graft union, which means that the base stem of the rose sticks out of the ground. Obeying these directions can ensure that your rose will die over the northern prairie winter.

Instead, plant the rose deeply, so deep that only a few little stubs of the top are above the original soil level. The graft union, or the base of the plant, should be as many as six inches deep. Planting deeply can make a Zone 4 rose hardy in Zone 3. Planting deeply also protects the rose from drying out as it grabs hold. Take care that the lightest soil of all (it can be mostly peat) is mounded above the graft union.

The properly planted bare root rose will end up looking like a mound of peat the size of a gopher pile with a few stubs of stem sticking out. As the weather warms, the rose's new shoots will burst forth through the peat and the plant will be in full, spectacular bloom by late-June of its first season.

Pruning roses

All of the complex instructions on pruning tea roses in warmer climes can be thrown out the window on the northern prairie. Ignore them. They are designed to correct problems we don't have.

Do not prune hardy roses at all in the fall. Leave them stand and let the leaves and snow gather at the base to provide the most effective winter protection possible.

The first task of pruning a hardy rose in the spring is to get rid of the dead stems. Dead stems will emerge from winter a dark brown. If all the stems above the soil are black, get rid of them all and wait for new shoots to come from below the soil. Some people can't resist digging down a little in early spring to see if there is some green left on the branches. If there is green, the rose has survived and will grow up quickly to look substantial again by late June.

Typically, even hardy roses die back a little at the tips over the winter. Those tips can be cut off in early spring for appearance's sake.

The second task of pruning roses is *to do no harm.* Hardy roses bloom much more on last year's wood than on the new shoots. Therefore, if some of last year's wood is still healthy, by all means leave it in place, even if the branch comes out at an odd angle. If a renegade branch is unbearable, cut it off after the first bloom to improve the rose's general shape.

Shaping a rose into a round ball by trimming back live stalks will only reduce the bloom. If you intend to cut off the bloom, why plant a rose?

Tea roses, if you choose to fiddle with them, have to be cut back in the fall in order to prepare for whatever measures one plans for winter protection. Any exposed branches will die, anyway.

Dealing with disease

Roses are more prone to leaf disease in warmer, more humid climes. Even so, leaf disease can take off in the north when the humidity is high, or if the roses are watered overhead.

There is one, easy, affordable solution: Purchase a can of rose spray at the big box store and start spraying your rose's foliage in early June. Spray every few weeks. If you only have a handful of roses, one can of spray should get you through the entire season.

The reward? If we have a late fall, you might see roses blooming their hearts out under your eaves in early November.

Ortho Rose Spray is *systemic*. It goes through the leaves and into the system of the plant, inoculating it against disease. Most rose sprays also contain an insecticide, which will kill aphids and other leaf-nibbling pests at the first bite.

If rose foliage gets spotty, or yellow very late in the season, do not panic! The general health of the rose is unlikely to be affected. Consider spraying next year to avoid a repeat performance.

It is probably best not to make tea out of the rose hips if you have sprayed the rose throughout the season with systemic rose spray.

Fertilization

Roses benefit from annual applications of 10-10-10 or ammonium sulfate as much as any other plant does on the plains. Concentrate fertilizing in the early part of the season to encourage the plant to harden up before winter.

Specialized rose fertilizers are not necessary and are unduly expensive.

There are many silly ideas about rose fertilization that involve household products, such as Epsom salts, or kitchen waste, such as banana peels. The grain of truth in these off-beat ideas is too small to do any good at all.

Dead-heading roses

Yes, it does help to cut back the spent blooms. Doing so prevents the development of the rose hips, which contain the seeds, and which signal to the rose that it has finished its job for the season. Dead-heading spent blooms will encourage further bloom. Leave the last bloom to develop the hips late in the season for some good winter interest.

The complicated instructions on rose pruning, designed to encourage tea roses to re-bloom for commercial purposes, are neither necessary or practical for hardy roses.

Climbing roses

There are no true climbing roses hardy for the northern plains. However, the hardy "William Baffin" grows vigorously enough to be trained to a trellis. Its stalks can grow to nine feet in length.

Miniature roses

Miniature roses are cute as the dickens and often irresistible when blooming in the greenhouse in spring. They are not winter-hardy, however, and would have to be buried in order to make it through winter.

Cheating

Some people try to cheat our climate by growing a non-hardy rose in a pot and bringing it inside over winter. However, roses need a cold period to survive. The only way this can work is if you can store the potted rose in a cellar that is close to freezing throughout the winter. You can bring the pot upstairs in March to give it an early start, but be aware that this is a low-percentage endeavor.

A few extraordinary varieties

Because the rose world changes so fast, a thorough list of rose varieties available would be obsolete soon after the ink dries on this book.

However, there are some varieties which persist through the decades, and deserve consideration:

William Baffin

Introduced by the Morden Research Station in Manitoba, the William Baffin is a vigorous rose which is perfectly hardy. It can be used as a large hedge, or to fill a big spot on the hot side of the house. It can sport over 500 blooms on a single mature bush. However, the Baffin is so vigorous that it can spread by sending up suckers. Don't hesitate to cut it back to about two feet!

Tropicana

The Tropicana tea rose is a favorite of the author's, and has shown more hardiness than other tea roses. You will need to cover Tropicana, but the orange blooms are spectacular and do not shatter quickly. And what a scent!

Knock Out!

Introduced by breeder Will Radler, the Knock Out® rose, and its successors in the Knock Out series have taken the rose world by storm. They are disease resistant, put on a great show, and if planted deeply enough, able to survive northern prairie winters.

The real old-fashioned roses   *Rugosa*

The Hansa rose, as well as those with "F. J. Grootendoorst" in the name, are real old-timers, the roses your great-grandmother planted. They bloom mostly dark pink, and their foliage is ruffley and soft-textured, not glossy and dark green.

Old-fashioned roses need good fertilizer to avoid yellowing of the leaves. They also will get disease more quickly in a damp year, and do not respond to sprays as well. However, there is nothing better for a cemetery planting, where the winds will likely whip enough to keep the disease from developing, and where benign neglect can allow them to thrive for decades. "You can't kill them with an ax!" said one old-timer.

Avoid frustration

To sum up, the larger rose world can intimidate the amateur gardener. Fortunately, growing exceptional roses is relatively simple on the northern prairie, if you follow a few rules:

•Ignore non-local instructions

•Seek out local advice from people who actually have a rose or two in their yard.

•Eliminate all roses which aren't Zone 4 hardy, or hardier

•Plant deep

•Use peat liberally

•Buy a can of rose spray, spray a few times per summer

•Fertilize roses as you would fertilize the rest of your plants

•Start small, with single rose plants spread amongst other plantings

•Learn to appreciate the beauty of roses as they appeared naturally on our prairie for hundreds, perhaps thousands of years!

CHAPTER 20

Annuals

More than trees, shrubs, fruits or even perennials, annuals are for *fun*. Experimentation is encouraged, and never costly. New varieties appear each year by the dozen. Dream big!

For the more sober, practical gardener, annuals provide season-long color and flexibility in design from year-to-year which cannot be beat.

Annuals are plants which do not usually survive the winter. Once they freeze out, they are done and you are free to clear the bed and prepare the soil for next season.

Some annuals seed themselves, and some plants which are considered annuals, such as pansies and dianthus, can occasionally come back the next season. Thus, the line between annuals and perennials is sometimes blurred.

Annuals can be planted in a mass, in which case they are called *bedding plants*. Such a use is more common in institutional plantings on college campuses, or in large display gardens that charge admission.

For the home gardener, a mass bed might be of interest. However, a mere sprinkling of annuals can add a spark of color to a perennial bed, with the added advantage that the annuals bloom all season long, whereas perennials have their day in the sun and then fade.

In addition to annuals used for splashes of color, each new year greets us with new novelty annuals of which a gardener might like to try only a single plant. For example, a twelve-foot tall castor bean in the center of a bed will draw the neighborhood's attention one season, but wear out its welcome in subsequent years as fast as a popular hit song sinks from number one on the charts. So, the savvy gardener finds a new novelty plant for next year and laughs at the neighbors who all planted castor beans—one year late.

One advantage to living in the north

For the northern gardener, annuals are a particular boon. Because they aren't around for the winter months, annuals don't care how cold it gets in January. What's more, the further north one goes, *the better the conditions become for growing annuals.*

Not only are the summer days longer in the north, but the nights are usually cool. The combination of long days and cool nights makes annuals stout and healthy.

In addition, blooms are actually a deeper, more intense color in northern latitudes. People who have been to northern Europe, most of which lies far to the north of the 49th parallel, or even to Alaska, can attest to the dramatic annual flower displays in those regions.

The most popular annual flowers for our area are petunias, impatiens, marigolds and geraniums, but there are *hundreds* of others on the market. Find your favorites through experimentation and reconnaissance.

Annuals vs. Perennials

The most common knock against annuals is that you must plant them every year. However, annuals cost only a fraction of perennials, and there is an advantage to being able to till your flower bed every year without having to worry about disturbing the roots of perennials.

Because annuals have no winter worries, they are the best option for pots. It is risky to use shrubs or perennials in planters, as they likely won't survive the winter.

When is the right time to plant annuals in the spring?

Planting annuals the first week of May is probably foolhardy. Planting annuals in the second week of May is a gamble which might pay off. Planting annuals the third week of May is a good idea. Planting around Memorial Day is about ideal, if you can still get the plants.

Planting the last week of May and the first week of June, if you can find the plants on the market, seems late, but it is not. By July, you won't notice much if any difference between those annuals planted early and those planted late.

If you are really restless to start planting, petunias, pansies and alyssum can take a little frost. Meanwhile, impatiens, coleus and celosia don't like cold weather at all.

How to plant annual flowers

Nearly all annuals prefer well-drained soil, and will thrive in a raised bed of peat or compost. Very few annuals, with the possible exception of pansies or alyssum, will thrive in heavy, saturated soil.

Most annuals will thrive in full sun. Impatiens are the primary annual for deep shade.

Do not try to plant annuals directly underneath large trees, particularly old evergreens. Place planters there instead.

Preparation

Start planning a new annual bed the fall before planting. Spray glyphosate on the grass where you wish to create an annual bed. Use the garden hose to experiment with various shapes for the bed. You may till three or four days after spraying, even if the grass isn't completely dead.

Add peat and 10-10-10 fertilizer to the area before tilling. Make sure the soil is loosened quite deeply. The soil should be tilled at least eight inches deep.

If it is difficult for you to dig a hole for a plant, it is also going to be difficult for the plant to grow in that soil. Well-tilled soil will make it easy to place the plant deeply enough, and will make it easier for the plant to send roots out into the soil. Improper planting in poorly tilled soil stunts plants all season.

Give annuals space

People tend to plant annuals too close to each other. Annuals explode with new growth, and if they are not allowed the room to grow, they can become lanky, stunted, and diseased later in the season. Planting annuals far enough apart, which usually means planting them as far apart as the plant is going to grow tall, can add an extra month of peak performance to the end of the season. Planting farther apart will also save money.

A newly planted flower bed should look quite sparse. Leave a saucer-like depression around each plant. A freshly planted bed of flowers should appear pock-marked with craters.

Each plant should be in a saucer the depth and size of a serving dish. This may seem excessive, but it is not. As the plant grows, the over-sized depression will disappear. Meanwhile, the plant will benefit from having the initial watering with fertilizer and subsequent waterings soak down slowly right around its roots.

Loosen the root ball

Most annuals come in *cell-pacs*, containers which have individual little compartments for each plant. Although it is easy to remove each plug from the pot, the plants tend to be completely root bound.

Squeeze the root ball and break up the root at planting in order to allow the roots to penetrate the soil. Plants which don't have the root ball loosened do not send their roots out into the surrounding soil during the season and will be less able to withstand drought as well as plants whose roots have been loosened.

If you purchase annuals in pacs with plants (usually four or six) grown together in a single compartment, the act of breaking apart the plants from each other will effectively loosen the roots.

243

Buy annuals green and stout

Ideally, annuals purchased at the greenhouse should be stout and dark green. Avoid purchasing annuals which have a lanky single stem with a bloom on top. Rather, seek out plants which are short, green, healthy and without much, if any, bloom. Such plants will establish themselves quickly in the garden and will outperform lanky starter plants by a large margin.

Purchasing healthy plants gives your garden a huge head start. Many plants arrive from the greenhouse lanky and a bit limp, particularly if they are purchased late in the season. Pinching back lanky plants will allow them to develop roots before putting on fresh foliage, and will lessen the trauma of having the root disturbed during planting.

A new dilemma: vegetative vs. seeded

Please read and absorb this boring section before you go to the greenhouse, and before you read the rest of this chapter. Please.

In the past decade, great strides have been made in breeding annuals. Many strains of old favorites have been developed which grow and bloom like they are on steroids.

However, most of these superior new breeds *cannot* be reproduced from seed, and must be propagated by cutting, tissue culture, or some other form of what is called *vegetative* reproduction. Therefore, they are more expensive. *Many times* more expensive.

Consequently, you will have a choice when you get to the greenhouse: Do you buy little coleus in four-pacs for a couple of bucks, or the big, sturdy coleus with a fancy name available for three times that price for a single plant?

A common question arises when a customer sees a beautiful *cutting-grown* verbena in a single pot for several dollars, while a few feet away are six pacs of *seeded* verbena for much less.

"Do you have these big ones in six pacs?" the customer asks, hoping to score a bunch of them without going broke.

"We certainly do not!" replies the slightly irritated greenhouse owner, who knows how much those cutting-grown super plants cost.

The answer? In this instance, at least, sound horticultural practice coincides with economic good sense: the *cutting grown* annuals are best for pots and planters, where their superior genetics allow them to perform well in the company of other plants. The *seedling* plants, although they will be smaller, are best used in the ground, where they can be spread out and will, cumulatively, make a better show from a distance.

Fertilize annuals from day one

The first watering after planting is crucial. It is important to water with fertilized water immediately after planting. The first watering packs the soil around the roots. The fertilizer introduced by the first watering, if it is done thoroughly, can last the plant the first month of the season.

Keep annuals out of the garage

More annuals die in the garage before planting than anywhere else. Annuals must have daily exposure to the sun, the breeze, and the cool spring air to prevent them from going into decline. They must also have daily watering. Even storing plants on a sun porch or indoors in front of a sunny window can cause them to get lanky. Instead, put them outside and bring them in the garage or the porch only if it threatens to freeze.

It is best to wait to purchase annuals until you are ready to plant. They are always better off in the greenhouse.

Annuals need more frequent watering

So intent are annuals upon pouring all of their energy into blooming and creating seed that their root systems are generally quite puny. Therefore, annuals must be watered frequently, and several of doses of water soluble fertilizer applied in summer will do them a world of good.

Get up early

Watering annuals in the early morning is best, especially if you use a sprinkler. Watering in the evening can cause droplets of water to remain on the plant throughout the night. Those droplets are an ideal breeding ground for disease. Watering in the morning means the droplets will likely dry quickly, before diseases can reproduce in the droplets, and before the hot sun of mid-day burns holes in the more tender annual blooms by using the water droplets as a prism.

At Bergeson Gardens, we run the sprinklers all night to avoid getting morning garden visitors wet. It is our belief that as long as the water is running over the plant and not sitting stagnant, disease is not forming. It is also our opinion that six to eight hours of sprinkling is needed to thoroughly soak annuals. In hot weather we might sprinkle for eight hours two nights per week.

Should I dead-head?

Removing the spent blooms (a process called *dead-heading*) on some annuals can keep them fresh and blooming throughout the summer. Geraniums, standard petunias, cosmos, dwarf dahlias, zinnias, marigolds and snapdragons are a few varieties which can truly benefit from the removal of spent blooms.

When to skip dead-heading

Impatiens and fibrous begonias take care of their own dead blooms. Trailing petunias produce so many blooms that dead-heading is impractical. Celosia blooms seem to last all season. And, it is impractical to deadhead plants with tiny blooms such as alyssum or lobelia.

How to dead-head, when you do

Always remove the entire bloom *including* the forming seed pod. By preventing the plant from producing seed, you encourage it to produce additional bloom.

Growing annuals in pots

Here are the rules for success with annuals in planters and pots:

•Change the soil in the pot or planter *entirely* each season. Soil in pots and planters deteriorates, and can become salty. Dump the old stuff out into the garden, where it will do no harm. Start with fresh potting soil, preferably made up of good, dark sedge peat.

•Beware of old bags of potting soil at the box stores, particularly if they seem heavy or dense. If you think the bag is left over from last season (if the label is faded, or there are several broken bags on the pallet), go find something fresh.

•Do not use field dirt, or soil from your garden for your pots. It is too heavy and will turn to rock.

•Make sure the planter or pot has a drain hole. If stagnant water sits in the pot—even if the water level doesn't reach the surface—plants will suffer and die.

•Drill holes in all planters which don't come with holes. If you made the mistake of buying a big ceramic planter without a drain hole, and drilling a hole might crack the thing, put big rocks in the bottom to collect the extra water and make darn sure you don't water so much that the water reaches soil level and is wicked upward.

•Add time-release fertilizer beads to the soil at the time of planting *and* fertilize pots frequently (weekly) with water soluble fertilizer. Potted annuals need a lot of food!

•Water only after a slight dry crust has formed on the soil on the top of planters.

•Fill the gap from the soil to the top of the pot (which should be at 2-3 inches) with water. Let it soak in for a few minutes. Repeat. Then repeat again. Even if water flows out the bottom of the pot in the first watering, it may not have saturated the soil. Repeated soaking ensures that all pockets of soil in the pot have become moist.

•Don't let saucers underneath pots sit full of water for days on end. The plant may drown from the water that is wicked up.

•Different pots dry out at different rates. Clay pots breathe, so they dry out faster than heavy ceramic. Black plastic pots get hotter than light-colored plastic pots. The only sure way to test if a planter or pot needs water is to stick a gloveless finger in the soil.

•If a pot tips over in the slightest breeze, it is too small for what is planted in it. Repot, or plant something different next year. Better yet, sell the pot for 50 cents at the fall rummage sale. Small pots are a curse.

The following list of annuals is incomplete. Hundreds of annuals not included on this list will work in our area, but the ones which follow are, in our opinion, the most useful and trouble-free. We include any special instructions specific to our area, and things we have learned growing annuals in Bergeson Gardens.

MAJOR ANNUALS

The following families of annual flowers have been around for decades and, although new variations of these old favorites are introduced each year, the basic types have performed well year after year. They are solid. They are easy. And they are not costly.

This is a subjective list, of course, chosen after years of experience. Other gardening professionals *will* have other favorites. But the new northern prairie gardener won't go wrong choosing from this list.

The descriptions of these flowers are meant to include instructions *specific for the northern prairie.* Cruising the internet for instructions, or watching cable television shows from the two coasts, or the South, can yield misleading, even damaging information about how to grow these very varieties. Make sure additional books or information you seek out come from the northern prairie and nowhere else.

The safest and best use of the internet (and of the empty hours during long winter evenings) is to find dozens of photos of each of the following varieties.

Most annuals prefer sun

It can be assumed, unless stated otherwise, that the following annuals require sunshine during most of the day.

Ageratum

With its distinctive powder-puff blue or white bloom, ageratum lend an old-fashioned touch to a flower bed. The shorter varieties work well as a formal border, while the taller varieties form a colorful and informal background.

Ageratum need constant moisture without being saturated. They will suddenly wilt if allowed to dry out. The do recover quite well once they get water again. Water underneath, as the fine-textured ageratum blooms look quite sad after getting doused.

Alyssum

The sturdy white alyssum, also known as "Sweet Alyssum," can continue to bloom and fill the yard with their sweet scent deep into the fall. Alyssum make a great border. In a hot spell, alyssum can fade, or fall victim to insects. If they begin to look bad, cut them back and they will revive when cool weather comes back.

To prevent an insect called the *leafhopper* from eating blooms on alyssum, mix granular systemic insecticide sold for houseplants in the soil around the alyssum at planting time.

New, *vegetative* (and therefore expensive) types of alyssum are amazing, but are best used singly in pots.

Purple alyssum are about one-fifth as showy as the white, and really aren't the best way to introduce purple into the garden. Alternating them with white sets the purple off a bit.

Amaranthus

Otherwise known as "Love-Lies-Bleeding," this old-fashioned plant has revived in popularity. It can grow to seven feet tall. Some varieties sport rope-like blooms which trail to the ground. Others hold their flower more uprightly.

Amaranthus produce seed by the million, many of which will come back next season. If it is any consolation, self-seeded Amaranthus are easy to kill with a hoe. If you thin the seedlings the next spring, you will have a showy bed of flowers for free.

Begonia, Fibrous

The fibrous begonia, otherwise known as *wax begonia*, creates a loud splash of color in mass plantings. Both the foliage, which can range from light green to dark maroon, and the bloom, which can be white, pink, dark pink, or red, will make a great show from a distance.

Although considered by many to be a shade plant, the fibrous begonia seems to do best in about half-a-day of sunlight.

Fibrous begonias should be planted no more than a foot apart in a mass bed, as they don't really take off upwards until they get a bit crowded sideways. We have had the best luck planting them 10-12 inches apart.

Newer, more vigorous forms of fibrous begonia appear on the market each season. They can grow to two feet or more, and really make a show. Amongst them are "Dragon Wing" begonias, which are cutting-grown and expensive, but which are simply spectacular.

Begonia, Tuberous

With their intense oranges, yellows, pinks and reds on a bloom with petals which are succulent and lush, the tuberous begonia are an old-time favorite for the shade.

Although the old-time tuberous begonias actually grown from a tuber are now primarily available only from specialty catalogs, new varieties of tuberous begonias grown from seed, such as the Nonstop, are increasing in popularity in area greenhouses.

Tuberous begonias are great for a window box in the shade, but do not water them too often. If the soil surface is continually wet, tuberous begonias can rot off at the base and simply disappear.

Hanging tuberous begonias will droop nicely over the edges of a basket, filling an important role on shady porches.

Tuberous begonia bloom stems are brittle and should not be subjected to high winds. The plant itself, however, is plenty tough.

Castor Bean

The enormous castor bean provides a touch of the tropics in northern gardens. The huge leaves on a plant which can exceed seven feet in height make a real statement.

If you can get some of the beans, seed them in the garden in early May.

Yes, castor beans are the source of the famous poison *ricin*. However, we know of no cases of pet-poisoning from castor beans yet. The spiky hard shell which contains the beans has, thus far at least, provided ample discouragement to hungry children. However, *do not allow children to eat them.*

Celosia

Included in the celosia family are the colorful *cockscomb*, which come in all colors and heights, the blooms of which look uncannily like brains, as well as the *Celosia plumosa*, which blooms in extremely bright flame-like plumes. In a good year, celosia will be a showstopper.

Celosia plants are fussy to get started, but hardy once established. It is particularly important with celosia to purchase small plants that aren't blooming. Celosia purchased with a bloom perform very poorly when transplanted into the garden, even if you cut the bloom off at planting.

Ideally, celosia are seeded late and planted near Memorial Day as scrawny little seedlings. Unfortunately, however, most producers have them blooming in early May, a practice which increases sales but stunts the celosia once they are planted in the garden.

Cold weather in June stops celosia in its tracks, and can sometimes affect their performance for the entire season.

Once the plants start growing, celosia require little care beyond watering. Their display improves every day until frost.

Cleome

The stately cleome forms a backdrop for an old-fashioned flower bed. Cleome sport non-stop cylindrical, spidery blooms, and come in white, pink and purple. The plant can grow to six feet, although four feet is more common. One pac of four plants will cover a large area. Plant them three feet apart for best results.

Young cleome look weak in the greenhouse and attract no impulse buyers. Their mid- to late-season performance justifies a purchase.

Cleome can seed themselves. Severely thin the seedlings as they sprout in spring to get another display next summer.

Coleus

Planted for the rich colored leaves, which come in dozens of variations, coleus have until recently been strictly suited for shade. In recent years, however, the introduction of sun-tolerant *vegetatively reproduced* varieties have made coleus more popular and useful than ever. Some of them grow to three feet wide and three feet across in the garden!

Coleus range in leaf color from lime green to dark maroon, with some fascinating orange shades as well. The bloom is worthless and can be pinched off as soon as it appears without hurting anything.

252

Cosmos

Consider seeding cosmos right into the garden. What a happy, fragile flower! Removing the spent pods keeps the cosmos sending out fresh bloom. Cosmos are a classic old-fashioned Grandma plant, and look best spread amongst other old-fashioned Grandma plants.

Dahlia, Dinner Plate

The larger dahlias, those which can reach six feet tall and produce dinner plate blooms in late summer, must be purchased as a tuber. The root does not survive outside in our winters, so will need to be dug up, dried out, and stored in the basement. With dahlias, the process is easy and usually successful.

Large-blooming dahlias often need staking to prevent them from tipping. Dinner plate dahlias feature a wild array of colors, are easy to grow, and can develop into an addictive hobby.

Dahlia, Dwarf

Dwarf dahlias are annuals which bloom all season. They come in a variety of stunningly clear colors. The plant's foliage is a rich, dark green. Dahlias bloom in the greenhouse in early spring, and thus are often purchased as a potted plant for Mother's Day.

To keep dwarf dahlias blooming all season in the ground, the dead blooms must be removed. Be careful, as the dead blooms look very similar to the new buds! Examine to see if the interior of the bud is brown (a spent bloom) or yellow (a new bloom).

Daisy

Just what is a daisy? There is no scientific answer to the question.

Generally speaking, daisies are wildflowers with a yellow center surrounded by a single layer of narrow white petals. However, there are many plants, domesticated and not, many unrelated to each other, which fit this definition, and which claim the name.

Some people consider rudbeckia, or "Black-eyed Susan" to be a daisy, too, even though its petals are dark yellow. Rudbeckia are related to, and perhaps synonymous with Gloriosa daisies, which are related to coneflowers, or *Echinacea*—and it goes on.

In short, do not send your non-gardening spouse to the greenhouse to pick up some daisies. You never know what you'll end up with.

Although the best daisy is still a wild daisy, gardeners might want to add a wild, old-fashioned touch to their garden with a domestic variety. The "Marguerite" daisy, which comes in yellow, white or pink, is the most common annual daisy on the market.

After their bloom fades, it is best to trim back the entire daisy plant about half-way with a hedge clipper to encourage further bloom. Marguerite daisies can put out a scent similar to pig manure, if you ever wonder what that foul smell is in the flower garden.

Datura

A stately annual also known as "Angel's Trumpet," the datura can reach three feet in height and five feet in width in the long days in the northland. Datura spreads its seeds liberally, so you will never need to purchase a second plant. Unwanted seedlings can be easily hoed away the next season. Most datura are white. Purple and yellow datura hesitate to open and are more a curiosity than they are equivalent to the white in vigor and appearance.

Dianthus

The annual dianthus, a member of the carnation family, often survives our winters if protected by snow gathered around its foliage. The surviving plants will produce a doubly spectacular display of bloom the next June. For this reason, do not remove your dianthus from the flower bed in the fall. You may get another year out of them!

Dianthus blooms can be solid-colored, or they can feature an intricate mix of different colors separated by fine lines.

Deadheading annual dianthus is necessary for re-bloom.

New taller versions of dianthus make for long-lasting cut flowers. "Amazon Neon Rose" and "Jolt Pink" bloom all summer. Due to their hard work all season, these excellent new varieties do not store up enough energy to make it through the winter.

Geranium, Zonal (*Cutting Grown*)

Zonal geraniums are so-called because of the band of darker color green on their leaves. They are *cutting grown*. They are tough. And they are what you want.

Geraniums provide the richest red of any flower. The magentas and lavenders are stunning as well.

Cutting-grown geraniums are simply the best potted plants for outdoor sunshine. Geraniums thrive in pots where their roots are continually drained and warm.

Although they work in the ground as bedding plants, geraniums do not make the impact on the landscape in the ground that they do in containers. Get more bang for your buck and use geraniums only in pots.

The spent blooms on cutting-grown geraniums must be removed or they will be overcome by mold and disease which can spread to the entire plant. To remove spent blooms, press a finger against the lump at the base of the bloom stem and bend the bloom down. The bloom will snap off easily at the base, leaving no remaining stem to rot. Any employee at a greenhouse should be able to show you how it's done.

For many gardeners, snapping off the spent geranium blooms from the pots on their front slab is a pleasant, oddly-satisfying, thrice-weekly chore. There's something good about that definite "snap."

For appearances sake, it is important *not* to water geraniums with an overhead stream of water. The blooms do not like being wet.

255

To preserve the tender blooms on this tough plant, pull your geranium pots into the garage when rain or storms are predicted.

Yes, there are less expensive *seedling* geraniums for sale at some greenhouses, but they are more suited for mass plantings in the ground than in pots. Rarely do seedling geraniums produce as many blooms as cutting-grown geraniums, and their colors are generally not as intense.

In the past two decades, the breeding of geraniums has taken an unfortunate direction for those of us on the prairie who have plenty of space. Because the market for blooming geraniums is best on Mother's Day, breeders have concentrated upon producing *compact* plants that produce a single, large bloom in early May. By doing so, the big breeders have forgotten that, Mother's Day aside, the real purpose of a geranium is to grow huge and be covered with bloom throughout the entire summer!

Pay attention to the tag. Purchase geraniums which are larger and rangier in habit for best results throughout the summer. Of course, if you have a small window box, the compact geraniums will be perfect.

Geraniums, Regal

Known as "Martha Washington" geraniums, Regal geraniums, with their old-fashioned azalea-like blooms, are another popular blooming plant for Mother's Day. But after that? They fade! Why? Because Martha Washingtons are fussy, fussy, fussy.

Blooming Regal geranium plants purchased for Mother's Day have been raised in exact conditions. Regals need night greenhouse temperatures in the low 50s, and day time heat which doesn't often exceed 70 degrees. They also need 14 hours of sunlight to initiate bloom.

The best hope to keep a Regal geranium blooming past its first bloom in spring—the bloom that got you to buy it—is to place the plant in a cooler spot in the yard and hope for a cool summer. Regals do not like sitting wet, so a clay pot is ideal. If you bring them in for winter, put them in a corner which gets cool at night.

Regal geraniums are a Grandma plant, and they worked well for Grandma because she had a drafty old house and knew just where to set the plant so it would not get too hot.

Geraniums, Scented

A few years back scented geraniums became all the rage, a fad which has since faded. At the time, several news articles made the rounds that claimed that scented geraniums, most prominently the *citronella*, would keep mosquitoes away from your deck. Alas, those articles were written by folks from areas where they don't have northern mosquitoes.

Scented geraniums smell good and come in fragrances which range from lemon to chocolate. They also get quite large, and need frequent cutting back. If you preserve and plant the cuttings, your house will soon be overwhelmed with scented geraniums.

Although they exist in great variety, the best way to find odd scented geraniums is to get a cutting from an enthusiast. You can meet them online. Exercise the same caution as you would when meeting strange plant people in person.

Impatiens

No, your great-grandmother didn't plant impatiens. They were discovered in Central America in about 1960, and have since enjoyed a meteoric rise in popularity due to their ability to produce colorful blooms in deep shade.

Although reputed to be a shade plant, impatiens seem to do best in about half-a-day of sunshine. Although they remain the single best blooming plant for shade, the use of impatiens should not be limited entirely to shady situations, especially given that new sun-tolerant breeds of all colors appear each growing season.

Impatiens should be planted *exactly* 12 inches apart to produce an eventual mass. Planting any closer is a waste of plants, and can cause impatiens to flop over mid-summer.

However, planting too far apart is also a risk. When we planted impatiens 16 inches apart, they didn't do as well as at 12 inches spacing. Then we discovered university research which indicates that impatiens *actually sense when they nearly touch their neighbor and put on a burst of growth in order to compete.* Yes, plants try to out-do each other.

Impatiens don't mind poor soil, but to get the most out of them, fertilizing regularly with a water soluble fertilizer is a good idea. If June is cold, impatiens may be slow to take off. Don't worry. Impatiens will explode into bloom in mid-July no matter what.

Impatiens last much longer in the northern latitudes than they do even as far south as Chicago, where they get lanky and flop over in August. In the far north, they look spectacular until the day before frost.

Many impatiens were wiped out by mildew in August of 2017. It is not yet clear whether this was a one-year phenomenon related to specific climactic conditions, or if it will get worse. New Guinea impatiens are not susceptible to the mildew. As always, try to water underneath and early in the morning.

Impatiens, New Guinea

A few years after the discovery of impatiens in Central America, a different breed of the genus was found in New Guinea which could withstand much more sun. The New Guinea impatiens also feature a larger, almost luminescent bloom. In addition, New Guinea feature darker, shinier, sometimes multi-colored leaves.

New Guinea impatiens, because they must be grown from cuttings, are more expensive than their Central American counterpart, and are most practical if planted in pots. Although the label will say they survive in full sun, one-half-day is about enough. They seem to thrive best in pots on the east step of a house.

Just like tuberous begonias, New Guinea impatiens will rot off at the base if the surface of the soil is constantly wet. Use light soil in the pot, and don't water until a crust forms on the soil's surface.

Lobelia

The deep blue of the lobelia blooms is particularly vivid when used in planters in combination with red geraniums. It is the most solid deep blue available in annual flowers, with possible competition from the difficult-to-grow larkspur.

Lobelia come in both trailing and compact forms. Both work well in planters. Lobelia don't do as well in the ground.

Many gardeners are frustrated that their lobelia don't make it through the entire season. To do so, lobelia must have consistent moisture. *Lobelia do not recover from getting dried out to the point of wilting.* Partial shade is ideal and takes the onus off the gardener to be there every day with the hose.

The compact "Crystal Palace" from England has been around for 130 years, long after the actual Crystal Palace for which it was named burned to the ground in London. It is the bluest of blue. Other colors include white, pink and lavender, as well as bi-colored blooms.

Breeders have introduced new, more vigorous *vegetatively reproduced* varieties of lobelia which are doubly strong.

Marigolds

Few people are ambivalent when it comes to marigolds. Some hate them, the rest love them. If you don't mind the orange and yellow color scheme, and you aren't allergic to the scent, marigolds are a showy and tremendously easy way to fill a large area in full sun.

Marigolds range in height from 8 inches to 2 feet. Plant as far apart as the tag says they will grow tall. If you plant marigolds too closely together they may become diseased, especially during a rainy summer. Avoid watering overhead, if possible.

If a single marigold plant does succumb to disease, pull it up and throw it out immediately to protect the rest.

In recent years, a primitive form of the marigold called the "signet" has returned to popularity. They have tiny yellow or orange blooms. Their foliage is especially scented with a twist of lemon.

Individual branches of signet marigolds may break down from the base, but the weakness seldom affects the entire plant.

Moss Roses   *Portulaca*

The very first annual to make a splash on the summer scene, the moss rose sometimes fades as the summer wears on. Adding fertilizer in the end of June keeps moss roses going longer than they otherwise would, sometimes through Labor Day.

Moss roses thrive in junky, gravely soil, and in hot, dry locations. The blooms pout a day or two after a rain, but revive nicely.

Pansies

Despite what their name might imply, pansies are tougher than most annuals.

Pansies love cool weather, but can keep going in the heat as long as they are wet underneath.

Pansies are one plant which can thrive in saturated, heavy soils. They work in partial shade, but they seem to perform best in a wet spot in open sunshine.

Pansy blooms get smaller as the season gets hotter. As fall arrives, the blooms increase in size, as does the general vigor of the plant. Pansies have been known to survive winter without losing the green to their leaves.

The variety of pansies to hit the market in the past two decades is astounding.

Because they love it cool, pansies thrive in greenhouses in the north early in the spring, putting on enormous blooms which often lure people to plant more of them than they should. Realize that pansies are a cool weather plant before going whole hog.

Petunia, Trailing

The introduction of the "Purple Wave" trailing petunia in 1995 changed flower gardening forever, and for the better. Since the arrival of the Purple Wave, dozens upon dozens of trailing petunias of various colors have been introduced under various trade names.

Each new trailing petunia has its own habit, strengths and weaknesses. Some grow more upright, some climb, some stay flat to the ground, some get lanky, others stay compact. Indeed, some varieties seem to need more fertilizer than others.

The strongest trailing petunia plants are those with purple or pink blooms. At the opposite end of the spectrum are the reds, always a difficult color to breed in petunias.

Trailing petunias work if planted in a flower bed, but truly excel where they are allowed to cascade over the side of a planter, or hanging basket.

Because they are what is called "heavy feeders," it is important to fertilize trailing petunias frequently. Use a mild mix of fertilized water at least once per week. In addition, we place time-release fertilizer beads in each pot at planting.

Trailing petunias cannot be allowed to dry out, especially when they are at their peak in August. During a hot spell, they need to be watered twice per day.

To give the trailing petunias enough soil, make sure you use 12 inch hanging baskets, not 10 inch. We even tried 14 inch baskets but found them too heavy to move around with ease. However, with a light soil mix, a 14 inch basket would be ideal.

If trailing petunias fade or get scruffy looking as the season wears on, (usually due to gaps in watering) cut the stems back to the edge of the pot. Within a couple of weeks, they will have recovered and will look fresh again. It is not practical to remove spent blooms from trailing petunias as there are simply too many.

Trailing petunias demand even more sunshine than standard petunias. They will not do their best hanging under an east or west awning. Trailing petunias do best if planted on the south side of the house, or hanging in the middle of the yard in full sunshine.

If you have a special summer event scheduled and would like to have a bunch of spectacular hanging baskets on the porch, consider growing the baskets out in the yard in the full sun and moving them to the porch a couple of days before the company arrives. Take full credit for your gardening genius as people ask, "How did you get those petunias so beautiful without full sun?"

Petunia, Standard

No plant provides a more vivid variety of pure color than the old-time petunia. For bed of mass color in full sun, plant petunias.

Make sure you plant petunias at least 12 inches apart. Planted any closer, petunias can decline—even rot—in August, especially in a wet season. If at all possible, do not irrigate petunias overhead, keeping in mind it is better to water overhead than to not water at all.

Deadheading standard petunias will encourage more fresh blooms, but make sure you pinch off the *entire seed pod*. Merely pulling the dead bloom out of the seed pod does no good whatsoever. Scissors are the best way to do the job right.

If the petunias you purchase are lanky with a single bloom on top, cut the plant in half at planting time.

If at any time during the season petunias become scruffy-looking, take a hedge clippers cut them in half. They will come roaring back.

Snapdragon

Although the seedlings are tender and soft at planting, snapdragons develop into one of the toughest annuals in the garden as the season progresses. The blooms of some varieties produce an intoxicating, jasmine-like scent. Snapdragons bloom soon after moss roses to provide early color in the annual garden.

The taller varieties of snapdragon can flop over in a windstorm or heavy rain. Take care to prop them up right away in the morning following a storm before they grow crooked.

If the first bloom of snapdragons is removed immediately after they fade, you may get a spectacular fall bloom as well.

Snapdragons are able to survive deep frosts with no apparent damage.

Verbena

Verbena love full, hot sun. The new *vegetatively reproduced* varieties of verbena bloom without ceasing all summer and can each fill a space more than two feet square. The popularity of verbena is on the upswing due to their low care requirements, toughness, and the intensity of their reds and blues. They also make for spectacular pots, planters and hanging baskets.

Verbena is one annual where the difference in performance between expensive *vegetatively* reproduced plants and their *seedling* counterparts is well worth the money.

Zinnia

Nothing more old-fashioned than a zinnia garden out by the driveway. The bright-hued blooms come on plants which vary from tiny to tall.

Consider seeding zinnia right in the garden, as they sometime balk at being transplanted from pacs. Zinnias come fast from seed.

It is wise to remove the spent blooms from zinnias. If dead blooms remain, the plant's new foliage will grow right around the old bloom— but the now-concealed bloom can become saturated with moisture and develop mold.

Late in the season, mold which originated in a single rotting bloom can suddenly consume the entire plant. Although that rot won't spread to nearby zinnias, it is best to remove the affected plant.

NOVELTY ANNUALS

Asters, Annual

Annual asters are not commonly planted in the Upper Midwest, perhaps because they bloom so late in the season. However, planning for fall aster bloom will produce reward in the form of compact, pastel-colored blooms much larger and fuller than those of the perennial aster.

Bacopa

It isn't easy to find a trailing, delicate white bloomer for planters. Bacopa fills the bill. Bacopa does need consistent moisture or it will fade, only to come back full force when cool weather returns. Breeding is increasing the size of the bacopa blooms almost annually. The purples, in particular, are becoming well worth trying. One plant is all that is necessary for a round planter of any size.

Calendula

Another daisy-like flower, the calendula sports clear-colored orange and yellow blooms. It prefers cool weather, and is used as a winter annual in Arizona. Plant calendula in part shade to get it through the heat of summer and it will produce another bloom as the weather cools towards fall.

Calibrachoa

Although only distantly related to the petunia, the relatively new calibrachoa derives its popularity from its minature petunia-like blooms, which come in an array of striking colors. Calibrachoa need even more fertilizer than petunias. They also require heat. Finally, they must dry out between waterings. Use in pots and fertilize frequently.

Canna

The stately canna is grown from rhizomes. Cannas can grow to five or six feet tall in the long, northern days. Their blooms range from pink to red to orange, and their large leaves range from green to maroon, or can be variegated with orange.

Canna rhizomes do not survive our winters in the ground, and thus are listed here as an annual. However, cannas can easily be dug and divided after frost, dried, and stored in a dry location. After a day of soaking, they can be potted in early spring to give them a head start, or the rhizomes can be planted directly in the ground.

Daisy, Gerbera

People love the clear, primary colors of the gerbera daisy, but growing them is a challenge. They require heat, and if kept too moist, they simply wilt up and die. Benign neglect in the watering department is a key. Do not plant them under sprinklers. Make sure they are grown in the lightest potting soil you can find.

Dusty Miller

Like all plants with silvery foliage, the Dusty Miller likes sunshine and can't sit in saturated soil. A hardy, easy to grow plant, Dusty Miller will continue to look good well after hard frosts.

Foxglove   *Digitalis*

In the northland, foxglove is best considered an annual. Its small, gloxinia-like blooms hang from a tall spire. Foxglove are used to produce the heart medicine "digitalis."

Fuchsia

Fuchsia like it cool, not too wet, and quite shady. Once you find the right spot for a fuchsia, you shouldn't have a problem getting them to flourish there every year. Fuchsia are easily reproduced by cuttings. Due to their dangling habit, they are only suitable for hanging baskets or pots.

Grass, Ornamental

Although the recent fad has been to plant perennial ornamental grasses, there are a few unique annual grasses which work well as the centerpiece of a planter, or in the garden.

As of yet, there are no maroon-colored grasses which make it through winter. However, the annual maroon grasses can grow over your head.

Annual grasses don't start growing until there is heat, so one usually has to purchase them as scraggly, unsatisfying, stunted-looking starters. Don't worry. They will burst forth soon enough!

"Purple fountain grass" has become an important centerpiece in planters. A single plant of "Vertigo" will get four feet tall and three feet wide for a massive daub of maroon in the garden.

Heliotrope

From Peru, the heliotrope is, due to its overwhelming scent, also known as "Cherry Pie Plant." The deep purple blooms work well if contrasted with bright yellows such as marigolds or rudbeckia. In cool weather, the heliotrope leaves will also turn deep purple. Heliotrope attract butterflies.

Kale, Flowering

Kale thrive in cool conditions. Ornamental kales can be striking in mass beds, or can be a novelty as a single plant. Heat will cause kale to lose their center and *bolt,* which means the plant sends up a long shoot which eventually blooms. Once they bolt, kale are useless as an ornamental. Ornamental kale are a little tougher to eat than kale varieties bred for eating.

Lantana

Snowbirds to the Southwest notice lantana planted everywhere on the desert, and sometimes try to replicate them back home. However, the lantana needs the desert heat to truly thrive! A basket on a hot, enclosed porch will do the best.

Lisianthus

Popular for its long-lasting, rose-like blossoms, lisianthus can prove difficult to grow in the garden. Its greyish-blue foliage provides a clue why: like most plants with silvery foliage, lisianthus must have full sun, and cannot stand too much moisture. We have had success by planting the lisianthus in a hot spot well out of the range of sprinklers.

Morning Glory

The old-fashioned morning glory vine can be seeded right into the ground in spring. Be sure to follow the instructions on the packet for softening (or nicking) the very hard seed shell.

University research has discovered a quirky way to get morning glory to bloom more prolifically, and it is a story worth telling:

Apparently, morning glory are meant to germinate a week or two before equinox, March 21. For whatever reason, to bloom most fully, morning glory *require* a couple of weeks where the days are shorter than the nights.

In the north, we plant long *after* March 21. To create a few short days for the young morning glory, it is recommended that one cover the plant with an upside-down pot for several hours per day when the seedling is at the two-leaf stage. After about a week of such treatment, the natural, longer days are fine. Oddly, that one week of short days can triple the eventual bloom!

Nasturtium

The tender-looking nasturtium, with its complex orange and yellow blooms, needs heat to take off. Its peppery-flavored blooms and leaves are good in salads and the blooms work as beautiful garnishes.

Nemesia

From South Africa, the striking nemesia prefer cooler weather. Cut them back if they start looking scruffy, and hope for repeat bloom in the fall.

Nicotiana

An ornamental form of tobacco plant, the nicotiana produces star-shaped blooms of white, red, yellow or pink. It ranges in height from 12 inches for the dwarf varieties to 6 feet for the *Nicotiana sylvestris*, which also produces a wonderful evening scent.

Osteospermum

Another candidate for daisy status, the unfortunately-named osteospermum snag early-season greenhouse visitors with their strikingly clear blooms. Ranging in color from white to purple to orange, osteospermum are unique in that their centers are purple with hints of bright yellow pollen.

Osteospermum often quit blooming in the heat of summer, only to roar back after Labor Day. It helps to know that they grow wild on the coast of California, flourishing with bloom in the cool winter ocean breezes, and hunkering down during the heat.

Rudbeckia

Otherwise known as "Black-eyed Susan," rudbeckia straddle the divide between annual and perennial. A perennial in less harsh climates, the rudbeckias are a wonderful annual in the north. We consider the "Goldsturm" a perennial, although it would be worthwhile planting as an annual.

The "Goldsturm" and other rudbeckia make a grand show for the last half of summer, well into the autumn. To characterize the color, I recall a garden visitor with poor eyesight who mistook a distant mass bed of rudbeckia for a school bus.

Salvia   *Salvia farinacea*

Formerly called "Rhea" salvia, the "Evolution Violet" adds a powder blue bloom to the garden.

Salvia   *Salvia splendens*

Red salvia planted in a mass can be the brightest mass of red in the garden. Mix them with white petunias. The blooms are irregular and not meant to be viewed up close. However, because they are held proudly above the plant, they make an impact from a great distance. Other colors of this type of salvia, such as cream and deep purple, are novel, but not as showy.

Red salvia form a tiny part of the massive salvia family, which is related to mint and sage. In the northland, red salvia is well-known as an annual, but in warmer climes there are dozens of types of salvias which don't appear related to our red.

Vinca, Flowering

Most of the northern prairie lacks the summer heat needed to get the flowering vinca to bloom and thrive. Let the hotter parts of the country have this bedding plant. They need it!

Ugly ducklings

Annuals can be divided into cool-loving and heat-loving groups. The gardener who understands this can save money in the greenhouse by understanding what they see when they arrive there in early May.

"What a relief it is to see color after our long, drab winter!" we say as we walk into the greenhouse. But, because greenhouses in the northland are quite cool, especially at night, during early spring, the plants which are thriving are the cool-loving plants: pansies, osteospermum, Regal geraniums, nemesia, and the like.

The temptation is to fill up one's cart with that which is blooming. The risk is that you will fill your garden with plants which decline with the increase in summer temperatures!

So, mix it up. Purchase some of the ugly ducklings such as annual grasses, cleome, castor bean, celosia—heat-loving plants which look scrawny and color-less in the greenhouse in early spring, but will explode with growth and color when it gets hot.

CHAPTER 21

Perennials

What is a perennial?

In our area, a realistic gardener might define a perennial as a plant which *might* make it through the winter. The hardier perennials, old favorites like iris, peonies, hosta and daylilies, are virtually certain to make it through forty-nine out of fifty winters. But others, such as Shasta daisies, are less dependable, yet still worth the effort.

Perennials lend an old-fashioned, English air to the garden. They tend to be loose and informal, and work best if arranged loosely and informally in the broader landscape.

Perennials inspire loyalty in those who plant and care for them. My grandfather compared the pleasure of seeing perennials sprout in the spring to getting together with old friends.

Perennials vs. shrubs

Perennials are distinguished from *shrubs* by the fact that tops of perennials die back to the ground every winter. Shrubs are considered *woody plants*, because their stems survive the winter and shoot out new growth from the tips in the spring. Perennials are considered *herbaceous,* because they die back to the ground and must start fresh from the base come spring.

Why perennials come back year after year

Perennials survive winters because they devote much of the growing season to storing away resources underground. Their roots, tubers, bulbs or rhizomes—the name of the underground part varies from plant to plant—are far more developed than are the roots of annuals.

Because so much of the perennial's yearly cycle is spent storing away nutrients for the winter, the bloom time lasts for only a portion of the growing season. Even the best perennials are unlikely to bloom for more than four-to-six weeks. Some perennials can repeat their bloom if the dead blossoms are removed before seed pods form. However, there is no such thing as a perennial which blooms all season.

The importance of thoughtful design

Design is more important with perennials than with annuals. If you make a mistake with annuals, you have a clean slate next spring. With perennials, you hope to get it right the first time so you don't have to move them.

One should pay attention to the various blooming times of perennials in planning. You want some color all summer, so you want to mix perennials with a great variety of bloom times. Tossing in a few annuals between the perennials ensures color all season.

Because perennials usually bloom and then are finished for the year, it is unwise to plant masses of a single variety of perennial. Day lilies and ornamental grasses are an exception.

The wrong reason to plant perennials

Many people want to plant perennials to reduce their annual workload, to "get this bed planted and be done with it." Bad idea! Perennials need tending. They need weeding. Some need to be divided every now and then. One type will get out of hand and overwhelm its neighbor. Another will stubbornly refuse to grow in one spot but thrive in another.

Perennials are for the patient, the observant and the persistent. Over the long haul, they are neither less expensive nor less work than annuals.

However, everybody should have some perennials—because they are *fun!*

Buy a few perennials from the garden center, but also exchange them with friends. Develop your perennial garden slowly, over time.

PURCHASING PERENNIALS

Purchasing perennials

Spring is the best time to plant perennials. The selection at local nurseries is the best at that time, and spring planting allows the plants to become established before the onset of winter.

There are two ways of purchasing perennials: bare root or potted. Bare root is more economical, and in many cases a better practice, but retail establishments which stock a broad selection of bare root perennial plants are rare.

Bare root plants are most commonly ordered from mail order nurseries.

Beware! Not all mail order nurseries are reputable. Fancy guarantees mean nothing. Some of the plants arrive dried up, even dead.

Yes, most companies replace the plants, but you've just wasted one growing season learning your lesson. You generally get exactly what you pay for, and the replacements are often as dead as the original. Check the reviews online.

When purchasing potted perennials at a nursery, avoid picking out plants in bloom. Purchase stout, green, healthy looking plants and wait for them to bloom in their own time. Perennials in the greenhouse in pots have usually been forced ahead of their usual seasonal schedule by the warmth of the greenhouse.

Do not set such plants out until the last danger of frost is past. Once established in the ground, however, perennials come up slowly in accord with the season and one need not worry about them.

PLANTING AND CARE OF PERENNIALS

Do not break up the dirt ball

Unlike annuals, perennials don't like their root disrupted at planting. Leave the root ball intact, especially on tender plants such as clematis.

Winter warmth and wet kills perennials

In the heavier soils of the northern prairie, a wet fall followed by a heavy snow cover before the ground freezes can lead to roots of the plant being saturated in unfrozen ground for much of the winter. This can lead to root rot.

To prevent root rot, use plenty of peat or compost at planting time, enough to raise the beds above the ground level through the addition of peat or other organic matter. Do not water the perennials late in the fall.

The right kind of raised bed

It is better to mound soil to create a raised bed rather than putting down timbers or brick walls, which allow frost to come into the bed from the side. Any wall higher than a foot risks making the soil in the bed colder.

Winter cover or no winter cover?

Allow perennials to be covered naturally by leaves and snow. Leave all perennials standing (except peonies and iris) going into the winter in order to gather more leaves and snow around their base.

Covering perennials with a thick layer of straw can kill them off by encouraging rodents, mold, and rot. If you have already covered them thusly, make sure to remove the cover as soon as possible in spring.

Preparing the ground for a perennial bed

Kill off the grass with glyphosate. Wait a few days. Till. Add bag after bag of peat or organic matter, either placed on the surface or tilled in.

With perennials, it is especially important to add phosphate (in the form of bone meal, 10-10-10 fertilizer, or superphosphate) *before* the bed is tilled and planted.

Deadhead perennials for better appearance, longer life, sometimes another bloom

Only select few perennials can be prodded into producing a second bloom (of admittedly inferior quantity) by cutting off the spent blooms.

Even so, deadheading perennials is a good idea. Energy which would be spent producing seed will then be put into improving the root, which will make the plant more likely to survive the winter. Deadheading gets rid of blooms that have become ugly. Many perennials turn into attractive green shrubs once the spent blooms are removed.

Fertilizing established perennials

Established perennials can always benefit from an annual spreading of 10-10-10 fertilizer, spread at the rate prescribed on the bag.

Do not subject perennials to heavy doses of nitrogen, especially doses such as one finds in lawn fertilizers. Too much nitrogen can cause lanky growth, and require that plants be staked, while at the same time limiting the bloom.

Ammonium sulfate applied in moderation gives perennials a tremendous boost, and is not so potent as to create problems.

Dividing perennials

Very few perennials *require* occasional dividing to maintain their health. Most of the time, dividing is merely a method for reproducing perennial plants.

Division is usually best done when the plant is dormant. Use a good, sharp butcher knife for the best results. Wash the root or tuber of the perennial off with a hose so you can see clearly what you are doing.

Divisions must include both shoots *and* roots in order to survive.

With the more vigorously spreading perennials such monarda, hosta and phlox, it is possible just to dig out a chunk of shoots with a spade and plop the chunk in the ground at its new location. Water well after planting, and consider cutting back the tops to lessen the strain on the root system as it resets in its new location.

With peonies and other perennials with a more centralized root system, one must dig up the whole clump, wash off the soil, and make each cut only after careful consideration. *The goal is to have a proportionate number of shoots and tubers on each division.*

DISEASES AND INSECTS ON PERENNIALS

After perennials finish blooming, it is common for their foliage to look scruffy and get spots, or turn yellow. Don't worry. Diseases which threaten the life of perennials are very rare.

Diseases that show up on a perennial's foliage late in the season are usually harmless. The plant will come back the next year with fresh new growth, and perhaps the conditions will be different and the disease will not occur.

Same goes for insects. Most insects which show up on perennials are more companions than enemies.

As with all plants, perennials which are well-spaced are less susceptible fungal infections. Perennials, like all plants, prefer to be watered underneath the foliage. Do not water overhead unless you do so early in the morning, which will allow the leaves to dry quickly.

Cut peonies back to the ground in the fall to prevent disease from progressing from the foliage down into the root. Do the same for iris.

When perennials die out in the center

Autumn Joy Sedum, Miscanthus grass, garden mums, and Moonbeam coreopsis sometimes die out in the middle of the plant. This means the plant could benefit from division. It also can mean the plant is sitting too wet, in too much shade, or has too much nitrogen.

MAJOR PERENNIALS FOR OUR AREA

The following perennials have been selected as the best for our area due to their hardiness, usefulness in the garden, and ease of culture. The list is not complete, as perennial enthusiasts will quickly note.

However, these favorites have proven themselves over time to be almost sure bets for the beginning gardener as well as useful to the experienced gardener. Those new to gardening will find plenty of varieties within these categories to keep them busy for many years to come.

The following perennials have been alphabetized according to the name which seems most often recognized by area gardeners, a flawed system to be sure.

Artemisia *Silver Mound*

Also known as "wormwood," the silver foliage of the *Artemisia* provides a summer-long accent in the perennial garden, or the more formal landscape. The most popular variety in our area is the *Artemisia nana*, commonly known as "Silver Mound."

Silver Mound thrive in hot, sunny locations. They survive drought. They require little care. They are from the sage family, so they prefer desert conditions.

Silver Mound grows to about two feet across, sometimes a little more. It forms a dignified, compact mound of up to twelve inches in height.

If the season is wet, or if they are in richer soils, the Silver Mound may open up in the middle. *Cut the plant back to about a third of its original height.* The plant will look scruffy for a while, but will soon bush out with fresh foliage and look as good as it did in June.

To refresh old silver mound plants, dig them up and divide them when they are dormant, taking out the old woody center. Silver Mound should not be planted where the soil remains wet over winter, as they are susceptible to root rot.

Silver Mound are one of the hardiest, most useful perennials we have. Use them to contrast with plants with darker foliage or blooms.

Astilbe

Astilbe are one of the very few perennials hardy in our area which bloom where shade prevails. Astilbe can withstand sunshine, but must have moist, well-drained soil. Growing astilbe in a raised bed of peat in medium shade is ideal.

Also called "false spirea" due to a leaf which is similar to the dwarf spirea, the astilbe sends plume-like bloom stalks above the foliage which range in height from one to four feet. The blooms can last for much of the summer, and colors include pink, white, lavender and red.

If planted in raised beds, Astilbe are perfectly hardy in our area. They must not sit moist over winter. Astilbe are not very common in gardens in our area, but they should be planted more often. Getting rid of the old bloom will allow the attractive foliage to show for the remainder of the season.

Divide the woody astilbe crowns in the spring every 3-4 years to keep the plants vigorous.

Baby's Breath   *Gypsophila*

Baby's breath are a favorite for their clusters of tiny white or pink blooms. Ideal in flower arrangements, Baby's breath can be dried to last even longer.

Baby's breath can be difficult to keep going in our area. The secret to a long life: the plant can never sit wet, and must be placed in a well-drained, even a dry location.

Baby's breath absolutely require full sun, and may die out in a wet summer if not in a well-drained location.

Baby's breath roots go very deep, therefore they are very difficult, if not impossible, to move once established. Give each plant plenty of room as the plant can span up to five feet wide by late summer.

Bleeding Heart   *Dicentra*

Bleeding heart are a sentimental favorite for beside a shady back step. Their pink or white blooms form a perfect heart, with a droplet hanging from the bottom of the bloom. Their tender foliage is a dusky blue-green from spring through July.

Bleeding heart prefer deep shade. If planted in sun, they will turn yellow and go dormant earlier in the season.

Bleeding heart are one of the first perennials to shoot up in the spring, and they are usually in bloom by late May or early June, before most other plants kick in.

After the bleeding heart stops blooming, its foliage slowly fades until by August it is virtually all dead. Do not be alarmed. Simply cut away the dead stems and leaves. The plant will come back next year.

Bleeding heart have no noticeable disease or insect problems.

Never risk root rot by covering a bleeding heart for winter. They are hardy.

In addition to the common bleeding heart there are the less common "Luxuriant." Luxuriant bleeding heart can bloom all season, and require less moisture than the common. Their leaves are deeply cut and lacy, and the plant is about one-third the size of the common bleeding heart.

Like the common, "Luxuriant" bleeding heart cannot sit wet for long periods.

Garden Mums   *Chrysanthemum*

Mums are an important staple for fall bloom. They are not completely dependable as a perennial on the northern prairie. Expect occasional winter kill.

A natural, or gardener-assisted covering of fallen leaves can support mums in getting through the winter, but care should be taken that the covering does not become matted and wet enough to cause rot. Remove the cover early in spring.

Be careful to select early blooming varieties of mums, as the late bloomers will be caught by early frosts. Young mums may be pinched back about an inch during the spring and summer to encourage bushy growth.

Mums need drainage, and their slightly silvery foliage is a reminder that they can take a little drought.

Mums which show exceptional vigor can be profitably divided.

Dozens upon dozens of garden mums are on the market, with new varieties appearing each year. *Make sure the mums you purchase have an established history in our area.* The surest bets are those introduced specifically for the northern plains.

Clematis

Clematis are famous for their spectacular summer display of purple blooms. Although there are hundreds of varieties of clematis available nationwide, from vining to shrub types, from white to red, the purple "Jackmanii" outshines them all in our area, and has for decades.

Vining clematis may require a little help to get the vine started on the trellis each spring. The old vines must be pruned away. Once established, a clematis can bloom for decades.

Clematis like their root kept cool. Perhaps for this reason, they are reputed to grow best on the east side. However, if the root is protected by mulch, or if the lower part of the plant is shaded by small shrubs or other plants, clematis will thrive on the west wall of a building as well.

Establishing a clematis vine can be difficult, but by following a few basic guidelines, success can be within reach for any gardener.

•Dig a large hole, even as deep and wide as two feet if you really want to do it right. Fill the hole with peat or organic matter. The object is to create an ideal place for the root to spread out and remain healthy for twenty or more years.

•Strip the leaves off the bottom three inches of the vine you purchased. *Be sure not to disturb the root ball when you remove the pot, or when you are planting.* Then, plant the top of root ball about three inches deeper than the soil surface, filling in soil three inches up on the stem.

•Keep the vine trimmed to about six inches in height the first season. Pruning will force the plant to develop the all-important root.

A trellis is necessary for a clematis, but it needn't be fancy. A swatch of chicken netting attached to the wall is sufficient. A chain link trellis works well.

Clematis in our area will die back to the ground in most winters. Some people have had luck laying the entire trellis on the ground, vines and all, and covering it up with leaves, or even a carpet. If the vine stems survive the winter, the display of bloom the next spring will be earlier and more spectacular.

Start with the purple "Jackmanii," which is spectacular enough to be considered a staple of the northern prairie yard, and add other colors as novelties.

Coral Bells   *Heuchera*

Coral Bells bloom for several weeks starting in mid-June. If planted in a mass, Coral Bells dark pink blooms create a striking effect from a distance at a time when many of the perennials have not yet started providing color. The tiny bell-like flowers droop languidly from the end of a long stem, and are ideal for a miniature kitchen table arrangement.

Coral Bells are now being used as much for their foliage as for their bloom. Most of the *Heuchera* family variations come to us from Europe where Coral Bells are a favorite.

Heuchera varieties with darker leaves tend to do better with some shade and are not generally as hardy. The old-fashioned, green-leafed "Splendens Scarlet" is the most reliable and provides dependable bloom to boot.

Coral bell roots are fibrous and shallow, and form a tight crown. The plant can *heave*, or push itself out of the soil in late winter during periods of alternately warm and cold weather. Good snow cover helps prevent heaving, as does a layer of peat added to the soil around the plant.

Frequent division of the crown will help prevent the heaving and will keep Coral Bells from forming such a tight clump that it kills itself off.

Daylily *Hemerocallis*

Daylilies come in hundreds of varieties, with new colors added every year. They are hardy, dependable and low-maintenance. Daylilies work well in a mass, especially in a large institutional setting. Although each individual bloom only lasts one day, more come all the time.

Daylilies can benefit from division. The dwarfed Stella d'Oro blooms more if it is divided every year. However, many institutions simply let their daylilies grow year after year, and they still do fine.

Daylilies are can be divided most any time, but late summer is best. Cut back the foliage to four to five inches when dividing. Plant the crown, the point where the root meets the stem, about an inch below soil level.

Daylilies like sun, but are tough enough to survive in part shade.

Delphinium

Delphinium come in many colors, but their blues are exceptional—the deepest blue available in the perennial world.

Traditional delphiniums have a small mound of foliage at the base, and send up large flower stalks in June, with some stalks reaching as high as seven feet. Along the stalks are hundreds of small blooms which, taken as a whole, form impressive vertical towers of color.

The bloom stalks are hollow and weak, and when they grow to be particularly large, they must be staked or they will tip over.

Deadheading the large blooms immediately after they fade will encourage smaller side blooms, which can provide color well into the summer. Cutting the whole plant back almost to the ground after the first bloom can result in a fall bloom of inferior quality.

Delphinium can be short-lived, but dividing them every three years or so can prolong their life. Divide in early spring, just after the sprouts start to show.

A hot, dry summer is hard on delphinium.

If planted in a moist spot in the heavy soil on the northern prairie, the delphinium may decline and die more quickly. As always, adding peat will improve matters.

Dianthus

A delightful, tundra-like plant, the perennial dianthus forms carpet of very fragrant, delicate, heavily-scented blooms. Dianthus need sun, but can tolerate average to poor soil. The more silvery the dianthus foliage, the drier the soil they prefer. The dianthus with more silvery leaves do not spread as fast as those with darker green leaves.

Dianthus are one plant that does better in the alkaline soils of the northern prairie than it does elsewhere.

Purple coneflower   *Echinacea*

Echinacea root is used for medicinal purposes, but the drooping, daisy-like blooms are what most interests the perennial gardener. The petals of the flower are colorful, and the central cone of the flower is also striking, with the pollen providing a vivid yellow accent.

Echinacea are native to the prairie and are thus resistant to drought. They grow in poor soil. They need full sun to do their best.

In part shade, echinacea get lanky. Saturated, heavy soils kill the plant.

Echinacea can put on a second bloom if their first bloom is removed as soon as it fades.

The purple-flowering varieties are hardy. The white flowering varieties are less so, and can benefit from some winter cover. The covering should not become wet and saturated or it will cause the echinacea crown to rot. As usual, a good layer of snow is the ideal cover.

Ferns

Ferns are a stately filler for shady spots, particularly dark coves on the north side of the house. Although ferns do spread, they seldom become a problem. With adequate moisture, ferns can stand a little sunshine.

The "Ostrich" fern is the tallest, reaching four or five feet. The fronds unravel in a predominantly vertical pattern. The "Lady" fern, a native in area woodlands, has delicate, lacy leaves which are held horizontally.

More a novelty, the "Maidenhair" fern has a delicate, bluish foliage on dark stems, and only grows to two feet. It makes a nice accent for the shade bed.

Definitely a novelty, the maroon and silver-leaved "Japanese Painted Fern" is cold-hardy, but does not like alkaline soil. Plant it in straight peat.

Grasses, ornamental

Ornamental grasses provide a great year-around display. Although they are a recent development in gardening, ornamental grasses are proving to do better on the northern prairie than in woodlands and elsewhere. Makes sense!

It is important to leave the grasses standing in the winter, not only to gather the snow around the base, but also to gain the aesthetic benefit of the beautiful fronds of grass. Cut the old foliage back on the first warm day of spring.

"Karl Foerster" grass is the most frequently planted. It grows to 4-5 feet with a strictly vertical habit. It seems to be the best grass for the heavy soils. It is the most formal and dignified of the ornamental grasses.

"Flame Grass" *Miscanthus sinensis var. purpurescens* forms gracefully drooping white plumes which almost sparkle in the sunshine in the winter. Miscanthus grass has not been as reliable as the Karl Foerster. One cluster will die out over winter, another a few feet away will survive.

Miscanthus sometimes can die out in the middle, which may be the plant objecting to too much nutrition or moisture.

Blue Oat Grass stays confined in a clump, and is planted more for its foliage than the seed heads. The stringy, tough blue foliage forms an upright tuft which grows to 18 inches.

Panicum is a tall, airy blue foliaged grass which is not as immediately striking as other varieties, but cherished by those with subtle tastes.

The menu of grasses is likely to expand. Their toughness and winter beauty seem to ensure that they will become a staple in the northern yard. Plant them in groupings of three for a pleasing, natural look.

Hosta

The shade-loving hosta is so popular and broadly used that some people resist planting them. Yet, there is no better foliage plant for the shade. With *thousands* of varieties on the market, you are likely to find at least one you love, and which is unique.

Hosta range from two inches in height to some which exceed four feet. The leaves can be green, blue, yellow, even gray. Leaves can be solid-colored, or feature striping which forms intriguing patterns. In addition, the leaves vary in texture. The combinations of traits are endless, and one is sure to catch your eye.

Some are bred for the scent of the blooms, which can rival orange blossoms in sweetness. If you find the bloom stems to be a distraction from the foliage, however, you may remove them without hurting the plant.

One does not have to be hooked on hosta to find them useful in the landscape. Any shady spot is a candidate for a bed of hosta, and sometimes hosta is the only plant which will do the job.

Hosta are a favorite meal for slugs, which are especially a problem on smooth clay soils after a rain. If you see holes in the leaves, spread commercial slug bait on the ground underneath your hosta. The slug bait advertised as pet-friendly is also organic and quite harmless to all.

An even more organic solution: Bury empty tuna fish cans with their lip even with the ground level and fill them with beer. The slugs will be drawn into the beer and drown, a sobering lesson for us all.

Divide hosta almost any time except for June, which is when their leaves are most fresh.

Iris

The stately iris blooms in late spring or early summer. The peculiar heavy sweetness of the iris bloom's scent brings back memories for many people.

A few iris varieties can bloom again in the fall.

Iris come in an astounding variety of bright colors including black, deep purple, blue, purple, white, yellow, even tan.

Iris grow from a fleshy root called a rhizome which resembles ginger root. It is common for the roots to show. *Do not cover the visible roots with mulch.*

Iris roots should be planted very close to the surface. Iris do well in dry areas, and can be planted or purchased at any time. They need at least six hours of sunlight per day.

Iris can benefit from being dug up and divided every three or four years. They can be divided at any time after they bloom. Throw out any roots that look dried up and old.

Cut back the fan of leaves halfway at transplanting to lessen the strain on the root as it establishes.

In addition, it is a good practice to cut established iris foliage back halfway in late summer to discourage the iris borer, a worm which enters the tips of the leaves and works its way down to the root. Clean up iris foliage thoroughly in the fall to deprive the borer eggs of winter habitat.

Iris, Siberian   *Iris sibirica*

Most often purple, the Siberian iris loves wetlands. If you have a water feature, plant Siberian iris nearby. The blooms are smaller than the traditional iris.

Lamium   *Dead Nettle*

Lamium is a dependable and attractive ground cover which grows well in shade or part shade. It grows where nothing else will, particularly in the sterile ground beneath large evergreens. Hardy ground covers which grow in shade are rare in our area, making lamium of great value.

Common lamium, more properly known as *Lamiastrum,* is the most vigorous of the varieties. It will spread to fill an entire area, but can be easily kept in check at the edge of that area with a mower. Lamium do not spread in the pernicious manner of Snow-on-the-Mountain.

In June, lamium send up white, pink, or lavender blooms which are not of great interest. It is the variegated foliage which makes lamium interesting and worthwhile.

Lamium are so hardy that the leaves often keep their green over winter; it can appear as if they start in the spring where they left off in the fall.

Monarda   *Bee Balm*

Monarda is a native plant from the mint family. Its leaves can be used in tea and its flower petals as an accent on salads. But the best feature of Monarda is its mop-like bloom, which can last for several weeks in late July before fading. Monarda, like its counterparts in the mint family, spreads vigorously, so it is best to give it plenty of room.

Most Monarda develop mildew on the foliage late in the season. The plant is strong enough to ward off the affliction, which is primarily cosmetic.

Monarda should have full sun. Avoid overhead watering to lessen the problem of mildew. They seem to spread faster in shade, and get more disease problems.

Peony

For the old-time gardener, the powerful scent of peony blooms is an integral part of late June. A peony bush can last for most of a century.

After blooms have faded and the thousands of fallen petals have dried up on the ground, the remaining seed pods may be trimmed off and the peony will function as an attractive dark green shrub for the rest of the summer.

288

Although peonies respond well to division, it is not necessary. Divide peonies in early September. Cut back the stalks to the ground, dig up the root clump, wash the dirt off the root with a hose, and carefully slice the root into partitions which each contain both tubers and a new sprout.

Peonies should be in full sun. If established peonies stop blooming, it is usually because trees have come to shade the plant over the years. It is then time to dig them up and move them into the sunshine.

Like all plants which grow from tubers, peonies love bone meal or the fertilizer form of phosphate. Mix such fertilizers in the soil underneath and around the peony before planting.

Do not plant peonies too deeply, or they will not bloom. Take care to plant them no more deeply than they were before. If the root purchased has a shoot or two, they should be barely covered, and then only with light soil.

Peony flowers can be so large that the stalks tip, especially after a rain. Either stake the blooms, or surround the plant with a wire peony cage.

Consider single-blooming varieties if you don't wish to stake the heavy double blooms for support every year.

If peony buds rot and don't open, they are infected with peony blight, otherwise known as *botrytis.* The best way to prevent such disease is to cut the peony foliage back to ground level in the fall, a requirement which makes peonies one of the very few perennials which should be cut back before winter.

Ants which sometimes infest peonies do no harm. They are merely collecting the sugar droplets produced by the blooms.

There are hundreds of varieties of peony. Some have thicker stalks, some bloom double, others single. There is even a yellow peony on the market, but they are so rare that each tuber can cost as much as $500.

Phlox, creeping

Creeping phlox bloom in early May. The bloom forms a carpet of lavender or pink, depending upon the variety, and lasts for a couple of weeks. Do not cover in the winter, as creeping phlox can develop mold underneath any covering.

Phlox, upright

Upright phlox are a true old-time staple, producing blooms of pure, bright colors in July.

Plant them out in the open so they get plenty of air circulation to prevent mildew. "Miss Lingard" is more resistant to mildew than other phlox, and blooms early and often. Cut off the early bloom after it fades for a re-bloom later.

Upright phlox spread by the root. It is easy to move a clump elsewhere to form a new patch.

Rudbeckia   *Black-eyed Susan*

Rudbeckia are usually considered an annual in our area, but the relatively new "Goldsturm" has survived several winters on the northern prairie. No rudbeckia are completely hardy, but the long bloom-time makes them worthwhile to use even if they turn out to be an annual. Do not cut back the dead foliage before winter, as the dead blooms have winter interest and the foliage will gather snow around the base to protect the root for winter.

Sedum

Sedum are dependable and easy to grow. The sedum family ranges from upright, shrub-like plants to creepers. All have thick succulent leaves which allow them to survive hot and dry conditions. Sedum are ideal for raised rock gardens in the hot sun.

"Autumn Joy" is the classic upright sedum. After bursting out of the ground at the first hint of spring, the Autumn Joy grows into a compact upright oval, about 30" tall. In late summer, Autumn Joy put on broccoli like bloom heads which match the blue-green hue of the foliage. As fall proceeds, the hundreds of little blooms open to a soft pink.

The bloom color, as well as the foliage, turns to a deep mahogany pink. If left standing into the winter, the stems and blooms provide some winter interest.

Some upright sedum eventually die out in the middle, which is a sign that they should be dug up and divided. If subjected to excess moisture or nitrogen, upright sedum can weaken and flop over. A hot, dry location is best.

Creeping varieties of sedum are dependable and hardy, and can be used as a ground cover in hot, dry, gravelly situations.

New sedum are being introduced with increasing frequency. So far, the primary variety dependable enough for landscape use should be the Autumn Joy. Other varieties, which vary greatly in height and leaf color, may be used as accents in a perennial garden, but are not recommended in large numbers.

MINOR PERENNIALS

The following perennials are worthwhile, but need some special care of one sort or another. Perhaps they need a perfect spot, like the Baby's Breath, or perhaps they require work to prevent them from spreading like wildfire, like the Joe-Pye weed, or perhaps they are difficult to start, like the Monkshood, or perhaps they bloom gloriously for a short time but look awful after that, like the Oriental Poppy. All of these minor perennials are worthwhile, but they simply don't qualify for mass plantings essential to the larger landscape.

Achillea *Yarrow*

A grouping of yarrow provides color and a striking horizontal texture to the garden. The flowers, pincushion-like masses of tiny blooms, make for a striking and lasting cut flower.

Yarrow is known to spread. However, some new varieties such as "Coronation Gold" are more likely to confine themselves to a clump.

Newly planted yarrow require water, but once established, yarrow tolerate drought and poor soil well. As indicated by its silvery foliage, yarrow prefers hot sun.

After yarrow blooms fade, they can be removed with a hedge clipper leaving the attractive foliage to provide texture to the garden for the remainder of the summer.

The variety "Pearl," with masses of double white flowers, can be regarded as a sturdier alternative to Baby's Breath.

Yarrow are totally hardy, and clumps of it can be easily moved with a spade.

Ajuga *Bugleweed*

Ajuga is one of the most dense and compact ground covers available to the northern gardener. It will grow in a variety of conditions, from mostly sun to mostly shade. It grows thickly enough to crowd out nearly all weeds.

From the mat of dark foliage, the common ajuga sends up five-inch shoots of blue blooms in late May. Those flowers should be removed after they fade to allow the foliage of the ajuga to shine.

Due to its proven hardiness and vigor, common ajuga, with its glossy purple leaves, should be preferred over varieties with variegated leaves.

Alchemilla   *Lady's Mantle*

The charm of Lady's Mantle lies in the dewdrops which gather on the furry leaves during morning dew or after a rain. The surface of the leaves acts as if it has been waxed, causing moisture to form large drops which sparkle in the sunshine.

Lady's Mantle prefer a moist spot where there is somewhat less than full sun. The green flowers work well in some arrangements, but don't show up very well in the garden.

Lady's Mantle are used for a border in perennial gardens in partial shade. For maximum enjoyment of this plant, place it where you pass by frequently in the early morning.

Allium   *Ornamental Onions*

Allium bloom at the same time and with the same color as Dwarf Lilac—in early June. Allium are sometimes sold as bulbs. They come back year after year with their striking softball-sized bloom held two feet up by a long stalk.

Other varieties of ornamental onion feature odd foliage and varying colors of bloom. The various forms of allium are minor perennials which thrive in poor soil, and in hot sunshine.

Aquilegia   *Columbine*

Columbine are found in the wild in our area. Like many plants found native in the woods, they are a bit stubborn about growing in the garden, and can be short-lived.

Native columbine have an orange and yellow bloom, which opens in June. Cultivated varieties come in variations of the colors of red, blue, yellow, and pink. The blooms can last for the better part of a month.

Columbine prefer light shade, but will grow in the sun if provided good moisture. Columbine are susceptible to root rot, so it is essential to plant them in well-drained, lighter soil. A raised peat bed is ideal.

Deadheading the spent columbine flowers will not promote a new bloom, but it will prevent the seed pods from scattering hundreds of seeds around the general area. If allowed to set seed, the native varieties can form a beautiful mass.

Asclepias   *Butterfly Plant*

The butterfly plant is in the same family as the common milkweed. *Asclepias incarnata,* a hardy native variety, thrives in *wet* areas, grows to three feet and blooms mauve.

Asclepias tuberosa, the plant most gardeners think of as Butterfly Plant, has a deep root and thrives in *dry* conditions. It blooms a brilliant orange.

A deep root makes it unwise to attempt to divide butterfly plant.

Asclepias tuberosa is one of the last perennials to sprout in the spring. Be patient. Once they are fully leafed out in a pot they are easy to replant, but it is a trick to get bare root *Asclepias tuberosa* to break dormancy. To avoid the difficulty of getting the dormant plant to sprout, purchase asclepias as potted plants.

Asters   *Asteraceae*

Although fall-blooming asters thrive in road ditches and native prairie all over our area, domesticated varieties seem to do better in town than in the country, perhaps due to the protection of the buildings.

The aster's daisy-like blooms are delicate, tend towards powdery pastels in the pink and purple family, and can feature bright yellow centers.

Plant perennial asters in a sunny area, perhaps against the south side of the house, preferably under the eaves for frost protection.

Campanula   *Bell Flower*

An old-time perennial, the Campanula blooms in June, and provides wonderful early summer color of a blue hue second only to delphinium.

Campanula can spread to form a large patch. If you have a massive old house, a wild patch of tall campanula in the back yard is most appropriate.

Shorter varieties such as the "Blue Clips" form a compact mound, and can work in a more formal landscape.

Campanula will do well in partial shade. Remove the faded blooms to induce possible re-bloom.

Daisy, Painted   *Tanecetum coccineum*

Because it prefers well-drained, acid soil, the Painted Daisy is not a long-lived proposition in our area. However, planted in a raised bed of peat and fertilized consistently with an acidifying fertilizer, the plant can provide several years of pink, red and white blooms.

Daisy, Shasta   *Leucanthemum*

People simply won't stop planting the Shasta Daisy despite their borderline hardiness. They are a short-lived perennial. However, there is no dependable comparable white daisy perennial for our area.

Shasta Daisy put on a good show the first season. The Shasta often returns the second year, but can become weaker and smaller each year thereafter. Divide them every spring to potentially improve their longevity.

Eupatorium   *Joe Pye Weed*

As the name implies, Joe Pye Weed can become a weed. Avoid the common form of this plant. A striking large perennial, the Joe Pye Weed produces millions of seeds. The cultivated varieties "Bartered Bride" and "Gateway" are far less invasive.

Joe Pye prefer moist soil, and will wilt in the hot sun if they are not moist underneath.

Gas plant   *Dictamnus*

From the citrus family, the Gas Plant provides a stunning white or pink bloom, held proudly over the glossy green foliage in late June before most annuals and other perennials have started to show. Once established, Gas Plant is as hardy and dependable as any shrub.

Do not try to move or divide the plant once it has settled in, however.

The gas plant's status as a minor perennial comes from the difficulty finding them on the market.

Gas Plant are so named due to the not unpleasant but undeniably fuel-like fragrance given off by the flowers and the seed pods. The gas emitted by the dried seed pods can actually explode with a minor "poof" if a match is held near the pods on a still evening. Lighting the gas plant was one of the more memorable horticultural delights of my childhood.

Geranium, hardy

Hardy geraniums are completely unrelated to the annual geraniums in both appearance and genetics.

Hardy geraniums bloom various shades of lavender and pink in early summer. After the dainty, single purple or pink blooms fade, the foliage is mildly attractive, and can turn striking colors in the fall.

Hardy geranium spread to create a mass in partial shade, and are easily divided and moved to start new masses elsewhere.

Sempervivum   *Hen and Chicks*

Hen and Chicks are a favorite plant of children and eccentrics. Once you have one plant, you have all you ever need. A mat-like patch of Hen and Chicks can be striking.

To rid the Hen and Chicks of quack grass, rub the fronds of grass above the hen-and-chicks mat with glyphosate concentrate, taking care not to drip on or touch the plants.

There are many varieties of Hen and Chicks in the world, ranging from bulky to delicate. Due to a recent succulent fad, more and more are appearing on the market each year.

Hollyhock   *Alcea*

The most old-time plant possible, the hollyhock grows eight or nine feet tall and produces columns of the most striking blooms, single or double, ranging from pink to red, even green and black. A biennial, which means the plant grows one year without blooming before putting on its spectacular show the next season and then dying, the hollyhock should be allowed to seed itself or the patch will disappear.

Hollyhock are susceptible to leaf diseases. The ideal spot for Hollyhock is on an open south side of a building where the breezes and the heat will keep the disease from forming. Never place hollyhock under sprinklers.

Hollyhock can thrive in some pretty weak soil, even gravel.

Liatrus   *Blazing Star*

Liatrus are native to the prairie and are about the closest thing to a substitute available for the *lythrum*, which is now illegal. The Liatrus produces cylindrical lavender, powderpuff blooms about three feet in height. Liatrus grow from tiny bulbs. They cannot survive in overly wet conditions.

Lupine

On the northern prairie, domesticated lupine are short-lived, but put on such a stunning show while they live that they are worthwhile. Lupine are very vigorous in early spring, putting on their colorful columnar blooms as spring turns into summer. They come in a stunning mix of blue, pink, red and yellow.

Lupine benefit from a raised bed of peat. They work well on the east side of a house, where they are shaded from the hottest of the sun. Lupine become scruffy later in the summer, which is what you expect from perennials which bloom early.

Nepeta   *Catmint*

Nepeta are an effective source of a taller, bluish color. They spread and sprawl and are not appropriate for a formal setting. They need full sun and prefer a drier location. Even the shorter varieties will spread (though not uncontrollably) to form a nice mass. The perennial variety is not to be confused with "catnip," which spreads with obnoxious vigor.

Peony, Fern Leaf

Sometimes called the Memorial Day peony due to their tendency to bloom on that holiday, fern leaf peony are a favorite for cemeteries.

Because they grow to a divisible size so slowly, the Fern Leaf peony are high priced and difficult to find on the market. So far, attempts to reproduce them through tissue culture have failed.

A Fern Leaf peony can last decades in the cemetery. They do best in full sun. Their deep, wine-colored blooms contrast with delicate bright ferny foliage. They thrive on neglect.

Fern Leaf peony lose their bloom in early June. Their foliage dries up and dies by mid-August, after which one can safely mow over the area where they are planted.

August is also the time to dig up the tubers for division and replanting. Fern Leaf Peony tubers are especially brittle and should be handled with care. Wash the dirt off the clump with a stream of water, and be careful to divide the root in such away so each division has both a tuber and two or three shoots.

Planting Fern Leaf peony too deeply, or in shade, can cause them not to bloom.

Poppy, Oriental *Papaver*

The luxuriant deep green foliage of the Oriental Poppy bursts out of the ground in early May. The round bloom heads open into a Georgia O'Keefe painting by the end of the month, with blooms of the most pure orange available.

Having fulfilled its function of introducing summer, the Oriental Poppy then goes into decline. The blooms fade. The foliage inevitably gets yellow and diseased. For this reason, plant the Oriental Poppy where it will make a show in the spring, but won't be noticed the rest of the summer. One gardener suggested planting it near a large *Gypsophila* (Baby's Breath), which will cover the unsightly poppy foliage with a mound of later bloom.

Pulmonaria *Lungwort*

The delicate pulmonaria is a cute plant for the shade. With distinctive spotted leaves which come in different colors, and its tiny little blooms, some pink, some purple, and some which change over the days from one color to another, the pulmonaria is a conversation piece, a novelty item to add a little variety to an odd corner of a shade bed which already has enough hosta.

Pulomonaria will burn up in the sun. Even in the shade, if the weather is hot and dry, the pulmonaria may go dormant.

Snow-on-the-Mountain   *Euphorbia marginata*

Viewed as a weed by many due to its propensity to spread by the root, Snow-on-the-mountain makes a decent, if overly vigorous, ground cover for deep shade. Contain it by spraying the edges of the mass with glyphosate.

The fringes of the leaves of snow-on-the-mountain can brown in the sunshine, or in dry conditions. Wait for next year.

Wildflowers

Wildflowers are more difficult to establish than one might think. Most of the wildflower seed mixes are multi-colored the first season, but die down to just white daisies after that. To establish a true native-prairie wildflower patch of any size requires professional assistance.

CHAPTER 22

Vegetables on the Prairie

Due to the long summer days, vegetables grow large and produce bountifully on the northern prairie.

And the flavor! Our tomatoes, for one, taste like nothing in the store.

It doesn't end there: Our cabbage can reach nearly twenty pounds per head. One short row of carrots can produce bushels. A couple of squash plants can fill your winter with the most nutritious comfort soup possible, squash soup—or for your sweet tooth, "pumpkin" pie (most pumpkin pies are made with squash, and nobody notices the difference).

Watermelon ripen over a long six-week stretch. Muskmelon (cantaloupe) develop flavor and rich color in the north unlike the tomatoes in the store.

Six plants of bell peppers and you will probably pick a peck like Peter Piper. Onions, even garlic: Northern salsa has become an area canning staple. What would great-grandma say about *that* development?

Our only limitation is the relatively short frost-free growing season. However, the three summer months are so intense due to the long days at our northern latitude that even if you don't plant your vegetable garden until June 1, you will have plenty to eat come August and September. In addition, breeding advances have dramatically shortened the season, particularly for sweet corn.

Information overload

Volumes of information about vegetable growing are accessible online, or in bookstores, or merely in the heads of long-time gardeners. Everybody has opinions.

And they're usually right.

Vegetables grow so well in the north that if Uncle Albert only plants potatoes under a full moon as he has for the past seventy years, he's going to get a huge crop of potatoes! No harm in letting him think it's the moon.

Fads and quack ideas come out each year. Upside-down gardening. Gardening in a wash tub. Straw-bale gardening. Square-foot gardening. Hydroponic gardening.

And it all works.

But for prairie gardeners, *none of it is needed*. Every television-promoted gardening fad is an attempt to overcome limited space, and if you have relatively unlimited space, why bother?

The basics

Success with vegetable gardening on the northern prairie *is not difficult* provided you adhere to a few basics:

•Plant vegetable gardens in full sun

•Add organic matter (peat) to the soil, as well as a general mild fertilizer

•Water frequently, if possible beneath the foliage

•Weed, weed, weed

That's it!

Other possible tasks will suggest themselves soon enough. Yes, a massive, over-grown tomato will benefit from staking. But if you don't get around to it, it will still bear. Yes, those carrots growing like hair on a dog should be thinned. Yes, you should probably plant fewer eggplant next year to avoid an eggplant invasion.

New vegetable gardeners should get their nose out of books like this as quickly as possible and go prepare their soil for this year's garden!

With vegetable gardening, sweat is more important than knowledge.

That said, this chapter will address some of the issues of particular relevance on the northern prairie, without debating the virtues of planting seed potatoes whole, or divided in half, or one eye per cut, or under a full moon.

Choosing and preparing the garden plot

Vegetables *all* love full sun all day. Shade of any sort and for any length of time during the day will hurt the garden. In addition, vegetables do not do well when competing with tree roots.

Vegetables cannot stand to sit under water for even a couple of hours following a rain.

Thus, a garden plot will ideally be situated on a high, well-drained, sunny spot. A source of water should be nearby, as vegetables require watering throughout the summer to do their best.

Tough weeds such as quack grass should be eliminated from the garden plot by spraying glyphosate and tilling well in advance of planting. Advance spraying with glyphosate will not harm the vegetable plants planted later.

Some people add peat to their garden each fall or spring, which has the effect of raising the garden. Raised beds grow tremendous vegetables, particularly when the soil added is organic matter such as peat or very old manure.

There is no harm in using planters or pots to grow vegetables, although the soil will dry out much faster when up and out of the ground during the heat of summer.

A balanced fertilizer, such as 10-10-10, should be tilled into the plot each season before planting. If your garden is already rich in nitrogen, balance the nitrogen with additional phosphate in the form of bone meal, or superphosphate.

If you add manure to the garden, make sure it is so old that it is the consistency of loamy soil, and does not smell. Realize that old manure is full of weed seeds.

An excess of nitrogen reduces fruiting and can ruin root crops. Do not use lawn fertilizer on the vegetable garden, ever. And never use farm fertilizer.

Seeds vs. Transplants

Carrots, parsnips, radishes, spinach, corn and beans are almost always planted by seed directly into the garden.

Tomatoes, peppers, and members of the cabbage family such as broccoli work best if planted as transplants.

Melons, cucumbers, squash and onions succeed both as transplants and if seeded directly into the garden. Transplants have a head start, but planting from seed is cheaper, and the delay in fruiting is less than one might think.

Starting vegetable seeds inside

Many people start their own vegetable seeds inside and set the plants out after the danger of frost is past. Starting one's own seeds can be fun, and it can save money.

Most houses are too warm and have too little light for vegetable seedlings. The result is lanky, weak seedlings which don't adjust very easily to the outdoors when they are finally set out.

To make for stout plants grown inside, cooler temperatures, artificial light in addition to the sunlight which comes through the window, and even a breeze will help. Fancy expensive lights are not needed. Regular fluorescent lights are sufficient.

As soon as the weather warms, "harden off" the seedlings by putting them outside in the sunshine and breeze for several days before transplanting them into the garden. Of course, bring the seedlings inside during windstorms or freezing temperatures.

Rotate crops

All authorities on vegetables agree that vegetables should not be planted in the same place year after year. Insects, diseases, and even nutritional problems can be made much worse when the same crop is grown on the same spot every year. Ideally, vegetables should be planted in the same spot no more often than every third season.

May I use seed left from last year?

Seed decreases in germination percentage as it ages. Older seed, even if it germinates, can produce weaker plants. Seed quality is important to gardening success. Last year's seed will probably be okay, but seed more than two years old might be disappointing.

Choosing varieties

Area greenhouses usually have a good stock of the old favorites which have worked in our area for years and years.

However, there are thousands of vegetable varieties. No greenhouse can be expected to carry them all. Find what works. Talk to other gardeners. The vegetable world changes year by year. Old favorites sometimes develop problems. New varieties don't always live up to their hype. If it works for you, stick with it until it goes away.

Watering

Vegetable gardens need about one inch of moisture per week. Watering by hand does little good. Soaking the garden once per week with a sprinkler *in the morning* is the best strategy, unless your soil is very sandy in which case more frequent watering will help, and will certainly never hurt.

Wetting the surface of the soil daily does more harm than good. Dig down into the soil after you have watered to make sure that the moisture penetrates deeply. Soaker hoses have the advantage of not wetting the foliage, and therefore do not encourage disease.

Weeding

Weeding is a must. Don't plant what you can't weed. Weeds increase disease. They choke out the veggies. They reflect badly on the gardener's character. And they look awful.

Adding peat or compost will make weeding much easier by softening the soil surface.

Weeding can be made easier by weeding soon after the crust forms on the soil following a rain. If the soil is as soft as it should be, long sweeps of the hoe will kill thousands of weeds barely visible to the eye. Waiting two weeks will multiply the necessary work by at least ten times.

Do not use chemical weed control in the vegetable garden. Do not spray herbicides *anywhere near* the vegetable garden during the growing season, particularly broadleaf lawn weed killers. Soft-leaved vegetables are more sensitive to spray than any other plant in the yard.

Furry Pests

The most formidable pests in the northern vegetable garden are furry animals, usually deer, but frequently rabbits, woodchucks, and when the corn ripens, raccoons. There are no easy solutions. An electric fence a few inches off the ground can keep out rabbits and raccoons, but it takes a seven-foot high fence made of chicken netting or of seven electrified wires to insure that the deer stay out.

Ammonia based sprays smell unpleasant enough to repel deer, woodchucks and rabbits—if they are not already in the habit of eating in that area. Ammonia sprays using household ammonia mixed as you would for cleaning do not hurt the vegetable plants, and can be sprayed on and around the plants without harming the plant or fruit.

Most of the household remedies, such as human hair or bars of soap, work some of the time, which means none of them work *all* the time.

Insects

Insects in the vegetable garden cause consternation, sometimes panic. Sprays work, but not always. Some insects such as the Colorado potato beetle have developed immunity and require new insecticides every few years. Organic farmers pick potato beetles off the foliage, or use vacuums, and it isn't as difficult as it sounds.

Do not use just any insecticide on the garden. Make sure the chemical is labeled on the bottle for use on plants which will eventually be eaten. Be careful. We don't want our grandchildren to have eyes in the middle of their forehead.

There are non-chemical methods of insect prevention and control. Tilling the soil in the fall turns up beds of insect eggs which will then be killed by the cold. White *row cover*, a form of cloth designed for gardens, thrown over plants from the cabbage family will prevent worms by keeping away the white butterflies which lay eggs on the plant. Grubs and cutworms which go after young plants can be prevented by adequate tilling in fall and early spring.

Diseases

Various tomato diseases cause the bulk of disease complaints in the northern garden. These problems are discussed later in this chapter. Disease on other vegetables are less frequent and less troubling. For the most part, if the garden is placed in the open sunshine, if plants are spaced properly, and if overhead watering is limited to the early morning, diseases will not be a problem.

Fall clean up

Clean all foliage off the garden in the fall to prevent diseases and insects from breeding in the dead plant matter. Tilling the garden soil in the fall helps kill the eggs of potential pests. Till in new organic matter rather than tilling the old plant matter into the soil.

It is tempting to allow the garden to decline in late summer, but whatever weeding is done in late summer will decrease the number of weed seeds left to germinate next spring.

TOMATOES

Northern gardeners seem more passionate about tomatoes than any other vegetable. The first tomato of the season tastes the best, it seems. Tomato aficionados have well-developed methods for getting the first tomato to ripen by early July. Most of these methods include a lot of unnecessary labor. However, building fortresses of plastic around tomatoes that they planted far too early is a way for some area gardeners to work off the energy stored up over winter.

When is it safe to plant tomatoes?

This most common gardening question has a simple answer: Tomatoes should not be planted until after the last frost. Of course, you can never know the date of the last frost, but planting Memorial Day weekend, even though it seems late, is quite safe. Tomatoes planted before the soil warms up don't make much progress anyway. They are probably better off growing in the greenhouse until the weather warms. Tomatoes take no frost whatsoever.

Avoid common tomato problems

Tomato leaf diseases occur when conditions are right. Diseases occur when moisture is allowed to stay on the leaves for more than a couple of hours. To prevent moisture from gathering, give tomatoes plenty of space. Make sure they are planted in full sun. Plant them where they will get plenty of breeze. Perhaps stake them, or grow them in a cage to keep the foliage raised above the ground. Place grass clippings around the base of the plant to keep the soil from splashing up on the leaves during watering or rain. *Never use grass clippings from a lawn which has been sprayed with herbicide.* Water them in the early morning so the foliage dries quickly. Water underneath the plants rather than overhead if at all possible.

The spores which produce tomato leaf disease are ever-present. The above measures can prevent those spores from taking off and causing disease. By the time the leaves have started to deteriorate, it is probably too late to address the problem with sprays. *Prevention is the best cure for tomato leaf diseases.*

Fertilizing tomatoes

Too much nitrogen will cause tomatoes to produce lots of green growth and few fruits. Avoid planting tomatoes in manure, and avoid fertilizing with fertilizers high in nitrogen. A balanced garden fertilizer such as a 10-10-10 can be tilled in to the soil before planting for best results. If the soil is already rich in nitrogen (an old barnyard), add superphosphate only to help create a balance between the two elements.

Purchasing and planting tomatoes

Try to purchase stout, short, dark green plants. If tomato transplants are long and lanky, pinch off the lower leaves and plant the tomato several inches deeper than it was in the pot. If the plant is very lanky, the tomato can be laid in a trench leaving the top six inches of the plant exposed. Pinch the leaves off the buried portion of the stem. The tomato will develop new roots along the buried portions of the stem. It is not wise to pinch the tips of tomatoes back on most varieties.

Plant tomatoes in a depression at least the size of a serving dish and fill the depression with fertilized water after planting. Remember, tomato plants grow to be huge in the north due to all the sunshine—give each plant a space at least six feet wide.

SWEET CORN

To aid in pollination, it is best to plant sweet corn in blocks with rows of different varieties next to each other rather than in one long row. Plant one row each of three or four varieties with staggered ripening dates to prolong your season. Harvesting the corn just before the meal will insure the sweetest tasting corn, as the sugar in the kernels turns to starch rapidly after harvest.

SALADS AND GREENS

Leaf lettuce from area gardens is scrumptious, but head lettuce seldom forms heads once the hot weather hits. Spinach is best seeded early and used before hot weather hits. Another seeding in August can produce a fall crop. Celery is seldom rewarding for gardeners in our area.

Greens like prolonged cool weather. Plant them, realizing that the same cool conditions which hinder fruiting vegetables *help* the leafy vegetables.

POTATOES

Potatoes are raised by planting seed potatoes. Potatoes sold as seed are generally certified disease free and have not been treated, as many supermarket potatoes have, to prevent the eyes from growing.

If the ground is too cold, the newly planted seed potatoes will rot. A rule of thumb: if you can stand to sit bare-bottomed on the ground for one minute, it is warm enough to plant potatoes.

One pound of seed potatoes should produce ten pounds at harvest.

ROOT CROPS

If you don't have time to individually sow the seeds of root crops such as beets, carrots and parsnips, thinning the seedlings after they emerge is essential to getting roots of any size later in the season. Eliminate the weak plants first, then take out enough remaining seedlings so each plant has at least two inches of space.

ONIONS

Set onions produce an early crop, but produce onions which don't keep very long. For keeper onions, plant seedlings, which are available in bundles or in pacs. They look frail and floppy, like individual strands of grass, at planting, but they quickly rise to the occasion producing big, firm onions.

COLE CROPS

Cole crops are members of the cabbage family, namely broccoli, cauliflower, brussels sprouts, cabbage and kohlrabi. Cole crops tend to have powder blue leaves, and they have separate requirements from other vegetables.

Cole crops are usually started inside. Because cole crops can take a little frost, it is safe to put them in the northern prairie garden the week after Mother's Day. Cole crops grow better in cool weather. A hot summer can cause cole crops to bolt, which means they develop more bloom than fruit. There is nothing to be done. Brussel sprouts are the cole crop most vulnerable to hot weather, which causes them to produce loose heads which taste pretty bad.

MELONS

To get ripe melons before the first frost, it helps to start melons inside in early May for setting out into the garden after Memorial Day—or purchase transplants.

Melons respond to warm soil, and can grow faster if planted in a plastic mulch. Simply lay down a three-foot wide strip of clear poly on the row, burying the edges with soil. Cut a cross into the plastic in order to plant the melon. Plastic mulch heats the soil and keeps down the weeds.

Melons planted in cold ground can rot off at the base and simply disappear. It does not pay to plant melons in the ground too early.

Muskmelon fruit are ripe when the stem easily separates from the fruit. Watermelons are ripe when you thump them and they sound dull, like you are thumping your shoe, instead of sounding hollow.

CUCUMBERS

Cucumbers can become bitter if they 1) lack adequate sunshine 2) lack adequate water and 3) lack adequate nutrition. With those three problems remedied by proper soil preparation, weeding and watering, cucumbers will produce prolific crops on the northern prairie.

SQUASH AND PUMPKINS

Squash and pumpkins transplants—or seedlings—should be planted late in May. They will take off with hot weather, but not before. Allow plenty of space, as much as ten feet per hill. During our long summer days, squash and pumpkin vines *travel.*

PEAS

The most common problem with peas on the northern prairie is the seed rotting in cool, wet ground when planted early. Wait until the ground warms. A later, second planting of peas can yield a second crop.

BEANS

Plant beans in the garden as per directions on the package. Wait for crop.

PEPPERS

Peppers thrive in a hot summer, but heat isn't absolutely necessary. Their increased popularity, due to the salsa craze, has led to the introduction of dozens of new varieties. However, one should always start with the good old green pepper. They are so good off the plant that you can eat them like apples!

GROUNDCHERRIES

Please find one of these plants (all you need is one) and help preserve the grand northern prairie groundcherry tradition. Make grandma proud.

You can save the seed—one little fruit contains hundreds of seeds—from year-to-year.

Groundcherry fruit can be used in chutneys. Or, simply pop the beautiful, marble-sized fruit out of its husk right in the garden and enjoy the completely unique, butterscotch flavor.

313

SUMMARY

This chapter is short for a reason: the best knowledge of vegetable gardening comes from trial and error. Each gardener comes up with their own set of rules, and usually all of them work—no matter how goofy.

Following the above basic principles will give every vegetable plant *the best chance* of not just surviving, but thriving, and bearing bountifully.

New vegetable gardeners should simply dive in and get to work. Successful vegetable gardening on the northern prairie is not complicated. More than anything, it is good exercise.

CHAPTER 23

The Prairie Lawn

First, let us quash the expectations of lawn perfection created by golf courses and professional ball fields. High-class golf courses have perfect turf because they are maintained by full-time professionals with degrees in turf management who work daily to keep their dominion perfect. No homeowner can expect to replicate those results without similar effort and knowledge.

In fact, nobody should want to. Because golf courses and ballfields must drain quickly after irrigation and rain to allow for quick resumption of play, they must be watered, and treated with chemical fertilizers and herbicides, at a frequency that would wear a homeowner out. The perfection attained with such constant care comes at a high cost in time, money and chemical.

For the homeowner on the prairie, attaining and maintaining a beautiful lawn is much easier. Most of the original prairie consisted of grasses, after all.

Lawn success can be whittled down to the following:

•Start with good soil

•Fertilize moderately each year

•Water deeply when needed, at a rate of at least 1 inch per week.

The above three steps work to create healthy grass. Then, additional benefits flow: *Healthy grass will choke out most weeds.* Yes, if your lawn is fertilized and watered properly, and growing in good soil, you need not use chemical weed killers.

Preparing the soil before planting a lawn

Grass is tough, but it doesn't grow just anywhere. A healthy layer of at least four inches of top soil is necessary for grass to truly thrive. Planting grass or laying sod on hard clay or junky gravel doesn't work.

When building a new home, make sure your contractor understands the need for topsoil. Sandy loam is ideal. Any soil which forms hard lumps is a poor investment, and a sign of negligence on the part of whoever hauled it in.

The soil should be carefully graded. Make sure the land slopes away from the house *before* you establish a lawn!

Eliminate clumps either with a garden rake or by going over the lawn with a roller behind a tractor. Such implements are often available for rent.

Effort expended picking the tree roots, junk and rocks before seeding the lawn saves money, heartache and time later when the mower hits hard objects.

If you choose to put in a sprinkler system, do so before the lawn is seeded.

Fertilizing before planting

It is a good idea to till 10-10-10 fertilizer into the soil before planting the grass or seed. Phosphorous and potassium work best if mixed into the soil rather than being applied from the top. Additional nitrogen in the form of ammonium sulfate (20-0-0) can be applied just before seeding or sodding.

Seeding vs. Sodding

Sod provides an instant lawn, but is much more expensive and more work than planting a lawn from seed. Many people assume that sod will grow anywhere, but the soil must be just as prepared for sod as it is for seeding. *Daily watering during the first season is essential to the survival of sod.*

When is the best time to seed a lawn?

The simplest and most effective time of year to seed a new lawn is early to mid-September. The weather has cooled, but with some moisture, the grass will still sprout enough to power through the winter.

With September seeding, there is far less chance that hot weather will dry out the soil and cause the young, shallow-rooted lawn to die. A lawn seeded in September will be thin and wispy in late October, but by June you will have to start mowing, and by July or August the lawn can look fully established.

The second-best time to seed a lawn is early spring, as soon as the soil can be worked without forming lumps. May is a particularly good time to seed small areas, cover them with straw and use a sprinkler to get the grass established. Such spot-seeding can look mature by mid-July.

What type of grass seed mix works best?

In sunshine, Kentucky bluegrass works the best on the northern prairie. For shadier areas, purchase a special shade mix that contains creeping red fescue.

How deeply should the grass seed be planted?

Grass seed can be spread on the surface and raked in with a leaf rake.

How thickly do I spread the seed?

Kentucky bluegrass can be seeded at a rate of 1-2 pounds per 1000 square feet. Fescue mixes, which contain larger seeds, should be seeded at roughly 4 pounds per 1000 square feet.

Overdoing it a bit hurts nothing but your pocketbook, as long as the grass seed is evenly distributed.

Bluegrass seed requires some exposure to light in order to germinate, so do not rake the seed in too deeply—not more than one-half inch.

Care in the weeks after seeding

If you seed a lawn during the hot summer months, or if you are unable to water the newly seeded lawn regularly daily, it is best to spread straw over the freshly seeded area. Straw shades the young grass, and also preserves the moisture near the soil surface. After a few weeks, the straw can be removed, or you may simply grind up the straw with the mower and allow it to settle into the lawn.

New lawns seeded in the spring or summer require daily watering during hot sunny weather. It is best to use a sprinkler.

On a new lawn, take care not to leave the sprinkler on so long that the soil begins to erode and the grass seed is carried away in the run-off.

Early on, water often—as in daily, but not for a long time each watering. This will allow the grass seed to germinate without washing it away. The soil surface should not be allowed to form a crust between waterings during this crucial early stage.

As the lawn establishes itself, leave the sprinkler on long enough for the water to reach several inches below the surface. Dig down to see how far the water has penetrated. Water less often. Deep watering encourages the roots of the grass to penetrate deep into the ground.

Lawns need about an inch of water per week to stay in peak condition.

Initial mowing

Mow for the first time when the fine grass gets to be about three inches high. Mowing early on is important as it helps give grass an advantage over the weeds due to the fact that mowing *strengthens* grass but *weakens* most weeds.

Fertilizing established lawns

Fertilizing with nitrogen makes a huge improvement in a lawn's vigor and color. Ammonium sulfate is the most affordable and safe way to fertilize lawns. Lawn fertilizers are always high in nitrogen, as that is what grass needs.

One fertilization per year is better than none. At the very maximum, a lawn can absorb four pounds of nitrogen per 1,000 square feet per year, applied at a rate of no more than one pound at a time. However, more than two applications of fertilizer is probably excessive.

Grass should be dry when the fertilizer is applied to prevent the granules from dissolving on the leaves.

Recent research indicates that it is best to wait until early summer when the grass is growing vigorously for the first application of fertilizer.

CONTROLLING WEEDS

Mowing a lawn regularly and fertilizing with nitrogen will eventually result in the grass crowding out other weeds. Grass generally prevails if given the chance as most broadleaf weeds are unable to compete with healthy grass.

Weeds will increase during drought if the lawn is not watered. Weeds can also dominate grass in poor, rocky soils.

Dandelions and Other Broadleaf Weeds

The only quick way to get rid of dandelions in one's lawn is to use a broad-leaf herbicide. Such a chemical is best applied in May.

Broad-leaf herbicides can seriously injure or kill trees, shrubs, annuals and perennials. For that reason, it is best to apply the herbicide after the weather has warmed, but before trees and shrubs have put on leaves, before perennials have begun to sprout, and before annuals are planted.

There are several types of lawn weed killers on the market, including granular "weed and feed" mixtures. Such mixtures of fertilizer and granular herbicide can be effective if spread evenly.

Never apply weed and feed mixes to a flower or vegetable garden.

However, please consider not using the weed-and-feed mixes. They are volatile and do not store well. Who knows what fumes they give off in the garage. Fertilize with pure fertilizer, and if you find it necessary to use broadleaf herbicides, do so separately, and in a targeted manner.

The risks of broadleaf weed killers

Broadleaf herbicides have done a tremendous amount of harm to trees, shrubs and garden plants over the years. The chemicals are volatile, and if the weather is right they can move around to other areas of the yard even hours *after* the spray has been applied.

Broadleaf herbicides are difficult to wash out of the sprayer. Even the slightest residue can hurt tender-leafed annuals such as tomatoes. We have seen instances where an entire yard of shrubs and trees have been killed by a sprayer which wasn't thoroughly washed.

We are not blindly opposed to all chemicals, but broadleaf herbicides sprayed on lawns have done so much damage to trees and shrubs over the years that the responsible home-owner might consider just getting along without them all together.

Creeping Charlie

There is no known effective way to get rid of the tenacious creeping Charlie except to kill off the entire lawn with herbicide and start from scratch. Broad-leaf herbicides to not touch the plant.

A solution of Borax and water was once rumored to work, but if you put on a little too much, it will kill the lawn. Borax also lingers in the soil. It is no longer recommended.

When we encounter things we can do nothing about, it is just as well to learn to live with them. Such is the case with creeping charlie. It has pretty, purple blooms and somewhat attractive round leaves. Some savvy types have renamed creeping charlie "ground ivy." And what a scent when you mow it!

Clover

Broad-leaf herbicides are not effective on clover. It is best to accept clover in one's lawn and enjoy it. Sprays which control the clover family are dangerous to shrubs and trees.

Moss

Moss generally grows where grass wouldn't grow anyway, therefore the presence of moss does not mean that grass is being crowded out.

Moss is beautiful, and impossible for the gardener to purposefully establish. Enjoy it where it appears!

Mushrooms

Mushrooms usually pop up where there is some decaying wood, such as where a tree stump has been ground up. It is not worthwhile to apply fungicide. When the weather gets dry, the shrooms will go away, and in a few years the wood will have decayed to the point where mushrooms won't grow.

One can hasten the decay process by applying a nitrogen fertilizer such as ammonium sulfate.

Find pictures online of the distinctive shaggy-cap mushroom, which can flourish on lawns in late summer. Once you have identified them, *fry them up for breakfast.*

Rival Grasses

Quack grass is set back and soon overwhelmed by bluegrass when the lawn is consistently mowed, fertilized and watered.

Crabgrass, distinguished by its broad blades which radiate out from a central crown, is common in some parts of the country, and can become a problem in our area during a hot, dry summer. Crabgrass killer can be applied in the first part of May. However, watering and fertilizing will encourage the bluegrass enough to manage the problem nicely without chemical.

CREATURES

Really Green Spots

Dogs, by repeatedly adding nitrogen in concentrated places, create spots of vigorous, dark green grass. Spread fertilizer to even things out.

Nightcrawlers

Nightcrawlers (big earthworms) make mounds in the lawn which can make it difficult to walk on the lawn, or even mow it. There is no legal chemical cure for nightcrawlers, but they do tend to move on after a year or so.

In fact, a certain amount of worms are good for lawns. One can rake down the mounds with a harrow, or some other implement. The problem of an occasional mass infestation is troubling, but temporary. Encourage neighbor children to dig and sell the nightcrawlers for bait.

Grubs

Grubs themselves create little lumps in the lawn, but the real problem arises when the skunks come to dig up the grubs for dinner. Wait for the problem to go away, which it will, once the skunks do their job.

LAWN MAINTENANCE

Growing grass in the shade

It is very difficult to get a good stand of grass in areas where there is less than 50% sunlight throughout the day, particularly under the shade of trees, which also rob the grass of nutrients with their roots. Grass mixes containing fescue are best for shade. It also helps to let the grass in the shade grow to about three inches rather than keeping it short. Taller grass will have more leaf area to collect more sunlight, and probably will be healthier. If grass refuses to grow, consider a ground cover such as *lamium.*

Lawn clippings and leaves

It is always better to grind up the leaves and grass clippings and let them settle into the lawn than to put them in a pile off to the side.

Aerating

On heavy, hard-packed soils, a lawn can benefit from aeration. Machines can be rented. If open spots of ground appear where nothing is growing, not even weeds, aeration may be the solution.

Late-season mowing

Some people like to let the grass grow longer after Labor Day. More leaf surface means stronger roots going into winter.

Winter damage

Lawns can emerge from the melting snowpack looking pretty rough. There may be spots of mold. Circles may be dead due to winter-time dog or husband leakage. Don't worry. The lawn will quickly recover.

If by the end of May a spot is still barren, then it may be time to rake the area enough to loosen the soil and add some seed.

On the northern prairie, there is never any reason to spray fungicides on home lawns.

324

Starting over

If you have an infestation of weeds which just won't go away, or if the weeds are resistant to herbicide, or if the grass just doesn't seem to get going, it may pay to kill of the entire lawn with glyphosate and start over. That would be a good time to add some better soil as well.

Take your time with this project. Allow the weeds to regrow a time or two between glyphosate applications for better long-term results.

A

Acer · 110
Acer ginnala · 147
Acer negundo · 119
Acer platanoides · 110
Acer rubrum · 12, 110
Acer saccharinum · 111
Acer saccharum · 111
Achillea · **292**
Aesculus glabra · 117
ageratum · **249**
Ainus hirsute · 124
Ajuga · **292**
Alcea · 297
Alchemilla · **293**
alder, Prairie Horizon · **124**
Allium · **293**
alpine currant · 62
  foundation planting · 129
  north side · 27
  trimming · 134
alyssum · **249**
amaranthus · 68, **250**
Amelanchier · 222
American Bittersweet · **195**
American cranberry · 151
ammonia · 78, 83, 307
ammonium sulfate · 42, 43, 51, 71, 275
  application · 43
  arborvitae · 167
  lawn · 317, 320
  maple · 111
  roses · 236
  spruce · 160
  tree stump · 322
Amur chokecherry · **118**
  sapsuckers · 82
Angel's Trumpet · 254
annuals · 2, 5, 53, 76, **240**
  bedding plants · 240
  cool- vs heat-loving · 270
  cutting grown · 244

dead-heading · 246
disease · 57
fertilizing · 245
glyphosate · 242
landscaping, uses · 131
north side · 27
novelty · **264**
planting · 242
pots · 247
seed · 244
self-seeding · 240
vegetative reproduction · 244
watering · 245
when to plant · 242
wind · 29
anthracnose · 61, 116
aphids · 64
apple tree varieties
  Centennial · 200, **205**
  Chestnut · 200, **206**
  crabapple · 199
  dwarf · 200
  Goodland · **207**
  Haralson · **206**
  Honeycrisp · 12, 112, **207**
  Red Duchess · **209**
  Sweet Sixteen · **209**
  Wodarz · **209**
  Zestar · **208**
apples · 198, 199
  calcium deficiency · 208
  chlorosis · 33
  dwarf · 13
  fertilizer · 200
  fire blight · 200, 204
  flavor · 3
  frost · 202
  fruit size · 203
  fungus · 208
  iron deficiency · 200
  latex paint · 208
  maggots · 58
  north wind · 11
  pollination · 202

protection · 203
  pruning · 204
  russeted · 206
  soil pH · 33
  sun scald · 199, 207
  water sprouts · 204
  wormy · 203
apricots · **213**
  buds · 9
  Moongold · 214
  north wind · 11
  Scout · 214
  Sungold · 214
  Wescot · 214
Aquilegia · **293**
arborvitae · **164**
  American · **166**
  cedar-apple rust · 168
  dwarfed globe · **166**
  fertilizing · 167
  Holmstrup · **166**
  Little Elfie · 166
  Little Giant · 166
  planting · 167
  pyramidal · 20, 129, **164**
  red spider mites · 167
  Siberian · **169**
  Techny · 20, 128, **165**, 168
    hedge · 178
  winter burn · 168
Aronia · 138
artemisia · **277**
Asclepias · **294**
ash
  anthracnose · 116
  black ash · 25, **115**
  emerald ash borer · 25, 109, 115
  green ash · 11, 60, 61, 88, 99, 109,
    115, 186
  mountain ash · 24, 59, 60, 82, **102**
asparagus · 26, **217**
aspen · 20
  quaking · **116**
  Swedish columnar · **123**
aster yellows · 63
Asteraceae · **294**
asters, annual · **264**
asters, perennial · **294**
  foundation planting · 130
astilbe · **278**
  north side · 27

Autumn Blaze maple · 12, 110, 112
Autumn Joy Sedum · 276, 291

B

baby's breath · **278**
bacopa · **264**
Bailey Nurseries · 2
barberry · 130, **136**
bare root · 17, 88, 91
  hedges · 181
  planting depth · 92
  watering · 51
bark
  black · 122, 190
  bronze · 118, 219
  cambium layer · 79, 105, 201
  corky · 120
  damaged · 83
  glossy black with white · 122
  orange · 30, 172, 188
  protection · 79, 93
  red · 190
  smooth · 11, 79, 180
  white · 31, 117
  white-striped · 219
basswood (linden) · 86, 90, 109
  American · **103**
  boulevard · 24
  European · 103
  European, Norlin · 104
  sapsuckers · 82
beans · **313**
beaver · 80
bee balm · 288
  See also · monarda
begonia · 2
  fibrous · **250**
  tuberous · 64, **250**
  wind · 29
bell flower · 294
  See also · *Campanula*
Berberis · 136
Bergeson Ash · 88
Bergeson Dogwood · 141
Bergeson Gardens · 246, 248
Bergeson Nursery · 208
Betula papyrifera · 105
Betula pendula · 107

birch
    bronze birch borer · 105
    clump · 106
    cutleaf weeping · **107**
    Dakota Pinnacle · 107
    white paper · **105**
    winter interest · 31
Bittersweet, American · **195**
Black Hills Spruce · 163
black knot · 63
Black Walnut · 86, **123**, 215
Black-eyed Susan · 254, **269**, **290**
    See also · rudbeckia
Blazing Star Liatrus · 297
bleeding heart · **279**
    foundation planting · 130
    north side · 27
    wind · 29
blood meal · 83
blueberries · 216, 222
Bordeaux mix · 60
botrytis · 13, 289
boulevards
    black ash · 115
    stress · 24
broadleaf herbicides · 34, 321
    2-4D · 70
broccoli · 3, 312
bronze birch borer · 105
brussels sprouts · 312
buckthorn · 68
bugleweed · 292
bur oak · 30
butterfly plant · 294
    See also · Asclepias

C

cabbage · 3, 312
cables, underground · 25
cactus · 5
calendula · **264**
calibrachoa · **265**
cambium layer · 79
Campanula · **294**
Canadian Red Chokecherry
    black knot · 63
canna · **265**

Caragana frutex 'Globosa' · 137
caragana, common
    hedge · 177
    windbreak · 191
caragana, globe · **137**
    foundation planting · 129
    hedge · 181
castor bean · 241, **251**
Catalpa · 86, **124**
catmint · 298
    See also · *Nepeta*
cauliflower · 312
cedar, red · **171**
cedar-apple rust · 168, 171
Celastrus scandens · 195
celosia · **251**
Celtis occidentalis · 120
chemicals
    farmers · 54
    farmland · 25
cherries · **214**, **218**
    Bali or Evans · **214**, **219**
    buds · 9
    Carmine Jewel · 219
    Nanking · **218**
    Romeo and Juliet · 219
chlorosis · 33, 110
    chlorotic · 44
    See also · iron deficiency
chokeberry · **138**
chokecherry, Amur · **118**
chokecherry, red leaf · **118**
    black knot · 119
Christmas trees · 171
Chrysanthemum · 280
citric acid · 55
city water · 55
clematis · **196**, **280**
    Jackmanii · 280
cleome · **252**
clover · 322
cockscomb · 251
cole crops · **312**
coleus · **252**
Colorado Spruce · 163
columbine · 293
compost · 34
Concordia College · 103
Coral Bells · **281**
corn · **310**

Cornus · 140
Cornus alba · 141
Cornus alternifolia · 119
cosmos · **253**
cotoneaster · 59, **138**
   diseases · 138
   hedge · 177
   trimming · 134
Cotoneaster acutifolia · 138
cottonwood · 47, 86, 186
   foundation damage · 25
   hybrid · 113
   septic system · 25
   wind · 30
crabapple · 199
   apple scab · 108
   flowering · **107**
crabgrass · 323
cranberry · **218**
   American · **139**, 218
   Compact American · **139**
Crataegus · 124
creeping charlie · 321
Crystal Palace lobelia · 259
cucumbers · **312**
currant, Alpine · **140**
cutworms · 67

D

dahlia, dinner plate · **253**
dahlia, dwarf · **253**
daisy · **253**
   Gerbera · **265**
   Painted · **295**
   Shasta · 13, **295**
damping off · 64
datura · **254**
daylily · **282**
   foundation planting · 130
Dead Nettle · **287**
   See also · lamium
deciduous · 77, 88, 100
deciduous conifers · 173
deer · 76–79, 83
   fruit trees · 76
   shade trees · 76
delphinium · **283**
desiccation · 162

dianthus · **254, 283**
Dicentra · 279
Dictamnus · 296
Digitalis · 266
disease · 59
   anthracnose · 61, 116
   aster yellows · 63
   black knot · 63, 119
   botrytis · 13, 289
   Dutch elm · 61
   fire blight · 59–60, 98, 103, 108, 200
   fungus · 49, 54, 57, 61, 63
   leaf-drop · 61
   oak wilt · 62
   powdery mildew · 62
   prevention · 57
dogs · 84, 168, 323
dogwood · 20, 79
   hedge · 177
   pagoda · 23, **119**
      north wind · 11
   propane tank · 19
   windbreak · 190, 193
dogwood, Bergeson · 141
dogwood, red twig · **140**
   foundation planting · 128
   hedge · 180
   winter interest · 31
dogwood, variegated · **141**
   Ivory Halo · 141
   trimming · 134
drosophila
   Spotted Wing · 67
Dusty Miller · **265**
Dutch elm virus · 109

E

Echinacea · 284
Elaeagnus angustifolia · 122
elder, box · **119**
elderberry · 216, **220**
elm · 86
   American · 61, **109**
   boulevard · 24
   Dutch elm virus · 109
   Princeton · 61, 109
   Siberian · 185, 191
   St. Croix · 109

emerald ash borer · 25, 60, 109, 186
  black ash · 115
  green ash · 115
Engelmann Ivy · **194**
Euonymus alata · 142
Euonymus, "Burning Bush" · **142**
Eupatorium · **295**
Euphorbia marginata · 300
evergreens · 156
  ammonium sulfate · 45
  conifers · 156
  deciduous · 156, 173
  desiccation · 162
  non-coniferous · 156
  winter burn · 162
extension service · 1, 61, 67, 163, 216

F

fall cleaning · 58
fall color · 103, 110, 117, 122, 124, 135, 138, 139, 140, 142, 147, 149, 154, 177, 194, 195, 217, 232
fall fertilizing · 41
ferns · **284**
  Japanese Painted Fern · 284
  Lady · 284
  Maidenhair · 284
  Ostrich · 284
  wind · 29
fertilizer · 38
  acidifying · 33, 45, 111, 172
  ammonium sulfate · 42
  berry patch · 41
  bone meal · 40
  farm · 39
  flower beds · 41
  granular · 44, 51
  iron chelate · 44
  nitrogen · 39, 43
  numbers · 39
  phosphate · 39, 41, 43
  potash · 39, 41, 43
  potassium · 39, 41
  reproductive growth · 38
  spikes · 44
  superphosphate · 40
  urea · 39

  vegetable gardens · 41
  vegetative growth · 38
  water soluble · 51
fir trees · **173**
fire blight · 59–60, 98, 103, 108, 200
Flame Willow · 25, 193
flower beds
  fall preparation · 58, 72
  fertilizer · 51
  glyphosate · 70
  watering · 53
flowering crab · 3, 14
  boulevard · 24
  deer · 77
  fireblight · 59
  pruning · 97, 98
  seedlings · **189**
  sun scald · 11
Flowering Plum · 24
Forsythia, Meadowlark · **142**
  hedge · **177**
foundation
  damage · 25
foxglove · **266**
Fragaria · 226
Fraxinus nigra · 115
Fraxinus pennsylvanica · 115
friability, soil · 38
fruit trees · 87, 198–215
fruit, non-hardy
  blueberries · 4
  kiwi · 4
  peaches · 4
fuchsia · **266**
full sun, definition · 28
  annuals · 242
fungicide · 63
fungus
  anthracnose · 61
  black knot · 63
  cedar-apple rust · 168
  prevention · 49, 54, 57

G

gall · 66
garden mums · 276
gas plant · **296**

geraniums
    hardy · 296
    landscaping · 131
    planters · 18
    Regal · **256**
        See also · Martha Washington
    scented · **257**
    seedling · 256
    zonal · **255**
Gingko · 86
girdled trunk · 79, 82
Gleditsia · 124
glyphosate · 44, 69, 73, 94, 95, 164, 181,
    187, 223, 274, 296, 299, 325
    See also · Roundup
    vegetables · 304
    wicking · 70
Goldsturm · 269, 290
gooseberry · 216, **221**
    Pixwell · 221
    powdery mildew · 62
graft · **88**
    planting depth · 92
    roses · 21, 233, 234
    suckers · 98
grafting · 13, 87
grapes · **196**, 216, **220**
    Beta · 220
    flavor · 3
    King of the North · 220
    pruning · 10
    Valiant · 220
    viticulture · 220
grass, ornamental · 3
    annual · **266**
    blue oat grass · 285
    Flame Grass · 285
    Karl Foerster · 285
    Miscanthus · 285
    Panicum · 285
    perennial · **285**
grasses, undesirable
    crabgrass · 323
    quack grass · 322
groundcherries · **313**
growing medium · 37
grubs · 323
Gymnocladus dioica · 124
Gypsophila · 278

H

hackberry · **120**
hail · 60, 63
hardening off · 29, 306
Hawthorne · **124**
hedges · 176–82
    bare root · 181
    hedge-grade plants · 181
    planting · 181
hedges, formal · 176
    Alpine Currant · 176
    bridalwreath spirea · 178
    caragana · 177
    cotoneaster · 177
    dogwood · 177
    Meadowlark forsythia · 177
    Miss Kim dwarf lilac · 177
    Techny arborvitae · 178
    trimming · 178
hedges, informal · 179
    Amur maple · 180
    Canadian, Villosa · 179
    dogwood, Bergeson · 180
    dogwood, red twig · 180
    Globe caragana · 181
    lilac · 179
    potentilla · 180
    roses · 180
    spirea, old fashioned · 180
heliotrope · **266**
Hemerocallis · 282
Hen and Chicks · 297
    See also · *Sempervivum*
herbicides
    broadleaf · 34, 71, 321
    lawn · 70
    pre-emergent · 71
Heuchera · 281
hollyhock · **297**
Honeycrisp · 12, 112
Honeylocust · 86, **124**
honeysuckle
    aphids · 65
    common · 65
    vine · 65, **195**
    witch's broom · 191
hosta · 66, 275, **286**
    deer · 78
    foundation planting · 130

north side · 27
under trees · 28
humidity · 11, 62
hummingbirds · 195
hydrangea · 19, 45, **143**
ammonium sulfate · 45
blue · 45, 144
Limelight · 144
north side · 27
Pee-Gee type · 144
Quick Fire · 145
winter interest · 31
Hydrangea arborescens · 143
Hydrangea paniculata · 144
hydrangea, old-time
Annabelle · 143
Snowhill · 143

I

impatiens · 2, 242, **257**
deer · 78
New Guinea · 64, **258**
north side · 27
insecticides · 56
aphids · 64, 65, 139, 151, 236
aster yellows · 64
drosophila · 67
leafhoppers · 64, 249
roses · 236
spider mites · 67, 168
vegetables · 308
insects · 3, 56, 308
iris · 276, **286**
Siberian · **287**
Iris sibirica · 287
iron deficiency · 33, 43, 44
iron phosphate · 66
ironwood · **120**

J

Joe Pye Weed · 295
See also · Eupatorium
Juglans nigra · 123, 215
juglone · 123

juneberries · 216, **222**
juniper · **169**
cedar-apple rust · 168
juniper, spreading · 169
foundation planting · 128
Savin · 128, **170**
juniper, upright
Medora · **170**
Juniperus sabina · 170
Juniperus scopulorum · 170

K

kale, flowering · **267**
Kentucky Coffeetree · **124**
kohlrabi · 312

L

Lady's Mantle · 293
Lake Agassiz · 47
lamb's quarters · 75
Lamiastrum · 288
lamium · **287**
north side · 27
under trees · 28
landscape plan · 128
landscapers, professional · 22, 35
landscaping
corner · 20, 164
north side · 27
northeast · 105
south · 137, 165, 294, 297
west · 165
lantana · **267**
larch, Siberian · **173**
lawn · 316–25
fertilizer · 317
fertilizing · 320
herbicides · 70
maintenance · 324
peat · 36
phosphate · 40
seed vs sod · 318
seeding · 318
weeds · 320

leaf gall/warts · 66
leafhopper · 64
   alyssum · 249
Leucanthemum · 295
Liatrus · **297**
lilac · 14
   Japanese tree · 11, **121**
   landscaping · 134
   Villosa · **146**
lilac, Canadian
   Miss Canada · **146**
   Villosa · 179
lilac, common · **145**
   hedge · 179
   Pocahontas · 145
lilac, dwarf · **146**
   Dwarf Korean · 146
   foundation planting · 129
   Miss Kim · 147, 177
lily, day · **282**
   foundation planting · 130
lime · 42
linden · 103
   See also · basswood
lisianthus · **267**
lobelia · **259**
Lombardy poplar · 192
Lonicera x brownii · 195
lungwort · 299
   See also · *Pulmonaria*
lupine · **298**

M

Malus · 107, 199
manure · 37
maple · **110**
   ammonium sulfate · 44, 111
   chlorosis · 33, 110
   cracking bark · 112
   gall · 112
   sapsuckers · 112
   soil · 110
   soil pH · 33
   windbreak · 189
maple, varieties
   Amur compact · **147**

Amur maple
   hedge · 180
   landscaping · 134
   Autumn Blaze · 12, 110, 112
   ginela maple · 189
   Norway maple · 110
   Silver (soft) · 24, 110, **111**
      chlorosis · 112
      foundation damage · 25
      septic system · 25
      soil under · 28
      wind · 30
   Sugar (hard) · 11, 86, 110, **111**
      soil · 111
Marguerite daisy · 254
marigolds · **259**
Martha Washington · 256
   See also · geraniums, Regal
melons · **312**
memorial · 26
Memorial Day · 64, 137, 242, 252, 298, 309, 312
mice · 79, 81
micro-nutrients · 41
Minnesota, University of · 50, 90, 91, 122, 206, 207, 208, 209, 214, 221
   arboretum · 177
Miscanthus grass · 276
Miscanthus sinensis · 285
mites, spider · 66, 167
miticide · 167
mockorange · **148**
   Blizzard · 148
   dwarfed Golden · 148
   Minnesota Snowflake · 148
monarda · **288**
Moonbeam coreopsis · 276
Morden Research Station · 207, 238
morning glory · **267**
moss · 322
moss roses · **260**
Mother's Day · 253, 256
Mountain Ash · 24, 59, **102**
   sapsuckers · 82, 103
mulch · 13
mums · **280**
   winter · 13
mushrooms · 322

N

nannyberry · **148**
   landscaping · 134
nasturtium · **268**
nemesia · **268**
Nepeta · **298**
New Guinea impatiens · 64, **258**
nicotiana · **268**
nightcrawlers · 323
ninebark · 62, 130, **149**
   Diabolo · 149
ninebark, dwarf · 136
nitrogen · 74, 91
   deficiency · 26, 42
   dog urine · 84
   fruits and vegetables · 37
   manure · 37
   vegetative growth · 39
North Dakota State University · 107, 114, 124
Norway Poplar · 193
noxious weeds · 137
nutrients
   micro-nutrients · 41
   stealers · 44, 112, 174
nutrients, soil · 34
   fertilizer · 38
nuts
   black walnut · 215
   butternut · 215
   hazelbert · 215
   hazelnut · 215

O

oak · 20
   aphids · 65
   established trees · 117
   fungus · 65
   gall · 66
   oak wilt · 62
   pruning · 10, 62, 96
oak trees
   bur oak · 30, **121**
   northern pin · **124**
   red oak · 62, **124**
Ogallala strawberry · 227

Ohio Buckeye · **117**
olive, Russian · **122**
onions · **311**
onions, ornamental · 293
orchards · 4, 204
organic matter · 33
ornamental trees · 86
osteospermum · **268**
Ostrya virginiana · 120

P

paint, white latex · 11, 112, 208
pansies · **260**
Papaver · 299
parsley · 131
Parthenocissus inserta · 195
Parthenocissus quinquefolia · 194
pears · **214**
   Early Gold · 214
   Golden Spice · 214
   Ure · 214
peas · **313**
peat · 34
   aerate heavy soil · 34
   cautions · 36
   compost · 35
   fertilizing · 37
   flower beds · 36
   lawn · 36
   Minnesota · 34, 35
   moss · 35
   pH · 34
   sedge · 35
   sphagnum · 35
   weeding · 36
peony · 276, **288**
   botrytis · 13
   phosphate · 289
peony, fern leaf · **298**
peppers · **313**
perennials · 4, 53, 76, 79, 241, **271**
   bare root vs potted · 273
   center die-out · 276
   dead-heading · 275
   disease prevention · 287
   diseases and insects · 276
   dividing · 275

fall cleaning · 58
fertilizing · 275
foundation planting · 130
north side · 27
peat · 35
phosphate · 274
planting and care · 274
root rot · 9, 35, 274, 277
wind · 29
winter · 13
winter cover · 274
winter rot · 12
perennials, minor · 291
petunia, standard · **262**
petunia, trailing · 2, 51, **261**
pH · 62
Philadelphus · 148
phlox
creeping · **290**
upright · **290**
phosphate/phosphorus · 39
Minnesota restriction · 40
peony · 289
reproductive growth · 39
Physocarpus · 149
phytoplasma · 64
pine · **171**
burn · 157
Jack · 173
Mugo · **172**
foundation planting · 130
Norway · 173
Ponderosa · **172**
Scotch · 30, 156, 162, **172**, 188
fertilizer · 172
Pinus mugo · 172
Pinus ponderosa · 172
Pinus sylvestris · 172
planters · 18
plum tree varieties
Compass cherry · **212**
Gracious · 213
La Crescent · 213
Pembina · **213**
Pipestone · **212**
Sapalta cherry · **212**
Superior · 213
Toka · **213**
Underwood · **212**
Waneta · **213**

plum trees, flowering
Princess Kay · **122**
Rose Tree of China · **150**
plums · 198, **209**
black knot · 63
buds · 9
cherry-plum · 209
flavor · 3
frost · 211
hazards · 210
large-fruited · 209
north wind · 11
pollination · 211
rot · 210
shrub · 211
Toka · 211
wild · 210
Ponderosa Pine · **172**
poplar
hybrid · 24, **113**
Lombardy · 113, 123, 186, 192
Norway · 113, 193
Tower · **123**
windbreak · 186
poppy, oriental · **299**
Populus · 113
Populus tremuloides · 116
populus tremuloides 'erecta' · 123
populus x canescens · 123
Portulaca · **260**
potash · 41
potassium · 41
potatoes · **311**
nitrogen · 37
potentilla · **150**
hedge · 180
Katherine Dykes · 151
trimming · 134
Potentilla fruticosa · 150
powdery mildew · 62
power lines · 23
Prairie Horizon alder
wet soil · 25
Prestonian hybrids · 146
primrose
winter · 13
pruning · 96–100
grapes · 10
late-season · 10
water sprouts · 96
wind · 30

Prunus armeniaca · 213
Prunus cerasus · 214, 219
Prunus domestica · 209
Prunus maackii · 118
Prunus nigra Princess Kay · 122
Prunus tomentosa · 218
Prunus triloba · 150
Prunus virginiana · 118
Pulmonaria · **299**
pumpkins · **313**
purple coneflower · 284
purslane · 75
Pyrus · 214

Q

quack grass · 322
Quercus ellipsoidalis · 124
Quercus macrocarpa · 121
Quercus rubra · 124

R

rabbits · 79, 81, 83
raccoons · 83
Radler, Will · 238
raspberries, black · **224**
raspberries, purple · **224**
　Royalty · 224
raspberries, red · **222**
　Boyne · 223
　Caroline · 223
　floricane · 223
　Killarney · 223
　Latham · 223
　primocane · 223
　Red Wing · 223
　suckers · 223
raspberries, yellow · **225**
red cedar · 188
Red Lake currant · 62
Red Leaf Chokecherry · 24, 63, 86
Red River of the North · 123
Red River Valley · 2, 66, 191
Red Splendor · 108
　winter interest · 30

reproduction
　asexual · **88**
　cuttings · 244
　grafting · 87
　pollination · 88
　vegetative · 244
reproductive growth · 38
Rheum · 225
rhubarb · 14, **225**
　foundation planting · 130
Rhus · 154
Ribes · 221
Ribes alpinum · 140
rodents · 76, 79, 93
　voles · 12
root crops · **311**
rootstock · 88, 98
　dwarfing · 13, 200
　standard · 200
Rose Tree of China · 150
roses · 59, **228**
　bare root · 232
　bloom color · 230
　cuttings · 233
　disease · 3, 236
　fertilizing · 236
　foundation planting · 129
　full sun · 28
　graft, planting depth · 21, 234
　grafted plants · 233
　hardy · 229
　landscaping · 135
　own root · 233
　potted · 234
　pruning · 235
　scent · 230
　shrub · 5, 180
roses, climbing
　William Baffin · 19, 148, 180, 196, 237, **238**
roses, tea · 5, 228, **238**
roses, varieties
　F. J. Grootendoorst · 238
　Hansa · 230, 238
　Harison's Yellow · 231
　Knock Out · **238**
　miniature · 237
　Morden · 180
　Morden Blush · 231
　Morden Centennial · 231

old-fashioned · **238**
Persian Yellow · 231
Rosa glauca · 232
Therese Bugnet · 232
Yellow Rose of Texas · 231
Roundup · 69, 72, 73, 164, 181, 187
See also · glyphosate
row cover cloth · 308
Rubus · 222
rudbeckia · 254, **269**, **290**
Goldsturm · 269, 290
Marguerite · 254
See also · Black-eyed Susan
Rugosa · 238
Russian Olive · 190

S

Salix · 113
salt · 24
salvia · **269**
Salvia farinacea · 269
Salvia splendens · 269
Sambucus · 220
sapsuckers · 82
Amur chokecherry · 118
basswood · 104
maple · 112
Mountain Ash · 103
saskatoons · 222
See also · juneberries
sawdust · 26, 74
scion · 88
Scotch pine · 30, 156, 162, **172**, 188
Scots pine · 172
sedum · **290**
seedlings
hardening off · 29, 306
starting indoors · 305
windbreak · 87
Sempervivum · 297
septic system · 25
serviceberry · 222
See also · juneberries
shade · 28
impatiens · 28, 242, 257
lamium · 28
old-time hydrangea · 143
snow-on-the-mountain · 299

shade trees · 16, 19, 24, 30, 86, 89
spacing · 24
Shasta Daisy · 13, **295**
shelter belt · 184
shrubs · 4
bare root · 131
deciduous · 126
evergreen · 126
potted · 131
trimming · 134
watering · 133
yellow-leafed · 130
Silver maple · 44
Silver Mound · **277**
foundation planting · 130
slugs · 66
snapdragon · **263**
Snowball · **151**
Snow-on-the-Mountain · **300**
under trees · 28
soil · 3
compacted · 25
compost · 3, 34, 50, 73
ditch · 26
manure · 37
northern prairie · 32
nutrients · 33
organic matter · 3, 33, 34, 50, 69, 72
pH · 32, 38, 103
micro-nutrients · 41
sulfur · 42
salts · 34
tilling · 37
toxic · 25
under black walnut · 27
under evergreens · 27
under mature trees · 28
well-drained · 50
wet · 25
soil types
acid · 45
alkaline · 1, 120, 122, 156, 179, 191
clay · 36, 37
heavy · 33, 34, 37, 120
peat · 34, 37
poorly drained · 12
sandy · 33, 35, 47, 52
Sorbus · 102
sphagnum moss · 35
spider mites · 66
Spiraea · 152

spirea · **152**
  bridalwreath · 152
  bridalwreath, hedge · 178
  foundation planting · 129
  Renaissance · 152
  Tor · **154**
  Van Houtte · 152
spirea, dwarf · **152**
  Anthony Waterer · **153**
  Gold-leafed · **154**
  Goldmound · 130, 152
  Little Princess · 129, **153**
spirea, old fashioned · **152**
  hedge · 180
Spotted Wing Drosophila · 67
sprinklers · 48, 53, 54
spruce · **157**, 171
  bare root · 160
  Black Hills · **158**, 163
  burn · 157
  care · 164
  Colorado · **158**, 163
  disease · 163
  field-dug · 158
  moving · 160
  potted · 158
  seedling · 158
  shelter belt · 187
  soil under · 28
  spacing · 24
  tree spade · 159
  trimming · 160
  watering
      autumn · 10
  windbreak · 159
  winter interest · 30
squash · **313**
strawberries · **226**
  day-neutral · 227
  ever-bearing · 227
  June-bearing · 227
  Ogallala · 227
stump · 26
suckers · 98
Sugar maple · 44
sulfur · 42
  See also · ammonium sulfate
sumac · **154**
  staghorn · 154
  Tiger Eyes · 154

sun scald · 8, 11, 12, 78
  apples · 199, 207
superphosphate · 40
sweet corn · **310**
Syringa meyeri · 146
Syringa pubescens · 147
Syringa reticulata · 121
Syringa villosa · 146
Syringa vulgaris · 145

T

tamarack · **173**
Tanecetum coccineum · 295
Taxus · 174
Techny arborvitae · 20, 128, 165
Tilia · 103
tilth · 38
tomatoes · 58, 59, 62, **309**
  disease · 54
  nitrogen · 37
topping trees · 99
transplants
  wind · 29
tree spade · 100
trimming · 96
Trumpet Vine · 195
  See also · honeysuckle vine
trunk
  protection · 79
  southwest side · 8

U

Ulmus · 109
USDA hardiness zones · 1, 9, 199

V

Vaccinium · 218
vegetable gardens
  location · 29
vegetables · 5, 66, **302**
  ammonia · 307
  disease · 57, 308

fertilizer · 305
furry pests · 83, 307
insects · 308
planters · 304
raised beds · 304
rotate crops · 306
seeds vs. transplants · 305
starting indoors · 305
watering · 304, 306
weeding · 307
vegetative growth · 38
verbena · **263**
Viburnum · 139, 218
Viburnum lentago · 148
Viburnum opulus · 151
Viburnum trilobum · 139, 218
vinca · **269**
vinegar · 55
vines, annual
morning glory · 196
sweet pea · **196**
vines, perennial
clematis · **196**
vines, woody
American Bittersweet · **195**
Engelmann Ivy · **194**
grapes · **196**
honeysuckle · **195**
Virginia Creeper · **195**
violas · 13
Virginia Creeper · **195**
Vitis · 196, 220
voles · 12, 79, 81

Weigela, Red Prince · **154**
wildflowers · 300
William Baffin · 19, 148
willow · **113**, 190
compact · 79
Flame Willow · 25, 30, 114, 190, 193
Prairie Reflections · 114
pussy willow · 114
soil under · 28
Weeping · 30, 114
windstorms · 30
winter interest · 30
wind · 8, 11, 29, 30
windbreak · 19, 184
Amur maple · 189
caragana · 191
dogwood · 190
poplar · 186
red cedar · 171, 188
Scotch pine · 188
seedlings · 87
spruce · 187
weeds and grass · 72
willow · 190
windstorms · 97
winter interest · 30, 190
flowering plum · 122
sedum · 291
witch's broom · 65
woodbine · 194
See also · Engelmann Ivy
wormwood · 277
See also · artemisia

W

walnut
black walnut · **123**, 215
juglone · 123
water
alkaline · 33, 38, 55
water sprouts · 60, 98, 204
watering · 7, 46–55
autumn · 10
bare root · 93
weeding · 7
weeds · 68–75

Y

yard · 16
yarrow · 292
yellowing leaves · 110
See also · chlorosis
yew · **174**

Z

zinnia · **263**

CPSIA information can be obtained
at www.ICGtesting.com
Printed in the USA
LVOW08s0917130318
568974LV00001BC/1/P

9 781642 554861